RIGHTS AND REGULATION

RIGHTS AND REGULATION
Ethical, Political, and Economic Issues

Edited by
TIBOR R. MACHAN AND M. BRUCE JOHNSON

Foreword by
AARON WILDAVSKY

Pacific Studies in Public Policy

PACIFIC INSTITUTE FOR PUBLIC POLICY RESEARCH
San Francisco, California

Ballinger Publishing Company
Cambridge, Massachusetts
A Subsidiary of Harper & Row, Publishers, Inc.

International Standard Book Number: 0–88410–928–3 (CL)
0–88410–929–1 (PB)

Library of Congress Catalog Card Number: 83–11309

Printed in the United States of America

Library of Congress Cataloging in Publication Data

Main entry under title:

Rights and regulation.

   (Pacific studies in public policy)
   Includes bibliographical references and index.
   1. Industrial laws and legislation—United States. 2. Trade
regulation—United States. 3. Public policy (Law)—United States.
I. Machan, Tibor R. II. Johnson, M. Bruce. III. Series.
KF1600.R5   1983   343.73'07   83–11309
ISBN 0–88410–928–3   347.3037
ISBN 0–88410–929–1 (pbk.)

Cover Photo by: Richard Lee Kaylin
                 Visual Communications
                 1218 Washington Street
                 Denver, CO 80203

PACIFIC
INSTITUTE
FOR PUBLIC POLICY RESEARCH

The Pacific Institute for Public Policy Research is an independent, tax-exempt research and educational organization. The Institute's program is designed to broaden public understanding of the nature and effects of market processes and government policy.

With the bureaucratization and politicization of modern society, scholars, business and civic leaders, the media, policymakers, and the general public have too often been isolated from meaningful solutions to critical public issues. To facilitate a more active and enlightened discussion of such issues, the Pacific Institute sponsors in-depth studies into the nature and possible solutions to major social, economic, and environmental problems. Undertaken regardless of the sanctity of any particular government program, or the customs, prejudices, or temper of the times, the Institute's studies aim to ensure that alternative approaches to currently problematic policy areas are fully evaluated, the best remedies discovered, and these findings made widely available. The results of this work are published as books and monographs, and form the basis for numerous conference and media programs.

Through this program of research and commentary, the Institute seeks to evaluate the premises and consequences of government policy, and provide the foundations necessary for constructive policy reform.

PACIFIC STUDIES IN PUBLIC POLICY

Locking Up the Range
Federal Land Controls and Grazing
By Gary D. Libecap
With a Foreword by Jonathan R. T. Hughes

The Public School Monopoly
A Critical Analysis of Education and the State
in American Society
Edited by Robert B. Everhart
With a Foreword by Clarence J. Karier

Resolving the Housing Crisis
Government Policy, Decontrol, and the Public Interest
Edited with an Introduction by M. Bruce Johnson

Natural Resources
Bureaucratic Myths and Environmental Management
By Richard Stroup and John Baden
With a Foreword by William Niskanen

Water Rights
Scarce Resource Allocation, Bureaucracy,
and the Environment
Edited by Terry L. Anderson
With a Foreword by Jack Hirshleifer

FORTHCOMING

Fugitive Industry
The Economics and Politics of Plant Closings

Politics, Prices, and Petroleum
The Political Economy of Energy

Firearms and Violence
Issues of Public Policy

Money in Crisis
Government, Stagflation, and Monetary Reform

Forestlands
Public and Private

The American Family and the State

New Strategies for American Unions
The Economic Consequences

Political Business Cycle

Impoverishing America
The Political Economy of the Transfer Society

Rationing Health Care
Medical Licensing in the United States

For further information on the Pacific Institute's program and a catalog of publications, please contact:

PACIFIC INSTITUTE
FOR PUBLIC POLICY RESEARCH
635 Mason Street
San Francisco, California 94108

CONTENTS

FOREWORD
If Regulation Is Right, Is It Also Safe?

The distinguishing feature of *Rights and Regulation* is its concern with the moral aspects of regulation: is it right (or under what conditions would it be right) for government to regulate private enterprise? One question leads to another: does regulation provide the help it promises in averting dangers? More than any other volume I know on the subject of regulation, this collection shows that one can and does argue with moral imperatives. When imperatives conflict, as they often do, we look for ways of choosing among them by stipulating conditions of application or by seeing whether the consequences of following the opposing mandates would be more or less desirable according to other values held in common. This is precisely the sort of inquiry in which the authors of these essays have engaged. By intertwining facts and values, "ought" and "is," the book shows how questions of consequences may direct moral concerns and how moral awareness leads to new and interesting questions of fact. One (but by no means the only) strand of thought in *Rights and Regulation* raises the question of whether risk is reduced by attempting to deter danger before it occurs or by managing risk after it manifests itself.

The debate over regulation of risk reveals a strategic conflict between *anticipation* and *resilience*. Anticipation is a mode of control by central cognition; potential dangers are averted before damage is done. Resilience is the capacity to use change so as to better cope with the unknown; it is learning to bounce back.[1] Are risks better balanced, we may ask, by attempting to anticipate them or by trying to mitigate their effects after they have occurred?

A preoccupation with rejecting risk leads to large-scale organization and centralization of power in order to mobilize massive resources against possible evils. This size phenomenon becomes apparent when regulations drive out small drug companies that cannot afford years of testing. The probability that any known danger will occur declines because of anticipatory measures. However, there is an increased probability that unexpected dangers will prove catastrophic should they occur, both because resources required for resilient response have been used up in advance and because of inexperience in coping with failure.

Three Mile Island (I am aware it is used to "prove" everything) is a case in point. It occurred after (not before) large numbers of safety measures were retrofitted onto existing reactors. The idea was that by strengthening every part—pipes, valves, containment, alarms, and so on—the plants would be safer than ever. No effort was made to link the parts to the whole, in other words, to ask whether the relationship among parts was optimal in view of the hundreds of changes made. The point was to prevent failure. Training to respond to failure was minimal because that would have meant admitting things could go wrong. When the hundred or so warning lights and whistles went off, the staff became confused. The system lacked resilience because the staff had been taught to rely on anticipation.

Suppose something we have neglected turns out to be dangerous and that government seeks to protect people against this potential danger. Even so, anticipation is not necessarily the best policy. We might choose a few potential disasters to try to avoid, even at high cost. But when the expectation of catastrophe becomes common, priorities among the potentially preventable dangers must be established or else few resources will remain for responding to the unexpected. Knowing so little about whether a particular risk will materialize, we are in as much danger of harming as helping. How would government know which of an infinity of evils would be manifested?

1. W.C. Clark, "Witches, Floods, and Wonder Drugs: Historical Perspectives on Risk Management," in R.C. Schwing and W.A. Albers, Jr., eds., *Societal Risk Assessment* (New York: Plenum, 1980); C.S. Holling, "Resilience and Stability of Ecological Systems," in *Annual Review of Ecology and Systematics*, vol. 4 (Palo Alto, Calif.: Annual Reviews, 1973); and idem., "Resilience in the Unforgiving Society," no. R-24 (Vancouver: University of British Columbia, Institute of Resource Ecology, March 1981).

Many that now appear dangerous may actually turn out to be benign. Others may actually be a little dangerous but the consequences of trying to anticipate them may be much worse than letting them run their course. The most likely eventuality by far is that whatever happens will be unexpected. We might be better off, then, increasing our capacity to respond, our resilience, rather than dissipating our strength in efforts to ward off we know-not-what.

Yet it is the effort to get government to provide guarantees against risk that characterizes domestic developments during the twentieth century. If we substitute "security" for "safety," social policy for technology, the desire for protection is seen to be widespread. When one extends this protection to industry and its owners—"socialism for the rich"—insurance against adversity appears to be the ubiquitous phenomenon it is.

Thomas R. Haggard's "Government Regulation of the Employment Relationship" records a journey from resilience, characterized by common-law rules of tort, agency, and contract, to the growth of anticipation through regulation. The basic justification for employment regulations was the unequal bargaining power of worker and employer. Haggard argues that employers should not be held liable for their bargaining power, as it is not their fault that employees would rather work for them than for someone else. To this I would add that it has yet to be proved whether (or, more accurately, under which conditions) aiding workers to organize helps those who are worst off. By lumping all workers together, of course, they would undoubtedly gain bargaining power, though the question would still arise whether they might not benefit more from economic growth in the long run. Since their short-run income is likely to increase, however, there is every reason to believe that workers best able to organize will take advantage of those least able to organize—young people, minorities, immigrants. As a general rule, regulations help those who are organized: the children of those who are already plumbers do better than those whose families have no plumbers among them. No doubt the steel workers and the United Auto Workers have done well for their members by securing wages three to four times greater than those in the rest of industry but this is not the same as stating that wage and hour regulations help those who need it most. Anticipation as a method of social control helps those who get there "firstest with the mostest," because they decide in whose interest regulation is to be implemented.

In his discussion of "Substantive Due Process: A Doctrine for Regulatory Control," Norman Karlin examines the ideological basis on which anticipation is preferred to resilience or, as he puts it, the police power that justifies regulation is preferred against the Constitution that is supposed to protect property. It is hard to remember now, so harsh and vindictive has been the attack, that until the 1930s there was a doctrine of substantive due process protecting property rights. Under this doctrine, the courts assumed regulations affecting property rights produced initial harmful consequences so that the government, acting through the legislature and executive, had to accept the burden of proof in demonstrating that the property rights of individuals had been turned aside for good reason. Today, as Karlin shows so well, all this is taken for granted in regard to the due process requirements that have to be met whenever interference with freedom of speech or assembly is contemplated. This protection, however, has been taken away from property rights, which have been given an inferior place. Thus, regulation itself, based on the legislative police power, has become the embodiment of due process to be challenged only if there is some flaw in the way in which the public will is manifested, whereas restraints on expression have become subject to the same criteria of substantive due process that had heretofore protected property.

Observers of the American political scene will note that interest group activity flourishes as never before; by contrast, the economy, based on property rights, languishes. Once we understand Karlin's main points — political participation has been allowed to become resilient by applying due process against governmental intervention, whereas property rights have been subject to anticipatory regulation — the reason for the anomaly becomes evident: resilience outperforms anticipation.

J.C. Smith's elegant essay on "The Processes of Adjudication and Regulation, A Comparison" examines anticipation versus resilience under other names — regulation versus adjudication or criminal versus tort law. He is concerned about comparing mechanisms of social control, which he also calls "institutional paradigms . . . as methods of protecting people from the harmful consequences of action." Tort law enforces obligation by awarding damages as compensation in order to protect personal and property rights. Far from settling conflicting claims over rights, criminal law establishes certain behavior as so harmful that it incurs penalties stipulated in advance. Functioning after the alleged harm has already occurred, civil or tort law is essentially a mode of resilience; criminal law is anticipatory. Regulation is based on a criminal model.

Since regulation is a form of anticipation, it cannot wait for evidence from actual events. Thus, it does not correspond well to many particular circumstances within a general class of activities. Whereas anticipation requires bureaucracy to enforce standards, resilience is based on self-regulation by those closest to the scene who, therefore, have the best information about what is happening.

That anticipation is too much of a good thing is the position taken by Leland B. Yeager in "Is There a Bias Toward Overregulation?" He argues that "prospective costs and benefits escape accurate confrontation" because the benefits are received by well-identified individuals whereas the costs are dispersed among millions of taxpayers. The strategy of regulatory anticipation gains political support because it is active and positive, laying claim to doing good things for people, whereas a strategy of resilience depends on reaction to unknown events after they occur. "An economist sympathetic to the market can explain how entrepreneurs have incentive to seek unfilled wants and ways of filling them, but he cannot predict what unfilled wants are going to be filled and when." Yeager cautions that reliance on government "tends to freeze out alternative solutions," yet he fears that the safe subsidy of regulation will be preferred to risky exploration of new vistas.

The relationship between anticipation and resilience also may be traced through the various papers that raise the question of whether and to what extent regulation is morally permissible or morally mandatory. Should individuals be allowed to interact with one another on the understanding that the damage they do may be compensated for under the law later on? Knowing that they will be held liable, therefore, individual actors will themselves anticipate future damages, deciding to limit them in advance to the extent practicable. Thus anticipation becomes individualized, subject to the rules for providing remedies should mistakes be made. Or should the function of anticipation be collectivized so that the community, acting through the political process, imposes sanctions in advance of the damage to be done? If anticipation is collectivized, so is resilience, because the task of responding to untoward events now belongs to the bureaucracies that act for the people as a whole. Will the actions of individuals responding resiliently after the fact enhance the safety of society more or less than the actions of a government that has been trained to anticipate? Or is some combination of anticipation and resilience desirable?

In advocating "a constitution that protects each individual against coerced redistribution of wealth through the political process," M. Bruce Johnson, in his "Regulation and Justice: An Economist's Perspective," contends that by increasing transaction costs, regulation reduces the total available for everyone. "Individuals perceive that it is cheaper to use the political system than to redistribute wealth via the market. Politicians perceive that it is easier to remain in office by legislating redistributions of wealth from the large group to the concentrated special-interest groups." Johnson does not think it just for some people to "have more at the expense of less for everyone else." But that is exactly what a strategy of anticipation does; it reduces wealth to increase safety. If wealth and safety are connected, however, less wealth will beget less safety, in other words, "less for everyone else."[2]

Even if these contentions were ultimately shown to be correct, they could not be conclusive, for the proof must lie in the future. In the meantime, there is evidence that popular sentiment is turning toward anticipation. Opinion polls, election results, and jury awards suggest that the dividing line between voluntary and involuntary risks has been moving toward the latter, with "system blame" gaining on "individual responsibility," the seller rather than the buyer urged to beware lest penalties be incurred. Should that trend continue, tort law will prove disadvantageous to commercial interests. Then they too will seek protection from government, the broader the scope the better, so as to pass the penalties on to other people. A sign of the times is proposed federal legislation establishing uniform national standards for product liability and toxic substances under tort law. A complementary move would be to set up a broad "superfund" to cover not only direct damage and cleanup but also the costs of claims by third parties. And once indirect damage by third parties is included, efforts will surely be made, modeled on workmen's compensation policy, to reduce the burden of proof for claimants. All this would add up to national reinsurance, spreading the costs among millions of taxpayers. The liability of the nation would go up but incen-

2. See Aaron Wildavsky, "Richer Is Safer," *The Public Interest* 60 (Summer 1980): 23–39.

tives for consumers to act safely and for producers and sellers to provide safe products would decline. All interested parties feel better off, yet in the end, as Johnson warns, there is less to go around. Logrolling on risk—you insure me, I'll insure you—raises the premiums for everyone.[3] Regulation undermines resilience.

An effort at compromise is made by Judith Jarvis Thomson in "Some Questions about Government Regulation of Behavior." Though legal liability should adequately handle most cases of harm, she is concerned about "unintentionally harmful behavior." If there is a pattern to these events and if people affected do not have the resources to protect themselves, much like the worker who cannot find employment elsewhere, then she would, subject to some consideration of cost and benefit, favor regulation. The Goldilocks problem—how to get just enough but not too much—continues to elude us all. Knowing, nevertheless, that the fundamental choice is between anticipation and resilience should enable us to better choose where to draw the line.

Not one to mince words, J. Roger Lee, in "Choice and Harms," explicitly states that it is not the business of government to protect its citizens from harm, at least not all harms. The troubles people get into because they take their chances in interacting with others should not be regulated; only those harms that violate one's rights should be treated in this manner. Lee believes in voluntarism to the extent that he would prohibit the placing of burdens on individuals that they, themselves, have not chosen voluntarily to assume.

The responsibility toward future generations that Rolf Sartorius urges on government in his paper "Government Regulation and Intergenerational Justice" concerns variety. He fears that the operation of market forces will deplete natural resources, diminish the number and extent of animal species, and otherwise reduce the variety of life forms on this planet. I stress the use of variety as the motive for protecting future generations precisely because it is this selfsame quality that supporters of spontaneity in social life regard as their particular preserve. They prefer markets over bureaucracies, resilience over anticipation, largely because they believe bureaucracies enforce uniformity while markets encourage variety. The environmental movement has issued a fundamental challenge precisely

3. See Yair Aharoni, *The No-Risk Society* (Chatham, N.J.: Chatham House Publishers, 1981).

on the ground which market supporters thought themselves most impregnable – variety.

Can it be that markets sometimes destroy diversity while bureaucracies preserve differences? Yes, but . . . . When Joseph Schumpeter speaks of the "creative destruction" of capitalism, he means that it both does away with the old and brings on the new at greater rates than before. Some products lose out in competition but many new ones take their place. The balance must be in favor of markets as modern life is far more differentiated, in other words, more diverse than before. But how do bureaucracies, which specialize in the uniform application of rules, come to be considered as champions of diversity? By taking certain lands or species "out of the market," the hierarchy that runs the bureaucracy seeks to preserve a present form of life. Limiting preservation to a few forms, this is unexceptionable; no one ever said everything should be traded. But as the extent of preservation increases, the resources available to support new diversity are bound to decrease. How will a society devoted to preservation through regulation cope with new conditions when its diversity has diminished precisely because it is unwilling to allow old forms to fail? It is precisely the capacity of markets to encourage failure that is the key to their success; they are resilient because they create diversity to respond to emerging conditions. What markets pass on is not the entire past, as if it were all an heirloom, but a generalized capacity – knowledge, diversity, wealth – to respond resiliently to change.

As a good critic should, Randall Dipert, in his "Reflections on the Rights of Future Generations," has conceptual fun with the argument about responsibility to the future. Evidently, future generations are so numerous that they can always outvote present people; therefore it follows that by invoking the future one has ended the discussion, as it were, by majority rule. "It might thus seem," Dipert gets out his gentle rapier, "that we are violating the rights of these as-yet-unborn individuals by not engaging constantly in procreative activity." Can it be that the best way of protecting the rights of future individuals is not to give birth to them? "If all babies have the right to be born free of defects, then some babies' rights will be violated – by us, who allow them to exist." There may be obligations to future generations, but in Dipert's view these cannot be the same as those to the present population of planet earth.

Does it show greater concern for future generations to pass on life forms exactly as they are now, we may ask, or to send ahead a capacity to cope with the unexpected, thus enabling future generations to redesign their own lives? Is it true that anticipation through regulation will leave future generations better off than relying on resilience through markets?

Steven Kelman examines yet another aspect of regulation. In a luminous essay on "Regulation and Paternalism," Kelman makes the case that individuals may be better off by imposing restrictions on themselves through government regulation and that, for this reason, the main argument against restricting people's liberty in their own interest fails. To a point, the argument is persuasive: individuals may and do decide (think of Ulysses and the Sirens) that they would be better off restricting their choices. Soldiers may, in Thomas Schelling's famous example, burn their bridges behind them in order, by demonstrating their resolve, to increase their bargaining power. I have myself justified constitutional spending limits partially on the grounds that individuals, knowing the consequences of their actions will lead to larger total expenditures than they would otherwise prefer, may choose to make a prior standing decision on total spending.[4] So I concede, even embrace, the notion that experience may lead people to bind themselves in advance. But such a decision, as the spending limit example indicates, depends on a belief that over the largest number of cases the results will be better than if separate and different decisions were made as one went along. Is this true for regulation?

Kelman argues convincingly that there are many matters on which individuals lack information about harmful substances. He is also careful to say that in some cases regulation of these harms may turn out to be unwarranted but that is the price one has to pay for getting rid of the worst. Is it true, then, that governmental activity is geared toward using the knowledge of modern science – knowledge few individuals possess – to create priorities among possible dangers, choosing to eliminate or regulate those that promise to do the most harm? Since expenditures per accident or fatality averted vary from a few thousand to several hundred million dollars, this claim can hardly be substantiated.[5] There is also the discomforting fact that, in the past, with a minimum of regulation, morbidity and mortality

4. See Aaron Wildavsky, *How to Limit Government Spending* (Los Angeles and Berkeley: University of California Press, 1980).

5. John D. Graham and James W. Vaupel, "The Value of a Life: Does It Make a Difference?," *Journal of Risk Analysis* 1 (1981).

have shown dramatic improvement. Obviously, allowing things to go on as they were is far from deadly. Of course, everyone would like to pick out the eyes from the potatoe of life, choosing to regulate only those that will do considerable harm and leaving others alone so their unsuspected good may operate to our benefit. "We are not fully free," Friedrich A. Hayek warns, "to pick and choose whatever combination of features we wish our society to possess, or to . . . build a desirable social order like a mosaic by selecting whatever particular parts we like best. . . ."[6] How shall we come down, then, for a preponderance of anticipation or of resilience?

In analyzing the relative merits of anticipation and resilience, another concern is how important voluntarism should be as a moral priority. If voluntarism is the key, this requires an analysis of the degree of coercion in society, for others are quick to claim that individuals do not have genuine choice. In "On the Rationale of Governmental Regulation," Nicholas Rescher takes this position, though not without qualms. When there is "a clear and present danger," government should intervene, providing it can make a good case that the benefits outweigh the costs.

Alas, the history of the interpretation of the "clear and present danger" doctrine in the area of free speech would not give one hope that an operational definition of intervention will emerge. For it is precisely over the question of how immediate and how grave the danger is that disputes over regulation revolve. Exactly what Rescher fears—"the overall worsening of people's economic situation"—is exactly what is likely to happen as money is spent to guard against dangers that may or may not manifest themselves.

There is no need for Tibor R. Machan (see "The Petty Tyranny of Government Regulation") to make any compromise whatsoever because he believes that "regulating markets is regulating people" without their consent. In a word, regulation is wrong. He takes on the opposing view at its strongest, looking at a case in which most people would say government should intervene because of the importance of the possible harm and because individuals cannot know what they are getting. Machan contends that it is improper for government to force food producers to disclose the content of the food they sell. It is not in the producer's interest to harm consumers, and if inadver-

6. Friedrich A. Hayek, *Rules and Order*, vol. 1, *Law, Legislation and Liberty* (Chicago: University of Chicago Press, 1973), p. 59.

tent harm is done, tort litigation is available as a remedy. In the absence of proven danger, the imposition of mandatory content labeling trespasses against producers. Machan would not deprive manufacturers of "their nature as moral agents," that is, their liberty to choose and to take the consequences, unless and until it had been proven they had violated the rights of others. To the right that some suggest people have to drink clean water and breathe clean air (of course, these are matters of degree), Machan would oppose the rights of citizens to be free of the interference of others. Evidently, it would take a lot to convince him to place anticipation over resilience.

In conclusion, the approach I have taken to unify the concerns expressed by the authors of this volume is only one among many. Someone else might well have focused on the ways in which concepts of rights relate to regulatory activities. Certainly, readers who care about the rights and wrongs of regulation, such as its impact upon individual liberty and social justice, will find *Rights and Regulation* the best place to begin. For those readers who are also led to inquire into whether regulation of risk is likely to make us safer, thus justifying restrictions of individual behavior, the considerations adduced in this foreword may provide a start.

Aaron Wildavsky
University of California,
Berkeley

INTRODUCTION

Government regulation increasingly has become the subject of lively, and often bitter controversy. Whether appealing for reforms, piece-meal deregulation, or even a massive dismantling of the regulatory apparatus, critics of regulation have uniformly called into question regulatory performance. David Rockefeller, commenting on the current array of public problems and regulatory correctives, captured the flavor of these criticisms in claiming that "it is hard sometimes to tell the . . . problems from the programs . . . . It is worth considering whether our current national predicament does not derive from regulation itself: from a vast complex of powers, programs, and prescriptions that add up to the fundamental new problem of the contemporary age."[1]

This scrutiny of regulatory performance is an essential ingredient for any thorough assessment of the role that current regulation should play in relieving the social and economic ills that beset us. But evaluating performance is not enough. Regulation must be re-examined, not merely in terms of its accomplishments and its costs, but from a broader perspective, one that endeavors to comprehend its philosophical underpinnings. *Should* government regulate? If so, is all regulation justified on moral grounds? These questions are, of course, part of a still broader concern: what is the legitimate role of

1. *Wall Street Journal*, 13 June 1980.

government, and what are the proper means by which government should pursue that role? It was with these questions in mind that this volume was conceived.

The recent assault on regulation has generally steered clear of such fundamental theoretical questions. Critics of regulation have come mainly from the ranks of economists or political scientists. The former have focused primarily on cost-benefit calculations, claiming that, though the ends served by regulation may indeed be laudable, the costs of such regulations far outweigh their benefits. Political scientists critical of regulation have generally lamented the gross organizational inefficiencies and lack of accountability present in our regulatory network.

No doubt these are important considerations. Accumulated evidence supports the proposition that regulation as a method of executing good intentions has not worked in many instances. Examples of regulatory failure abound. Even in seemingly successful cases of government regulation, the success is often merely apparent. For example, the Food and Drug Administration, which prizes itself on promoting the safety, effectiveness, and even nutritiousness of foods and drugs, has in fact stifled innovation and consequently, has prevented the remedy of numerous medical ills.[2] Airline safety regulations have also come under fire from economists who argue that excessive concern with certain kinds of safety measures has resulted in higher prices for service that yields, at best, only marginal improvements in safety.

The claims about lack of accountability and organizational inefficiency are equally well founded. Many of the older agencies such as the Interstate Commerce Commission and the Federal Communications Commission have "tended to become as much the protectors as the regulators of the industries they oversee. . . . Policy is dominated by the 'iron triangle', a coalition of regulated interests, the regulatory agencies, and the congressional subcommittees overseeing the particular policy field" such that policies have worked to the advantage of established firms, insulating them from competition and, in effect, providing them with subsidies.[3] This cooperative relationship led "Nader's raiders" to "characterize the entire system of

---

2. David Leo Weimer, "Safe – and Available – Drugs," in *Instead of Regulation*, ed. Robert Poole (Lexington, Mass.: Lexington Books, 1981).

3. Carl P. Chelf, *Public Policymaking in America* (Santa Monica, Calif.: Goodyear Publishing Co., 1981), p. 243.

government regulation as being 'monopoly makers'."[4] Other agencies such as the Occupational Safety and Health Administration (OSHA) have produced such a maze of regulations that the regulations often contradict one another.

Contemporary defenders of government regulation concur with many of these contentions regarding individual agencies or particular regulations, but stress that opponents of regulation view the situation too narrowly. Economists, they argue, promote considerations of cost at the expense of justice and compassion. The goal of legislators who created OSHA was not so much to make the market more efficient — something that often served as a justification for the older type of regulatory bodies (e.g., the ICC or the FCC) — but rather to prevent the sort of producer and employer behavior that causes severe harm to people. The employee who is hurt while working in an unsafe workplace is due certain considerations, regardless of what they may cost.

Those who denounce the lack of accountability of the regulatory bodies, it is argued, fail to recognize that though this quality characterizes some of the older agencies, the newer agencies aimed at protecting the citizen's health and safety are not prey to narrow special interests. Regarding organizational inefficiency, proponents of regulation simply note that nongovernmental organizations are often inefficient, too, and that, in any event, some duplication of effort or overlapping of regulations should be tolerated in the effort to ensure that all facets of health and safety are secured.

Thus, defenders of regulation, in effect, argue that its critics just do not see the real issues. Health, safety, conservation, and so on, are absolute goals whose values are immeasurable. Efficiency is considered secondary, if not altogether irrelevant. As one defender of regulation argued, "How does one measure the efficiency of health research, of environmental protection, or even of occupational safety in an unambiguous manner? Efficiency is a foreign term in these and other areas of government. . . . The objective of building Chevrolet Vegas must pale before the goal of curing cancer."[5] If people have a right to health and safety, the provision of both should be assured to the best of our ability. Proponents of regulation perceive government

4. George J. Gordon, *Public Administration in America* (New York: St. Martin's Press, 1978), p. 332.

5. Kenneth J. Meier, *Politics and the Bureaucracy* (North Scituate, Mass.: Duxbury Press, 1979), p. 7.

as the only institution capable of providing these values in a comprehensive fashion. In short, they claim that some things should just be done—so long as they *can* be done and there is a chance to do them right.

Defenders of regulation have a point insofar as these issues have not been properly addressed in the recent literature on government regulation. Economists have their own methodology and frequently deny that those who criticize them speak meaningfully. Not only do most economists see their own fields as positive, value-free science, but many regard their methodology as the only road to truth about human affairs. Most have little patience with those who speak of justice, fairness, and compassion; these concepts are regarded by economists as ultimately subjective terms whose meanings depend entirely on the designation of the individual using them. Even noneconomist critics of regulation have tended to couch their arguments in terms of efficiency and organizational structure, sidestepping the philosophical and moral concerns at issue.

In contrast, the defenders of the newer type of government regulation (concerned with environmental quality, safety, health, and so forth) regard the consideration of values as indispensable. We wish to learn, after all, what we *should* do, what government policy *ought to be.* These are, of course, questions not only about what works, but also, and primarily, about what our goals should be.

These questions have become increasingly important in light of the seemingly uncontrollable impulse toward regulation that emerged in the 1970s. Regulatory activities now embrace broad social goals in addition to the traditional regulatory focus on antitrust or other economic concerns ushered in at the turn of the twentieth century, and expanded during the New Deal era. The regulatory explosion in the 1970s saw the creation of twenty new agencies in ten years compared with eleven during the entire span of the New Deal era. By 1980, "the federal regulatory role [had grown] until today virtually every aspect of people's lives—the food they eat, the air they breathe, the prices they pay, their working conditions, what they hear on the radio or see on television—is touched by federal regulation. Almost every facet of business activity is subject to scrutiny by one or more governmental agencies that have the power to inspect, review, modify, or reject the actions of private enterprise."[6] It is estimated that

6. Chelf, *Public Policymaking*, p. 239.

fifty agencies, employing over 100,000 people, spend $3 billion implementing over 60,000 pages of regulations.[7] Regulatory expenditures by 1979 were six times as great as expenditures just nine years earlier.[8] And these direct costs of maintaining the regulatory apparatus are dwarfed by the estimated costs to the economy. The Council on Environmental Quality, for example, "estimated that the regulations administered by the Environmental Protection Agency alone would cost the economy an additional $40 billion per year by 1984. . . . Murray Weidenbaum put the cost of compliance plus government administrative costs [of all regulation] at $102 billion for 1978."[9]

Clearly, this regulatory "growth industry" reflects an eclipse of limited government. Does it, in turn, mark the demise of a "free society"? Or does this expansion of government regulation represent a more meaningful freedom in which the rights of the public are protected from the license of industry? Do these regulations provide an atmosphere in which "higher" goals such as health, safety, and so on, can flourish?

To date, critics of regulation have not adequately addressed these questions. Critics and defenders alike have been at cross-purposes — engaged in a discussion of government regulation in which each accuses the other's arguments of irrelevance. This volume of essays emerged as a result of the editors' concern with this present state of government regulation studies. We found that an unusual number of scholars from a variety of disciplines shared that concern. Consequently, we asked a number of them to examine the topic from the standpoint of their individual specialties and interests. The resulting essays not only raise questions about government regulation but also discuss how to approach the topic in a constructive manner.

Though the essays represent diverse approaches and conclusions, they all share a commitment to look beyond the effects of specific regulations or particular regulatory bodies. In this spirit, each author has attempted to place regulation in a theoretical framework that establishes the proper bounds of government activity and assesses regulation in the context of that framework.

Legal scholars, philosophers, economists, and political theorists have contributed to the study. Some have argued that all regulation

7. Gordon, *Public Administration*, pp. 314, 335.
8. Chelf, *Public Policymaking*, p. 240.
9. Ibid., p. 246.

represents an unjustified intervention by government into the lives of individuals. Others have taken a less critical view, claiming that, in fact, moral considerations for the protection of individual rights not only permit, but require, some form of regulation. Our intention was not that uniform conclusions be reached. Rather, it was hoped that questions of rights and justice would be introduced into the discussion of government regulation, in part to escape the limits of piece-meal cost-benefit assessments, and in part to reintroduce the broader issues at stake in the relationship between government and people. What are the moral implications of regulation? What is the relationship of regulation to individual rights? How does regulation fit into our constitutional framework?

The essays are divided into five sections. In Part I, "Law and Regulation," the legal underpinnings of regulation are investigated. How did the explosion in government regulation arise out of a constitution devised, or so it is often presumed, to promote limited government? And is direct regulation or legal adjudication the best way to handle the problems that advocates of regulation allege must be addressed? Part II, "Political Economy of Regulation," presents two essays that investigate the conditions under which regulation has flourished and that propose standards by which the justice of regulation can be measured. In Part III, "Rights and Harms," two authors carefully consider the issues of what constitutes interpersonal trespasses and what are the limits of just response to those trespasses. In Part IV, "Rights of Future Generations," two authors examine the difficult question of the nature and extent of the claims future generations have on present generations and what those claims imply for current regulatory policy. In Part V, "Legitimacy of Regulation," three authors face head-on the moral implications of regulation. Does it promote or erode human dignity, justice, and fairness?

Throughout these essays we find an unusual concern with the moral aspects of government regulation. While not all contributors take the normative approach, and while there are clearly differences among those who do, the unifying element of this volume is its unique focus upon questions of justice and human rights as they relate to government regulation of business.

Thomas Haggard clearly takes a normative approach to the questions of whether government has the rightful authority to regulate the commercial aspects of labor, such as employment, hours of work, dismissal, promotion, and so forth. Haggard's attention to the natural-law tradition is quite unusual in the context of contemporary legal commentary on the government's role in the employment relationship.

Norman Karlin takes a rather different approach, mainly illustrating the jurisprudential concerns with the problems generated through government regulation. He outlines the historical background of regulation in terms of the demise, in his view unfortunate, of the doctrine of substantive due process. This demise had removed the limits on legislatures tempted to restrict the basic rights of market agents. The burden of proof for the validity of government regulation must rest primarily on those proposing it, contrary to present legal practice.

Professor J. C. Smith's contribution to this volume has the unique merit of showing why, from the standpoint of legal justice, government regulation is not an efficient and appropriate means for achieving the goals widely proclaimed to be the objectives of such regulation. Professor Smith argues that "the mechanism of social control of behavior through regulatory schemes, is itself, inappropriate for the uses to which it is put," and he proceeds to defend adjudication as an alternative to government regulation. Here we find the admission that the aim of government regulation is often commendable but the means are inadmissible in regard to a soundly conceived system of legal justice.

Leland Yeager's focus is still on the legal aspects of government regulation. Although concerned with some ethical issues, Yeager explores the question of whether contemporary political, juridical, legislative, and similar trends are unjustifiably predisposed toward the promulgation of both the ideology and the practice of government regulation. In other words, is the demand for regulation a kind of injustifiable prejudice? Much more healthy skepticism is required when the idea of government regulation is proposed as a solution to societal problems.

In line with neoclassical economic analysis, M. Bruce Johnson argues that, from an economic point of view, only individual preferences matter, nothing more. Within this perspective the Pareto optimality model is sound (as sound can be) and matters of justice — for example, considerations of fair distribution of wealth, related market conduct — are generally best left to the free market. The mere existence of coercion, through the introduction of government regulation, leads to the presence of a crucial element of injustice within the system. This could be avoided, even at the risk of other, occasional faults—market failures—by allowing the market to function through the choices of participants.

Contrary to Johnson, Judith Jarvis Thomson contends that on a case-by-case basis one could find many regulatory measures justifiable. Some regulation, at any rate, could be justified, especially if cost is borne by the general public. However, in many cases legal liability provisions would suffice to foster "good" behavior and prevent "bad" behavior in the marketplace. It is mainly negligent behavior that is difficult to cope with via liability provisions. In general, however, caution is required when considering the cost of government regulation.

J. Roger Lee takes a different view on roughly the same issues. He asks whether government ought to be in the business of protecting us from harms per se. His answer is that government ought to concern itself with rights violations, not with harms. Not all harms involve such violations. The determination of what prohibitions governments may impose must rely on a general theory of rights as well as on the idea of rational expectation. In short, hard cases must be based on what a reasonable person can expect from others in the way of caution, care, foresight, and so forth. On the whole, Lee defends the idea that a society ought to cherish voluntarism and prohibit the imposition of burdens not voluntarily assumed by participants in the marketplace.

Rolf Sartorius believes that governments have responsibilities toward future generations. He argues that these cannot be carried out without some government regulation in such areas as pollution, wildlife usage, depletion of natural resources, and so forth.

Randall Dipert presents a rebuttal to Sartorius's argument, maintaining that no *potential* beings have rights that override the rights of *actual* beings. At any rate, protecting the rights of actual beings is all the concern government needs to exhibit toward members of future generations.

Steven Kelman, too, endorses government regulation, but mainly on quasi-paternalistic grounds. First he observes that the bulk of government regulation is the result of people's choices to give up their right to choose in *some* instances. In these cases government regulation is not even paternalistic. Sometimes, however, there is clear justification for paternalistic government regulation, namely, in cases where such regulation would prevent people from yielding to severe temptation to do wrong.

Nicholas Rescher maintains that not only is government regulation feasible, but under circumstances pointing to a clear and present danger, it is desirable. When such circumstances arise, government regulation should be provided. But caution should also be exercised by requiring that government regulation be introduced only upon demonstration that benefits will result. Wholesale regulatory schemes in behalf of some ideal of equality (e.g., of wealth or welfare) can easily lead to the overall worsening of people's economic situation. The ideal of greater and greater productivity in a system should not be abandoned.

Tibor Machan develops a case for applying the current version of Lockean natural-rights theory to the moral evaluation of the institutution of government regulation. He holds, first, that no other rights system is tenable. In terms of such an updated Lockean system, government regulation functions somewhat akin to preventive detention. Such a preventive measure obstructs justice by imposing burdens upon market agents on grounds that they *might* possibly do something wrong. Machan maintains that the valid objectives of government regulation could be pursued — although success could not be guaranteed— via alternative market and legal measures (e.g., product approval centers and tort action, respectively).

Throughout the volume it is the normative elements, so widely ignored in the literature, that make this work unique. The readers will have to determine whether they value different goals, objectives, or principles more deeply than others. Since public policy, including the issue of regulation versus deregulation, is ultimately a matter of *what we should do,* what standards *ought* to guide our conduct, this work is clearly directed toward core issues.

In our efforts to organize the activities that led to this volume, we have been aided immensely by Kenneth S. Templeton, Jr., and A. Neil McLeod of Liberty Fund, Inc. in Indianapolis. We wish also to express our appreciation to the Reason Foundation for the support it gave to much of the initial work in the preparation of this volume. Many of the papers in the book would not have been as sharply focused nor attentive to particular nuances had their authors not had the benefit of comments from conference participants funded and hosted, respectively, by the above institutions.

In addition, we wish to express our deep appreciation to the Pacific Institute for Public Policy Research and, in particular, to the Institute's President, David J. Theroux, and Senior Economist, Charles W. Baird, for their immeasurable support and guidance in the course of preparing this volume. We also wish to thank the contributing authors for their enthusiastic cooperation in exploring the various topics. Needless to say, all the authors are speaking for themselves and not for any institution. Finally, we are indebted to Lynn Scarlett for her considerable editorial assistance.

Tibor R. Machan
Reason Foundation
Santa Barbara, California

M. Bruce Johnson
Pacific Institute for Public
    Policy Research
San Francisco, California

PART I

LAW AND REGULATION

Chapter 1

GOVERNMENT REGULATION OF THE EMPLOYMENT RELATIONSHIP

Thomas R. Haggard

INTRODUCTION

Despite the rhetoric (if not the partial reality) of the current movement toward deregulating the American economy, the employment relationship is and promises to remain one of our most thoroughly "regulated" economic activities.[1] This has not always been the case. With some exceptions, through the early 1900s employment relationships were for the most part governed only by the common-law rules of contract, agency, and tort. The purpose here is to examine from a historical perspective the competing jurisprudential, political, and constitutional philosophies that underlie this shift, with the emphasis on workmen's compensation and wage-and-hour legislation.

Before we can intelligently examine regulation of the employment relation, we must identify the "first principles" or premises upon which the subsequent criticisms will be based.[2] First, we begin with the proposition that, reduced to their most basic terms, "law" and

1. By "regulation" I refer only to the positive, unconditional commands of the legislature (or its administrative and executive agents) to private persons to do or not to do something within an economic context — pay a certain wage, for example, for a specified unit of work.

2. For a more complete discussion of this thesis, see Thomas R. Haggard, "The Right to Work — A Constitutional and Natural Law Perspective," *Journal of Social and Political Affairs* 1 (July 1976): 215–43.

"government" are simply instruments of physical force, and we will define them accordingly.[3] Similarly, we will define "rights" in terms of the moral claims we have against others that they act or forebear from acting, with it being permissible for us to use force or coercion to ensure that these claims are honored.[4] Conversely, our "duties" are to respect the moral claims of others, and a breach in that regard properly subjects us to a response of force.

Next, we will also assume that the proper as well as the exclusive function of government, as the political sovereign, is to vindicate the rights of each individual, through the enactment and enforcement of laws. Moreover, government has the same moral duty to honor the rights of individuals as any private person has (or would have, in a "state of nature").

In sum, once we have identified the substantive parameters of our individual rights and duties, we can then also identify the kinds of human conduct that the law, if it is to function within its proper moral limits, can legitimately regulate, prohibit, or require. What, then, are our moral rights and duties?

In the natural-law tradition, I maintain that human rights and duties flow from the fundamental nature of the human entity. From a conception of humans as essentially autonomous individuals who necessarily and properly live in society but who, through intelligence and volition, are ultimately responsible for achieving their own individual survival and salvation, one may deduce the fundamental, natural-law right of self-ownership—a right that enables a person to do whatever he chooses except violate the equivalent self-ownership rights of others.[5]

More specifically, and avoiding the complex analysis that underlies this equilibrium-of-rights theory, we will simply assert that the right of self-ownership is violated by only six basic kinds of human conduct, as follows: (1) The initiation of force (against person or prop-

3. "Government [acting through law], in its last analysis, is organized force." Woodrow Wilson, *The State* (Boston: D.C. Heath & Co., 1889), p. 572; Accord, Hans Kelsen, *What is Justice?* (Berkeley: University of California Press, 1957), p. 289.

4. Dr. Lawrence Becker provides this comprehensive definition: "The existence of a right is the existence of a state of affairs in which one person (the right-holder) has a claim on an act or forbearance from another person (the duty-bearer) in the sense that, should the claim be exercised or in force, and the act or forbearance not be done, it would be justifiable, other things being equal, to use coercive measures to extract either the performance required or compensation in lieu of that performance." Lawrence C. Becker, *Property Rights* (Boston: Routledge & Kegan Paul, 1977), p. 8.

5. See generally Murray N. Rothbard, *Egalitarianism as a Revolt Against Nature* (Washington, D.C.: Libertarian Review Press, 1974), pp. 58–60.

erty); (2) threats to use such force; (3) theft; (4) fraud; (5) breach of contract; and (6) high risk activities (those activities that have such a high probability of *eventually* violating another's right of self-owner-ship as to indirectly force the other person to take defensive mea-sures). These, of course, are the classically recognized ways in which one may "harm" another in the natural-law sense.[6]

In sum, the natural-law right of self-ownership entitles one to engage in any conduct *except* that which harms other persons. Con-versely, a person's right of self-ownership is violated by the "harm-ful" acts of others—but by nothing else! The individual is, thus, morally entitled to use physical force to resist harm by others or to obtain restitution for injuries and losses caused by such harmful acts, but if he uses force in any other circumstance he will have ini-tiated the breach of a natural-law duty. And finally, since law is sim-ply the surrogate of individual force, from a moral perspective only harmful acts can be made "against the law." With all of this in mind, we can now turn to the specific topic of government regulation of the employment relationship.

WORKMEN'S COMPENSATION LAWS

One of the first areas of the employment relation to be subjected to government regulation in this country was that involving the employ-er's liability for work-related injuries to his employees. The regula-tion in question, as contained in so-called workmen's compensation laws, was passed as a result of a rather massive dissatisfaction with the judicial or common-law rules governing such liability and with their underlying philosophical assumptions.

The common law governing work-related employee injuries was a combination of both tort and contract doctrines. As a matter of tort law, an employer was said to have an affirmative legal duty

> to use reasonable care in selecting suitable fellow employees, to promulgate proper rules which would minimize the risk of hazardous employment, to provide a safe place to work, to install safe appliances, to warn employees of existing dangers and to give instructions in how to avoid these dangers.[7]

6. See Richard Taylor, *Freedom, Anarchy, and the Law* (Englewood Cliffs, N.J.: Prentice-Hall, 1973), pp. 55–69.

7. William H. Simpson, *Workmen's Compensation in South Carolina* (Charlotte, N.C.: Dowd Press, Inc., 1949), p. 20.

If an employer was negligent by failing to exercise reasonable care in those areas and an injury proximately resulted, then such employer was deemed liable to the employee for compensation. The employer, however, had a number of defenses available to him in lawsuits of this nature. There was, first, the defense of contributory negligence, which would exonerate the defendant-employer of *all* liability if it could be shown that the plaintiff-employee's own negligence was also a "substantial cause" of the injury. Second, the law said that an *implied* term of an employment contract was that the employee assumed the risk of injury from ordinary dangers, or even extra-ordinary ones if the employee knew or should have known about them. And third, the law said that the employee also assumed the risk of injuries caused by the negligence or carelessness of fellow employees.[8]

Critics of the Common Law

The objections to this common-law scheme were manifold. The primary argument against it, however, was an emotional if not question-begging one, essentially claiming that large numbers of employees were being injured in industrial accidents. Under the common law the financial burden for this was, for the most part, being shouldered by the injured worker himself. Since this consequence was considered intolerable to a "progressive" and "morally sensitive" society, it was thus concluded that *something* had to be done to ensure that the cost of industrial accidents was borne by someone other than the injured worker himself.[9] We will return to this objection momentarily.

In a similar vein many critics maintained that the various common-law defenses described above were merely the devices by which "conservative" judges, intoxicated by the philosophy of laissez faire, contrived to promote fledgling American industries by wrongly insulating them from liability for their employees' injuries.[10] There does

8. See Crystal Eastman, *Work Accidents and the Law* (New York: Charities Publication Committee, 1910), p. 170.

9. See Harry A. Millis and Royal E. Montgomery, *Labor's Risks and Social Insurance* (New York: McGraw-Hill, 1938), p. 189.

10. See *Compendium on Workmen's Compensation, C. Arthur Williams and Peter S. Barth, directors of Compendium*, ed. Marcus Rosenblum (Washington, D.C.: National Commission on State Workmen's Compensation Laws, 1973), pp. 12–13 ("The courts con-

not seem to be any firm evidence of this bias, but the allegation was well received and is still repeated to this day.[11]

Of a more concrete nature, there were also a number of criticisms addressed to the procedural aspects of the common-law system.[12] It was argued that even employees with meritorious claims under the substantive law were often left less than fully vindicated because of the cumbersome nature of the procedures used in common-law litigation. Objections were raised with regard to the long delays, the allocation of the burden of proof, and even the reluctance of fellow employees to testify against the employer.

There were, in addition, the substantive objections. With respect to the contributory negligence defense, these may have had some merit, not only in the employee injury context but in other areas of tort law as well. It would seem that making contributory negligence an absolute bar to a plaintiff's recovery does not effect a proper vindication of individual rights. Despite the fact that in these situations the plaintiff has himself been negligent, the fact remains that the defendant has breached a duty he owed to the plaintiff, this breach has caused or contributed to the plaintiff's injury, and natural justice would suggest that the defendant thus be made to share in the cost of that injury.

Arguments against the assumption of risk doctrine, on the other hand, were less convincing. There were primarily two. First, critics seized upon the alleged economic justification, which assumed that the costs of these risks would be reflected in the employee's wages (thus mitigating against *additional* recovery from the employer).[13]

---

sidered the needs of developing industry to have priority over the needs of injured workers [and] many judges were management oriented. . . . "); Simpson, *Workmen's Compensation in South Carolina*, p. 22 (the common-law cases indicate "the desire of judges to encourage large industrial undertakings by making the burdens on them as light as possible.")

11. See Richard A. Posner, "A Theory of Negligence," *The Journal of Legal Studies* 1 (January 1972): 29–96.

12. See generally Eastman, *Work Accidents and the Law*, pp. 186–87; J. E. Rhodes, *Workmen's Compensation* (New York: Macmillan Company, 1917), p. 13; Abner Brodie, "The Adequacy of Workmen's Compensation as Social Insurance: A Review of Developments and Proposals," *Wisconsin Law Review* 1963 (January 1963): 59–60.

13. Justice Lemuel Shaw, for example, observed that "[H]e who engages in the employment of another for the performance of specified duties and services, for compensation, takes upon himself the natural and ordinary risks and perils incident to the performance of such services, and in legal presumption, the compensation is adjusted accordingly." Farwell v. Boston & Worcester Railroad Co., 45 Mass. (4 Met.) 49, 57 (1842). See also Murray v. South Carolina Railroad Co., 26 S.C.L. (1 McMul.) 385, 402 (1841), (Johnson, concurring): "No prudent man would engage in any perilous employment, unless seduced by greater wages than he could earn in a pursuit unattended by an unusual danger."

This theory, however, was said to be "unsupported by the facts," and probably correctly so.[14] Neither claim, however, is terribly important from the perspective of moral philosophy.

The second broad criticism of the assumption of risk doctrine claimed that since the employee's alleged consent to assume these risks was a result of the "inequality of the bargaining power" of the respective parties, such consent need not be recognized by the law.[15] In other words, because of this alleged inequality, the employment contract containing both express and implied terms need not necessarily be enforced according to those terms. Rather, a "fairer" set of rights and duties could be supplied by operation of law.

Inequality of Bargaining Power

This notion of an inequality of bargaining power, with the employee suffering the inferior position in comparison to the employer, is a recurring one and indeed may be the primary asserted justification for the regulation of employment terms that would otherwise be set by contract. It thus deserves some discussion.

Bargaining power has been described as "a vacuous concept of little analytical substance."[16] Even those economists who believe in the concept's utility cannot agree on what it really means or how relative bargaining powers are to be determined or measured. For our purposes, however, an explanation will suffice that is a fairly accurate, though simplistic reflection of what noneconomic commentators, at least, probably mean by the term.

One facet of the inequality in question apparently pertains to the relative intelligence, experience, and bargaining techniques of the two parties. But the question remains as to why the exercise of such a power or advantage by an employer should be considered a harm to the employee, thus justifying coercive restraints by the law. The natural rights philosophy outlined earlier presupposes that individuals will in fact differ in their inherent skills, in their training, and in the ranges of their experience; they are equal only in their natural lib-

14. Eugene Wambaugh, "Workmen's Compensation Acts: Their Theory and Their Constitutionality," *Harvard Law Review* 25 (December 1911): 130.

15. See Eastman, *Work Accidents and the Law*, p. 188.

16. Armen A. Alchian and William R. Allen, *University Economics* (Belmont, Calif.: Wadsworth Publishing Co., 1967), p. 420.

erty to use their skills, training, and experience to their best possible advantage. Put differently, the exercise of this bargaining advantage is a "right" of an employer and cannot, thus, be characterized as a harm to an employee however offensive we may find that kind of conduct from a higher moral perspective.

Inequality of bargaining power, however, also apparently refers to something more than the relative skills of the two parties. Many times it is used, rather, to refer to their relative "market positions." This, in turn, apparently means that A has a superior market position if A's alternative to contracting with B is relatively more advantageous to him than B's alternative is advantageous to B. For example, the employer's alternative to contracting with worker #1 is frequently to contract with a substantially identical worker #2; but worker #1's alternative to contracting with the employer may be not to work at all, or to work in another industry, or perhaps even in another town. Thus, the employer enjoys a relatively more advantageous alternative (to contracting with the worker) than the alternative available to the employee; supposedly, this gives the employer a superior bargaining power over the terms and conditions of the contract.

It is even harder here to see why the exercise of such a bargaining power should be considered a harm, subject to correction by the coercive office of the law. This is simply a matter of the availability and relative or comparative desirability of certain market alternatives—a matter over which the employer certainly lacks total control and for which he should not be held responsible. Is the employer to be faulted or blamed because a worker would rather contract with him than pursue whatever other alternative is available? I think not. Thus, the fact that the employee's consent to assume the risk of certain injuries was obtained by virtue of the employer's superior bargaining power is, standing alone, insufficient as a justification for later relieving the employee of that risk.

The Fellow Servant Defense

The final employer defense, that of the fellow servant rule, produced, by and large, the most opposition. As a form of assumption of risk, the fellow servant rule was opposed on many of the grounds previously discussed. But what seemed to incense the critics most was the fact that the fellow servant rule was also an exception to the general common-law rule of *respondeat superior*, under which the employer was generally liable for the harms done by his agents and employees to others. The question, however, is whether this exception was justified? [17]

The matter is not completely free from doubt. The South Carolina case to first adopt the fellow servant rule in this country had two strong dissents, and none of the arguments either way are particularly persuasive. [18] One need not, however, get unduly exercised about the fellow servant rule, or indeed the other facets of the assumption of risk doctrine. The courts, after all, were merely saying that this was an *implied* term of the employment contract, leaving the parties free to allocate these risks differently through express terms to that effect. [19] By the same token, placing the burden "upon the business, as it were, by a sort of implied contract that the employer, recognizing the risks necessary to his business, assumes the burden of compensating therefor," [20] would not be terribly objectionable — provided such an allocation of the burden could again be changed through an express term to the contrary. Unfortunately, however, the detractors of the fellow servant and assumption of risk doctrines wanted the presumption not only reversed but also made irrebuttable — in essence, taking it out of the hands of the contracting parties altogether and making it a politically imposed allocation of risk.

17. For a modern view that maintains it was justified, see Posner, "A Theory of Negligence," p. 44.

18. Murray v. South Carolina Railroad Co., 26 S.C.L. (1 McMul.) 385 (1841).

19. It is important to remember that assumption of the risk was a contract term "implied in fact" (based on the court's view of the probable intent of the parties) rather than "implied in law" (imposed by law regardless of the intent of the parties). Thus, the courts frequently indicated that an employer may expressly agree to assume the risks incident to employment which, under the common law, would ordinarily be assumed by the employees. See Rork v. Klein, 206 Iowa 809, 221 N.W. 460 (1928); O'Bierne v. Stafford, 87 Conn. 354, 87 A. 743 (1913). Posner, justifying the fellow servant rule in utilitarian terms, notes that "if the fellow servant did not accomplish an efficient division of safety policing functions between employer and employee, we would expect to find the parties abrogating the rule by contract. Yet the sample contains only one case in which the basis of a suit for injuries sustained by an employee was an agreement by the employer to indemnify him for accidental injury regardless of fault, rather than the employer's common law or statutory duty." Posner, "A Theory of Negligence," p. 71.

20. Lewis C. Williams, "Compulsory Workmen's Compensation Laws," *Case & Comment* 22 (September 1915): 298.

Employers' Liability Statutes

As a result of all these specific objections to the various common-law doctrines, in the late 1800s and early 1900s a number of states and the federal government passed so-called employers' liability statutes which modified or abolished one or more of the employer's three principal defenses.[21]

The reformers were not, however, satisfied with these steps. In the first place, the procedural unwieldiness of the common-law system remained a problem even under the new statutes. But more important, there was also still the matter of the unavoidable accident, employee injuries that were not the fault of the employer, fellow employees, the employee himself, or anyone else—injuries for which the law provided no relief even after abolition of the various defenses. It was thus determined that the entire common-law system had to be abandoned.

The ideological roots of the proposed substitute for the common law, the so-called workmen's compensation principle, trace back to the Prussian philosophical and political theories of the 1800s. Frederick the Great, for example, is reported to have believed that the state had the affirmative duty "to provide sustenance and support of its citizens who cannot provide sustenance for themselves. The state is entitled and is bound to take such measures as will prevent the destitution of its citizens."[22] Contemporary German political philosophers likewise argued "that many of the misfortunes, disabilities and accidents of individuals are ultimately social and not individual in origin, and that the state is therefore 'not to be negative nor to have a mere police function, but to be filled with Christian concern, especially for the weaker members.' "[23]

This "Christian concern" led to the enactment in 1876 of a voluntary employee accident insurance law; but the intended beneficiaries of this concern were unappreciative of the opportunity and the German worker's failure to participate made it clear, in the words of a later U.S. commissioner of labor, "that the most dependent class could only be reached by the strong hand of the state."[24] Participation was thus made compulsory!

21. Quoted in *Compendium on Workmen's Compensation*, ed. Rosenblum, p. 15.
22. Ibid., p. 15.
23. Ibid., p. 15.
24. Ibid., p. 15.

Intellectual Climate for Reform

Adoption of the workmen's compensation principle was slow in England and even slower in America, where the ideas of a limited state, of individual liberty, and of a laissez faire economic policy by government were deeply engrained in the social and legal fabric of the country. To the dismay of the social reformers of the early 1900s, the United States thus lagged far behind the countries of continental Europe in providing comprehensive compulsory accident insurance for its industrial citizens. But this was to change. Three elements of the newly emerging intellectual climate of the early 1900s contributed most heavily to the ultimate acceptance in this country of the workmen's compensation principle.[25]

There was, first, the philosophy of *humanitarianism*, evidenced by a growing concern for the physical welfare of one's fellow man. The plight of urban dwellers, and industrial workers and their families in particular, absorbed the attention of many compassionate people. The era thus saw a phenomenal growth of private charitable organizations and the development of a "social gospel" among the churches. The plight of the injured worker was naturally brought to light and much sympathy was generated on his behalf.

Second, there was the matter of *collectivism*. In the words of one recent commentator on the history of economic regulation, under the collectivist viewpoint,

> Society rather than the individual was looked upon as being *responsible* for many of the evils and problems of a "highly civilized and complex community." Collective [societal] action was necessary to control and supplement individual economic activity—to correct or prevent its abuses and to make it an instrument for the general welfare.[26]

Collective moral responsibility for industrial accidents was felt with special acuteness, as it was society at large that benefited from the vast material wealth generated by this injury-producing industrial system. Thus, while denying recovery to an employee whose work injury was totally his fault rather than the employer's could possibly be justified in "an entirely individualistic moral code," it was argued

25. See generally James E. Anderson, *The Emergence of the Modern Regulatory State* (Washington, D.C.: Public Affairs Press, 1962), pp. 7–12.
26. Ibid., p. 11 (emphasis added).

that a different result was to be reached "when considerations of social morality are introduced."[27]

These strains of humanitarianism and collectivism joined hands with the political philosophy of *progressivism* to thus provide a comprehensive justification for wide-ranging changes in industrial accident law. This is because the progressives, like Frederick the Great,

> viewed the government as an instrument to be used rather than shunned in their attempts to bring about economic and social justice. They believed the general welfare could best be promoted by substituting the *positive state* for the policy of laissez faire.[28]

This, of course, is the keystone in the argument for *any* kind of social legislation. The progressives of the era viewed government, not as a coercive force designed to restrain evil, but as a benevolent instrument for good—an institution uniquely capable, or so they thought, of getting things done in a speedy and efficient fashion, albeit through the use of force.

In any event, the movement toward the workmen's compensation principle was irresistible within this climate. In 1902 Maryland became the first state to adopt a state-supervised cooperative accident insurance fund. And by 1925 workmen's compensation statutes had been adopted in twenty-four states. The pace continued thereafter, although it was not until 1948 that Mississippi finally made it unanimous. What, then, are the substantive elements of this new approach to an old problem?

The Workmen's Compensation Principle

To begin with, the workmen's compensation principle jettisons entirely the common-law concept of "fault." As one early commentator put it,

> The naive notion that someone was negligent or at fault whenever an accident occurred, and that justice demanded merely the ascertaining of who had been guilty or at fault, has been abandoned. The presumption is in favor of assess-

---

27. Arthur Larson, "The Nature and Origins of Workmen's Compensation," *Cornell Law Quarterly* 37 (Winter 1952): 209.
28. Anderson, *The Emergence of the Modern Regulatory State*, p. 8 (emphasis added).

ing the cost upon the employer, not because he is personally responsible, but as a matter of social policy.[29]

Under the principles articulated in the first part of this essay, civil liability is necessarily limited to situations where one person has caused or is otherwise responsible for some harm to another. In the absence of such fault, there is absolutely no moral justification for using the force of law to require one party to pay compensation to another. Whether or not an employer has such a responsibility in the industrial accident context is a difficult question and one that the common law may not have adequately resolved. To abandon the idea of fault or responsibility altogether is, however, unacceptable.

A second essential component of the workmen's compensation principle deserving mention concerns the matter of actual recompense. Although recovery is virtually certain, the amount recovered is limited, which is to say that the injured employee is precluded from suing for the higher figure he might recover with the common-law tort measure of damages. In other words, "the right to benefits and amount of benefits are based largely on a social theory of providing support and preventing destitution, rather than settling accounts between two individuals according to their personal deserts or blame."[30] It is certainly objectionable to impose liability where there has been no breach of what might be called a natural-law duty—which is what the "no-fault" component of the workmen's compensation principle accomplishes. But equally objectionable is the notion of denying a person full restitution when a natural-law right has been violated—which is what the second component of the principle does!

In any event, in combination the two components of the compensation principle represent a so-called social compromise. In the words of the leading textbook on the subject,

> Compensation, when regarded from the viewpoint of employer and employee represents a compromise in which each party surrenders certain advantages in order to gain others which are of more importance both to him and to society. The employer gives up the immunity he otherwise would enjoy in cases where he is not at fault, and the employee surrenders his former right of full

29. Millis and Montgomery, *Labor Risks and Social Insurance*, p. 198.
30. Larson, "The Nature and Origins of Workmen's Compensation," p. 207.

damages and accepts instead a more modest claim for bare essentials, represented by compensation.[31]

On its face, this compromise sounds reasonable enough. But whether it should be imposed by law, rather than left to the discretion of the parties involved, is quite another question! Nevertheless, it represents the essence of the workmen's compensation principle.

The Supreme Court Response

It has been said that in America all great political and social issues eventually reach the Supreme Court for resolution on a constitutional basis. It should be no great surprise to learn, therefore, that so great a deviation from our common-law and natural-rights traditions as is reflected in the workmen's compensation principle would be challenged in the courts on the grounds of its alleged inconsistency with our basic charter.

The argument, in sum, was that these laws were simply beyond the scope of the states' police power—a power that is said to be implicit in the constitutional scheme. In the words of one early state court that held the workmen's compensation laws to be unconstitutional, "in order to sustain legislation under the police power, the courts must be able to see that its operation tends in some degree to prevent some offense or evil, or to preserve public health, morals, safety, and welfare."[32] This court could not see such a purpose in the workmen's compensation law and thus declared it to be unconstitutional.

The proponents of a limited police power failed, however, to explain adequately the theoretical underpinnings of their approach—as by reference, for example, to the notion that the police power is merely the device by which the state discharges its responsibility to vindicate the natural-law rights of each citizen. They thus left the door open to a constantly expanding conception of the police power—albeit working off the same definitional terminology of preserving the "public health, morals, safety, and welfare." Probably the broadest and most revealing restatement of the police power, which was relied on in another of the early state workmen's compensation

---

31. Wex S. Malone, Marcus L. Plant, and Joseph W. Little, *Cases and Materials on The Employment Relation* (St. Paul, Minn.: West Publishing Co., 1974), p. 48.
32. Ives v. South Buffalo Railroad Co., 201 N.Y. 271, 94 N.E. 431, 442 (1911).

cases, was that advanced by Justice Oliver Wendell Holmes, as follows:

> [I]f we have a case within the reasonable exercise of the police power, no more need be said [i.e. *a fortiori*, the legislation does not violate individual constitutional rights].
>
> It may be said in a general way that the police power extends to all the great public needs. It may be put forth in aid of what is sanctioned by usage, or held by the prevailing morality or strong and predominant opinion to be greatly and immediately necessary to the public welfare.[33]

In other words, rather than identifying individual rights by reference to some consistent philosophical system and then defining the scope of the police power by reference to those rights, the Holmesian approach identifies the police power by reference to so-called public needs (which is whatever the legislature says it is) and then recognizes as individual rights whatever is left untouched by the legislation! Obviously, workmen's compensation laws would be considered constitutional under such a conception of the police power, and this approach ultimately prevailed—not only in the workmen's compensation context but in other regulated areas as well.[34]

WAGE-AND-HOUR LEGISLATION

The second major aspect of the employment relationship to fall under the heel of regulation was that concerning wages and hours.[35] State regulation of wages has solid historical precedent. The labor shortage that resulted from the Black Death of 1348 led the English parliament to decree *maximum* wages for agricultural workers, thus depriving these workers of the bargaining advantage that they had over the landowners who were eager to bid for their services. Similar wage limits, designed to prevent the "exploitation" of employers, were common during the era of mercantilism and such legislation was even enacted in seventeenth-century America. All of these regu-

---

33. Nobel State Bank v. Haskell, 219 U.S. 104, 111 (1911).
34. New York Central Railroad Co. v. White, 243 U.S. 188 (1917).
35. See generally Harry A. Millis and Royal E. Montgomery, *Labor's Progress and Some Basic Labor Problems* (New York: McGraw-Hill, 1938), pp. 278–324, 517–34; John D. Hogan and Francis A. Ianni, *American Social Legislation* (Westport, Conn.: Greenwood Press, 1956), pp. 328–36; Frank T. deVyver, "Regulation of Wages and Hours Prior to 1938," *Law and Contemporary Problems* 6 (Summer 1939): 323–32.

lations were, however, swept away when the doctrine of laissez faire held reign in the late eighteenth and early nineteenth centuries. But the philosophy of regulation began to reassert itself around the middle of the century.

The first modern comprehensive minimum-wage statutes were passed in the various states of Australasia, beginning with New Zealand in 1894. The legislation was ostensibly designed to combat the alleged evils of "sweatshop" operations, of which low wages were but one component. The new laws thus compelled employers in the covered industries to pay "living" or "fair" wages, as determined by wage boards consisting of representatives from employers, workers, and the public. Britain followed suit with similar legislation in 1909. Again, it was the practice of "sweating" that precipitated the agitation for minimum-wage legislation in England.

Birth of the Minimum Wage

In the United States, public pressure to correct the evils of sweatshops and low wages began to intensify around the turn of the century. Some nonlegislative approaches to the problem were first made. The National Consumers League, formed in 1899, promulgated "fair house" standards calling for decent working conditions and a $6 minimum weekly wage. Employers who complied were entitled to put the fair house label on their goods and consumers were expected to buy only those goods that bore this label. The program, however, was ineffective. Encouraged, in comparison, by the reported "success" of the various Commonwealth countries in legislating a minimum wage, and armed with the heart-rending reports of the "muckrakers" on the poverty (and consequent vice) in which many women workers lived, the league and others began directing their efforts toward the passage of minimum-wage laws — limited, of course, to women. "Public opinion," the early proponents of the laws recognized, "was still too essentially individualistic — too thoroughly permeated with the philosophy of laissez faire, too inseparably wedded to the ideology of the preceding century — to tolerate regulation of the wages of male workers."[36]

---

36. Millis and Montgomery, *Labor's Progress and Some Basic Labor Problems*, p. 302. Oklahoma was the first state, in 1937, to include men in its minimum-wage law.

In 1912 Massachusetts became the first state to enact a minimum-wage law, and other states soon began to do likewise. The fear of unconstitutionality may have restrained some states from acting, but this was apparently resolved in 1917 when the U.S. Supreme Court, by a four-to-four vote, left standing an Oregon minimum-wage statute. By 1923, fifteen states, the District of Columbia, and Puerto Rico all had minimum-wage legislation. In that year, however, the Supreme Court declared the District of Columbia statute unconstitutional. Attempts were made to rewrite minimum-wage legislation in such a way that it could pass constitutional muster, but the Supreme Court rejected these efforts in a 1936 decision declaring unconstitutional a New York law that had taken the new approach. The setback was only temporary. In the following year, as a part of its overall capitulation to the New Deal, the Supreme Court upheld a Washington minimum-wage law, thus opening the door for further legislation.

By 1939, however, only an additional ten states had enacted minimum wage laws — all, with one exception, still limited to women and minors. Acceptance of the idea of a comprehensive minimum-wage law was undoubtedly slowed, in part, by the position of organized labor, at least in the early days. Samuel Gompers, for example, once wrote that "we want a minimum wage established, but we want it established by the solidarity of the working men themselves through the economic forces of their trade unions rather than by any legal enactment."[37] Industrial unions, on the other hand, were more amenable to the idea of the minimum wage, and in 1938 the United Mine Workers formally endorsed the idea.

The first federal involvement in wage regulation in the private sector occurred under the National Industrial Recovery Act of 1933. Under this act minimum wages were made a part of the codes that were formulated and approved for various industries. The NIRA was, however, declared unconstitutional in 1935.

Finally, in 1938, Congress enacted the Fair Labor Standards Act. This act provides comprehensive minimum-wage coverage and remains the primary legislation dealing with that particular matter. The constitutionality of the act was sustained by the Supreme Court in 1941. Until recently, public debate has focused on what the compulsory minimum wage should be and who should be covered, rather than whether there should be a compulsory minimum wage at all.

37. *International Moulders Journal* 49 (April 1913).

Regulating Hours

The regulation of hours was accepted in this country at a much earlier date than the regulation of wages. In 1847 New Hampshire passed a law mandating no more than ten hours of work a day for women. The statute, and others like it in other states, was apparently ineffective, and the first truly enforceable maximum-hour law for women was passed by Massachusetts in 1879.

The idea of a maximum workday was subsequently extended to cover some men, especially those in hazardous industries or in transportation, where public safety was at stake. Utah passed an eight-hour-day statute for miners in 1898. This provoked the first major constitutional attack, but the statute was upheld by the Supreme Court — a decision that encouraged other regulatory ventures by the states. The federal government itself, in 1907, got into the act by decreeing a sixteen-hour day for railroad workers. But maximum-hour legislation for men in other industries was declared unconstitutional by the Supreme Court in a 1905 decision, and organized labor was relatively indifferent to this kind of legislation for its male members, thinking it somehow unmasculine to whimper for shorter hours. Organized labor felt different about protecting women, however, and maximum-hour laws for them continued apace — their constitutionality being sustained by the Supreme Court in a number of cases. By 1939, forty-four states had maximum-hour legislation, five of which applied equally to men as well as to women; a number of additional states covered men in specific industries.

At the federal level the NIRA codes generally called for shorter working hours, as part of the "share the work" approach. But the primary federal involvement again came in the Fair Labor Standards Act of 1938, which provides comprehensive regulation of the hours of work for much of the American work force.

Wage-and-Hour-Law Debate

As was true with respect to workmen's compensation, the philosophy of humanitarianism played an instrumental role in the wage-and-hour-law debate. Workers, particularly women, laboring for long hours at "starvation" wages struck a responsive chord in the collective conscience of the era, especially when postured against the greedy evils of the profit system.

In addition, as in the case of workmen's compensation, what was essentially at stake was an attempted redefinition of the proper function of the state. In a revealing essay entitled "The Philosophy of Labor Legislation," W. F. Willoughby notes that political reform has two distinct tasks.

> It must convince the people, and their representatives, first, that the specific result sought to be accomplished is in itself a desirable one; and, second, that this result is one which can, and should, be accomplished through political action.[38]

Humanitarians and reform-minded economists had, he said, made the case for the desirability of wage-and-hour legislation; but the second task remained unfulfilled.

> Back in their minds the American public are still dominated by the dogmas of laissez-faire and individualism. . . . They still are influenced, though often unconsciously, by the doctrine that all resort to the state is to be deprecated. To the conception of the state as a powerful agent for the accomplishment of positive good they lend but a reluctant ear.[39]

Finally, the arguments in favor of wage-and-hour regulation reveal that a new conception of rights, liberty, and freedom was being postulated. Particularly assailed were rights of the old, natural-law variety—which, in the Lockean tradition, prohibited physical aggression or its equivalents (acts of harm, as previously defined), but otherwise left the parties to suffer or enjoy the consequences of their own voluntary relationships. One early text on the subject put it this way:

> "Rights" are recognized as relative, not absolute, things—things that are of social creation, not "inalienable." To dismiss the possibility of wage regulations in such an economic system with the glib pronunciamento that it is contrary to "natural law" is as great an intellectual sin as is the antithetical one of uncritical espousal of attempts to control without recognition of the distributive forces striving to work themselves out in the system of capitalistic enterprise; to say that such attempts are a "manifest violation of the sacred rights" of employer and employee is to expose oneself to the charge of

---

38. W. F. Willoughby, "The Philosophy of Labor Legislation," *American Labor Legislation Review* 4 (March 1914): 38.
39. Ibid., p. 39.

a social romanticism ill becoming one who professes realistic concern in the economic problems of the 1930's.[40]

In lieu of natural-law rights — which are essentially negative, namely the right of each individual to be left alone in the pursuit of his own happiness — the early proponents of wage-and-hour laws and other forms of social legislation came forward with a new concept of rights — essentially affirmative, namely *the right to be provided with something*. As was stated somewhat later in a Democratic party platform, that party promised to "reaffirm the *economic bill of rights* that Franklin Roosevelt wrote into our national conscience sixteen years ago," including "the right to a useful and remunerative job in the industries or shops or farms or mines of the nation" and "the right to earn enough to provide adequate food and clothing and recreation."

A parallel redefinition of "freedom" or "liberty" was also taking place at the time. In contrast to the view that "liberty signifies the absence of [impermissible] restraints imposed by other persons upon our own freedom of choice and action,"[41] the proponents of wage-and-hour legislation conceived of liberty more in the sense of being affirmatively provided with the economic means and opportunities that make choice "meaningful." This Willoughby called "real freedom" and "real liberty."[42] This same author also conceded

> that, in asking for the imposition of certain conditions, we are infringing to that extent upon the *theoretical liberty of contract*. But . . . we believe that we can maintain that such restrictions are far more than compensated for by the greater *practical freedom* in other respects conferred upon the people affected.[43]

Thus, wage-and-hour legislation was based on the belief that, in the interest of the state and out of a humanitarian concern for the individual himself, the civil society should insure the economic well-being of each individual, a freedom to which each individual and society have a rightful entitlement.

---

40. Millis and Montgomery, *Labor's Progress and Some Basic Labor Problems*, p. 279.

41. Edward S. Corwin, *Liberty Against Government* (Baton Rouge: Louisiana State University Press, 1948), p. 7.

42. Willoughby, "The Philosophy of Labor Legislation," pp. 39–40.

43. Ibid., pp. 41–42 (emphasis added).

Capitulation of the Courts

Again, however, this was not an idea that escaped vigorous attack at the constitutional level. Unlike the somewhat easy capitulation of the courts to the idea of workmen's compensation, the judicial acceptance of the regulation of wages and hours had a much rockier history. Indeed, judicial opposition to the idea is said to have marked an entire era of the Supreme Court—the so-called heyday of substantive or economic due process rights. Yet, calling it an "era" is somewhat misleading.

The conventional wisdom is that up until its total capitulation to the pressures of the New Deal, the Supreme Court was rigorous and consistent in upholding the constitutional liberty of contract against regulatory encroachments—for which the Court was the object of massive and continuing criticism, derision, and excoriation. To the extent that the early Court was a true defender of liberty of contract, the latter is of course unjustified. Unfortunately, the Court was not nearly as rigorous or consistent as its detractors would have us believe, and its early decisions reveal the seeds of the philosophies that eventually destroyed the Court as a defender of economic liberty.

Indeed, in the very first case in the area, *Holden* v. *Hardy*, decided in 1898, the Court sustained the constitutionality of a Utah eight-hour law for certain mine workers, and in doing so advanced practically all of the justifications that were, after some intervening rejections, ultimately to prevail on the issue as a whole.[44]

In *Holden* the Court began with the premise of the legal realists that law—including the penumbra, at least, of constitutional law—is a philosophically rootless but "progressive science" and consequently must "adapt itself to new conditions of society, and, particularly, to the new relations between employers and employees as they arise."[45] Determining the proper adaptation, moreover, is a function of the legislature.[46] The Court thus noted, with respect to the par-

---

44. 169 U.S. 366 (1898). See generally, Bernard H. Siegan, *Economic Liberties and the Constitution* (University of Chicago Press, 1980).

45. Ibid., p. 387.

46. With respect to the power of a legislature to "adapt" the liberty of contract out of the constitution altogether, the Court simply noted that "this right of contract . . . is itself subject to certain limitations which the State may lawfully impose in the exercise of its

ticular kind of work being regulated, that "these employments, when too long pursued, the legislature has judged to be detrimental to the health of the employees and, so long as there are reasonable grounds for believing that this is so, its decision upon this subject cannot be reviewed by the Federal courts."[47]

The Court, however, not only sustained as "reasonable" the finding of the Utah Supreme Court that long hours in the mines were hazardous to health; the Court went beyond that and provided additional affirmative justification for this kind of legislation. In a passage that reflects many of the ideological viewpoints previously discussed in response to the liberty of contract argument, the Court noted that

> [T]he fact that both parties are of full age and competent to contract does not necessarily deprive the State of the power to interfere where the parties do not stand upon an equality, or where the public health demands that one party to the contract shall be protected against himself. "The State still retains an interest in his welfare, however reckless he may be. The whole is no greater than the sum of all the parts, and when the individual health, safety and welfare are sacrificed or neglected, the State must suffer."[48]

The Court's reliance on an alleged inequality of bargaining power as a basis for setting aside the bargain, its emphasis upon "practical" as opposed to "theoretical" rights, its paternalistic concern for protecting the worker "against himself," and its open recognition of the superiority of the state or collective interest all speak for themselves insofar as the philosophical premises of the Court are concerned.

Given the breadth of the Supreme Court's holding and reasoning in *Holden,* one would have thought that virtually any maximum-hour law could have withstood constitutional scrutiny. Such was not the case however. Subsequently, in 1905, the Court struck down as unconstitutional a New York law limiting the hours of male bakery workers to sixty hours per week. *Lochner* v. *New York* represents almost as thorough an exposition on liberty of contract and limited

---

police powers," which "may be lawfully resorted to for the purpose of preserving the public health, safety or morals, or the abatement of public nuisances, and a large discretion is 'necessarily vested in the legislature to determine not only what the interests of the public require, but what measures are necessary for the protection of such interest.'" Ibid., pp. 391–92.

47. Ibid., p. 395.
48. Ibid., p. 397.

government as *Holden* represents the contrary—almost, but not quite, for some concessions to regulation are retained.[49] Justice Rufus W. Peckham, who had dissented (without opinion) in *Holden*, began the Court's opinion with the observation that the New York "statute necessarily interferes with the right of contract between the employer and employees. . . . ," and continued with the assertion that this "general right to make a contract in relation to his business is part of the liberty of the individual protected by the Fourteenth Amendment of the Federal Constitution."[50] If the statute was to be sustained, thus, the burden was on its proponents to show that it fell within the scope of the police power, which relates, Justice Peckham said, to "the safety, health, morals and general welfare *of the public.*"[51]

The Court first considered the statute purely as a piece of labor legislation and concluded that on that basis alone it could not be sustained under the police power.

> There is no reasonable ground for interfering with the liberty of person or the right of free contract, by determining the hours of labor, in the occupation of a baker. There is no contention that bakers as a class are not equal in intelligence and capacity to men in other trades or manual occupations, or that they are not able to assert their rights and care for themselves without the protecting arm of the State, interfering with their independence of judgment and of action. They are in no sense wards of the State.[52]

Implicit in that quotation is, of course, a rejection of the presumption of an inequality of bargaining power between employer and employees so frequently relied on by other courts and commentators as a justification for state intervention in the contracting process.

Viewing the statute then as a health ordinance, the Court first concluded that there was no necessary connection between the hours that a baker worked and the provision of clean and wholesome bread *to the public*—an apparently uncontested factual issue. If the Court had stopped there and said that this thus exhausts the possible police power justifications, all would have been well. In short, the Court could have said flatly that the state has no business interfering with the freely chosen actions and decisions of individuals that affect those individuals alone; and that contracts incorporating such a de-

49. 198 U.S. 45 (1905).
50. Ibid., p. 53.
51. Ibid. (emphasis added).
52. Ibid., p. 57.

cision do not involve a legally cognizable harm that is within the scope of the police power to correct. The Court essentially said that, but then qualified it by adding, "*unless* there be some fair ground, reasonable in and of itself, to say that there is material danger . . . *to the health of the employees*, if the hours of labor are not curtailed."[53]

By making this concession, the Court put itself in the totally vulnerable position of then having to determine that while there were some undoubtedly unhealthful aspects to being a baker, it was not *that* much more unhealthful than other occupations. By taking this approach, the Court opened itself to two objections: First, that the Court was simply wrong in its factual determination, as was argued by one of the dissents; and second, that this represents a substitution by the Court of its judgment for that of the legislature, an allegation that the Court denied, but unconvincingly. In sum, this made it easy for detractors to portray the *Lochner* Court in terms of a "super-legislature" bent on imposing its own ideological dogmas on the American people in conscious disregard of the growing evidence of the deleterious effects of such an ideology on the health and well-being of the citizens of the nation. That public image was ultimately made to stick; it led to the eventual demise of economic due-process doctrine; but the Court brought it on itself by deviating from a consistent theory of individual liberty under which what the individual does vis-à-vis his own health is entirely a matter for the individual to decide, not the state.

The dissent of Justice Holmes in the *Lochner* case is now frequently cited as reflecting the proper view. He starts off by asserting that "this case is decided upon an economic theory which a large part of the country does not entertain."[54] A careful review, however, of the majority opinion reveals no express references to any known economic theories, in the strict sense of the word; the *political philosophy* of liberty of contract is, of course, the basis of the decision, and this is apparently what Holmes had in mind—although one is shocked that he would place the concept of liberty of contract on the same level as, say, the theory of the business cycle.

Justice Holmes then goes on to show what a total and abject majoritarian he really was by asserting the unfettered "right of a majority to embody their opinions in law," however, "injudicious"

53. Ibid., p. 61 (emphasis added).
54. Ibid., p. 75.

or "tyrannical" they may otherwise appear to be—this, at least, with respect to the legislation of "economic theories," which encompasses the liberty of contract and who knows what other fundamental liberties![55]

Next, Justice Holmes dismisses as a "shibboleth" what has long been the cornerstone of most natural- and individual-rights theories, namely the maxim that "every man has freedom to do all that he will, provided he infringes not on the equal freedom of any other man."[56] That was Herbert Spencer's formulation; Holmes put it much more loosely.[57] In any event, Holmes's rejection of it is significant.

Finally, Justice Holmes returned to his thesis that the statute in question merely involved a matter of economic theory and in this regard he asserted that "a constitution is not intended to embody a particular economic theory, whether of paternalism and the organic relation of citizen to the State or laissez faire."[58] Or, as the Supreme Court, which as a body eventually succumbed to this theory of the economic neutrality of the Constitution, later put it: "Whether the legislature takes for its textbook Adam Smith, Herbert Spencer, Lord Keynes, or some other is no concern of ours."[59]

One must take sharp exception to this viewpoint. In the larger sense, of course, all human action is "economic." And if all that is required in order to justify legislative "experiments" (Holmes's term!) in this field is, as another celebrated judge claimed, the requirement that "the subject be one already fairly within the field of rational discussion and interest," then this would suggest that the legislatures are free to pattern social relationships in virtually whatever manner they desire![60]

Even if the economics toward which the Constitution is allegedly neutral is construed in its narrower, "production and exchange of

55. Ibid., p. 75.

56. Herbert Spencer, *Social Statistics* (New York: Schalkenbach Foundation, 1970), p. 95.

57. Holmes referred to it as "the liberty of the citizen to do as he likes so long as he does not interfere with the liberty of others to do the same," *Lochner* v. *New York*, 198 U.S. 45, 75 (1905), a formulation which sounds as if it is somehow sanctioning all kinds of wild and irresponsible behavior, a nuance that I suspect was not lost on Holmes when he paraphrased it in that fashion!

58. Ibid., p. 75.

59. Ferguson v. Skrupa, 372 U.S. 726, 732 (1963).

60. Learned Hand, "Due Process of Law and the Eight Hour Day," *Harvard Law Review* 21 (May 1908): 509.

goods and services" sense, Holmes's thesis is still unacceptable. It is true that the Constitution does not mandate, by name, any specific economic system. But what the Constitution *does* do is guarantee to every individual the freedom to do with himself and his property whatever he chooses, short of imposing harm (as previously defined) on other individuals; and the state is strictly prohibited from interfering with that freedom, its only function being to prevent and redress acts of harm by one individual against another. I would suggest that there is only one known economic system that is capable of existing under these stringent limitations on state power. It is sometimes called laissez faire capitalism; the "free market" is perhaps a better term. But whatever it is called, it is what the Constitution indirectly requires, for all other economic systems necessarily entail an impermissible use of state force in the acquisition and distribution of economic goods. Justice Holmes, thus, was simply wrong.

Holden and *Lochner* represent two radically different approaches to the question of government regulation; both involved the regulation of the number of hours that men could work. When the question of the regulation of the working hours of women arose, the Court thus had a choice. Unfortunately, in *Muller* v. *Oregon* the Court opted in favor of the *Holden* notions of paternalism, inequality of bargaining power, "real" rights, and the overriding interest of collective survival—all with a male chauvinist gloss that is chilling indeed to read today, given our greater sensitivity to the fact that women partake equally of the fundamental rights of all humanity.[61]

The Supreme Court and Wage Regulation

In any event, with the question of government regulation of *hours* left in a somewhat confused constitutional state, the Court next

---

61. The following excerpt is illustrative:

[H]istory discloses the fact that *woman has always been dependent upon man.* He established his control at the outset by superior physical strength, and this control in various forms, with diminishing intensity, has continued to the present.

. . . Education was long denied her, and while now the doors of the school room are opened and her opportunities for acquiring knowledge are great, yet even with that and the consequent increase of capacity for business affairs it is still true that in the struggle for subsistence *she is not an equal competitor with her brother.* Though limitations upon personal and contractual rights may be removed by legislation, there is that in her disposition and habits of life which will operate against a full assertion of

addressed itself to the question of the regulation of *wages.*[62] In this regard, the constitutional law counterpart of *Lochner* was the celebrated case of *Adkins* v. *Children's Hospital of the District of Columbia*, in which the Supreme Court struck down a women's minimum-wage law that Congress had passed for the District of Columbia.[63] One of the plaintiffs was a hospital employer, but the other was a woman who had lost her job because, for the services she provided, her employer could not afford to pay her the wage required by law!

The thrust and central premise of the majority opinion, written by Justice George Sutherland, was that this statute violated the substantive due-process guarantee of liberty. The Court noted:

> That the right to contract about one's affairs is a part of the liberty of the individual protected by this clause, is settled by the decisions of this Court and is no longer open to question. . . . Within this liberty are contracts of employment of labor. In making such contracts, generally speaking, the parties have an equal right to obtain from each other the best terms they can as the result of private bargaining.[64]

Implicit in that quotation is, arguably, a recognition that the concept of critical importance is equality of the *right* to bargain, not equality of actual bargaining position! In any event, the Court went on to assert that "freedom of contract is . . . the general rule and restraint the exception; and the exercise of legislative authority to abridge it can be justified only by existence of exceptional circumstances."[65]

Justice Holmes, in dissent, was full of his usual deference to the wisdom of legislatures. Liberty of contract he dismissed as being a

---

those rights. She will still be where some legislation to protect her seems necessary to secure a *real* equality of right. . . . Even though all restrictions on political, personal and contractual rights were taken away, and she stood, so far as statutes are concerned, upon an absolutely equal plane with him, it would still be true that she is so constituted that she will rest upon and look to him for protection; that her physical structure and a proper discharge for her maternal functions—*having in view not merely her own health, but the well-being of the race*—justify legislation to protect her from the greed as well as the passion of man. The limitations which the statute places upon her contractual powers, upon her right to agree with her employer as to the time she shall labor, are not imposed solely for her benefit, but also largely for the benefit of all (emphasis added).

208 U.S. 412 (1908), pp. 421–22.

62. See also Bunting v. Oregon, 243 U.S. 426 (1917).

63. 261 U.S. 525 (1923).

64. Ibid., p. 545.

65. Ibid., p. 546.

mere dogma having no firm constitutional basis.[66] And this was the view that ultimately prevailed.

West Coast Hotel Co. v. *Parrish*, which accomplished this turn-around, was only a part of the Supreme Court's ultimate capitulation to the New Deal.[67] In *Parrish*, however, the Court was faced with a Washington statute that pegged the minimum wage for women at a level "adequate to supply them the necessary cost of living and to maintain themselves in health" — the same standard that had been declared unconstitutional in *Adkins*. The majority opinion, sustaining the constitutionality of this statute, was written by Justice Charles E. Hughes. The overall flavor of his opinion is adequately demonstrated by the following quotation:

> In each case the violation alleged by those attacking minimum wage regulation for women is deprivation of freedom of contract. What is this freedom? The Constitution does not speak of freedom of contract. It speaks of liberty and prohibits the deprivation of liberty without due process of law. In prohibiting that deprivation the Constitution does not recognize an absolute and uncontrollable liberty. Liberty in each of its phases has its history and connotation. But the liberty safeguarded is liberty in a social organization which requires the protection of law against the evils which menace the health, safety, morals and welfare of the people. Liberty under the Constitution is thus necessarily subject to the restraints of due process, and regulation which is reasonable in relation to its subject and is adopted in the interests of the community is due process.[68]

That, in essence, writes liberty of contract, and potentially any other individual right, out of the Constitution altogether!

The Court then proceeded to justify this result by reference to some of the most antiliberty language the Court has ever used—namely, the opinion in *Holden* v. *Hardy*, reinforced by the chauvinism of *Muller*. The Court reiterated the inferiority, in bargaining power and otherwise, of women as employees; it reaffirmed the paternalistic function of the state in protecting people from their own indiscretions; it subscribed anew to the superiority of the interests the community and "the race" have in the health and well-being of their component parts, especially mothers; and it again favored "real" equality over more theoretical or jural equality.

66. Ibid., p. 568.
67. 300 U.S. 379 (1937).
68. Ibid., p. 391.

This case, thus, represents the end of an era in which liberty of contract struggled, ultimately unsuccessfully, to become a viable constitutional concept. It is apparent—in light of the exceptions to the liberty that were allowed by the Court, even at its strongest moments—that the Court was never really firm in its philosophical premises or consistent in their application. Eventually, the essential illogic of all the liberty of contract cases, some going one way and some going another, was used as a powerful weapon in the elimination of the concept altogether.

THE FUTURE PROSPECTS

So what does the future hold? The prospects for greater employment liberty are dim. Before the deregulation of the employment relationship can become a reality, a radical change in the intellectual climate of this country must first take place—a change that the proponents of a free society can effectuate *only* by being vociferous educators.

At the most abstract level, there must be a renewed understanding about the nature of rights and what the rights of man really are. The concept of rights is a powerful one, perhaps the most powerful of all human ideas, a necessary ally in any political movement of a basic nature. Until very recently, however, our thinking about rights had become extremely sloppy; the concept had degenerated into little more than a catalog of understandable human wants. At the popular level, it may still consist of this. But certain scholars are again beginning to think rigorously about rights, and it is within this rarified forum of philosophical debate that the movement must begin.

Similarly, there must be a return to the original American understanding of the true nature of the state and of the corresponding moral limitations on the functions that it can properly perform. We have gone through a period, corresponding with the rise and maturity of the regulatory movement, when government was extolled from pulpit and political stump alike as the great benefactor of mankind, as the only force capable of correcting the social ills that confront us, and even as the ultimate provider of material goods and services of indefinite variety. On the other hand, the popular disillusionment with government in vogue at the moment, from which the current deregulation movement draws much of its sustenance, is, I fear, somewhat shallow in its premises. It is more a reaction of annoyance and inconvenience, caused by the inefficiency, corruption, stupidity, and meddlesomeness of the current crop of politicians and bureaucrats than it is a reflection of a well-founded belief in the theory of limited government. Yet, that theory, even if in a popularized form, must be marketed and sold if deregulation is to be accomplished and have any permanence at all.

However, the educating task of the would-be deregulator does not end there. There are people who will express *abstract* intellectual assent to the ideas of individual rights and limited government, but who fear what they think may be the immediate *practical* consequences of deregulation of the employment relationship. They foresee a reversion to sweatshop conditions, starvation wages, 14-hour workdays, and armies of disabled industrial workers living on the meager charity of the community. Thus, the economist's tasks are: (1) to show (if such is the case, as I have reason to believe) that the workman's improved situation—allegedly effected by regulation—would have occurred naturally under the free market; (2) to identify the undesirable side effects of regulatory interference with the operation of that market; and (3) to otherwise demonstrate the feasibility of various free-market alternatives to regulation.

In the last analysis, however, the mere existence of the proper degree of freedom cannot alone ensure the kind of industrial society we would ideally desire. Take employment discrimination on the basis of race, for example—an area of current regulation not specifically covered in this paper. This is conduct that should not be coercively restrained by the state; it is conduct that many people will indulge themselves in despite strong economic incentives to the contrary; and yet it is conduct that, if pervasive, will destroy the stability, tranquility, and perhaps even the existence of the society in which it is practiced. It is also immoral. My final point, thus, is this: While the theory of the free society recognizes the liberty of men to be "evil" (in certain ways), it also presupposes that for the most part they will not exercise their liberty in that way; but that, rather, in their relations with one another, they will at least attempt to adhere to those higher tenets of morality in which regard for the "humanness" of another is the primary instruction. In short, as the state is relieved of its responsibility for achieving the "good society," that responsibility *must* be assumed by the individuals within that society.

Chapter 2

SUBSTANTIVE DUE PROCESS
A Doctrine for Regulatory Control

Norman Karlin

In 1937, with *West Coast Hotel Co.* v. *Parrish*, the era of substantive due process was brought to an ignominious end.[1] From then on, the doctrine was widely condemned. Efforts at revival were strongly resisted and quickly denied. That substantive due process continued to thrive under assumed names and a forced distinction was mere detail. The exigencies of the day required its demise. When that demise came, it was celebrated for what it was, a political event of the first magnitude.[2] Nonetheless, in yielding to what were presumed to be the political realities, the Court surrendered economic principle.[3]

1. 300 U.S. 379 (1937). The decision was anticipated in *Nebbia* v. *New York*, 291 U.S. 502 (1934), in which New York's milk price control regulations were upheld. Attacks on the doctrine of substantive due process were based on the notion that the Court, in reviewing the substance of legislation, was placing on the law its ideological imprimatur – an ideology, it was claimed, having no source in the Constitution and independent of constitutional requirements and directives. Holmes's dissent in *Lochner* v. *New York*, 198 U.S. 45, 90 (1905) is, of course, among the most famous.

There was also the "jurisdictional" objection to the doctrine; but even Justice Louis Brandeis agreed it was settled " . . . that the due process clause of the Fourteenth Amendment applies to matters of substantive law as well as to matters of procedure." Whitney v. California, 274 U.S. 357, 373 (1927) (Brandeis, concurring).

2. See generally William Leuchtenburg, "The Origins of Franklin D. Roosevelt's 'Court-Packing' Plan," *Supreme Court Review* 347 (1966).

3. Although there is an immense literature on the subject of substantive due process, there is little discussion of the economic consequences of the doctrine. In *Nebbia*, note 1, for example, what justification is there for showing a preference for producers and distributors of milk at the expense of consumers? During a severe monetary contraction, raising prices and lowering production is hardly antidotal. See text beginning at footnote 56.

THE DEMISE OF SUBSTANTIVE DUE PROCESS

In abandoning the doctrine of substantive due process, the Court drew a distinction that enabled it to separate property rights from individual rights.[4] It has continued to protect the latter—and today these remain relatively free from legislative interference.[5] As to property rights, however, the Court abdicated its responsibility, which then enabled the legislative branch to proceed without restraint. Under such circumstances it was probably inevitable that regulation would grow, finally to the point of absolutely diminishing returns.[6]

Today the economy is characterized by lagging productivity and continued inflation. Unless some institutional limiting device other than self-restraint is imposed on the Congress, the situation will only worsen.[7] It may then become apparent that cause and effect are rooted in the distinction separating rights. By then, however, it may be too late; and rights, both property and individual, will have succumbed to the regulatory process.

Prior to 1937, the main institutional device employed to hold regulation in check was the doctrine of substantive due process. Operationally, this doctrine imposed the burden of justification on those who favored government interference and expansion, and thus

4. The distinction was made in Justice Harlan Stone's famous footnote 4, *United States* v. *Carolene Products Co.*, 304 U.S. 144, 152–53 (1938). As to the validity of the distinction see footnote 24.

5. See text beginning at footnote 27.

6. This is not to suggest that for a long time regulation had positive, albeit diminishing, returns. It would depend on the regulation. But as this paper points out, the doctrine of substantive due process functioned as an instrument of restraint and forced those enacting regulations under the police power to demonstrate need, a burden not easily discharged. Accordingly, under the restraining influence of substantive due process there was far less regulation and its impact on production was significantly less damaging.

The incredible extent to which regulation has intruded on the economy has been comprehensively documented by Murray L. Weidenbaum. See Weidenbaum, *The Future of Business Regulation* (New York: Amacom, 1979) and Weidenbaum, *Government-Mandated Price Increases, A Neglected Aspect of Inflation* (Washington, D.C.: American Enterprise Institute for Public Policy Research, 1975).

7. As to the notion that legislators are able to police themselves if the policing is against their self-interest, see M. Bruce Johnson, "Planning Without Prices: A Discussion of Land Use Regulation Without Compensation," in *Planning Without Prices*, ed. Bernard H. Siegan (Lexington, Ky.: Lexington Books D.C. Heath & Co., 1977), pp. 88–97; Michael Granfield, "Concentrated Industries and Economic Performance," in *Large Corporations in Changing Society*, ed. J. Westin (1974), p. 145. *Journal of Law and Economics* 18 (1975) is devoted in its entirety to the topic, "economic analysis of political behavior."

functioned within the judicial structure as a limitation on legislative power. When the failure to find justification was translated into judicial overreaching, the Court was accused of lacing its decisions with ideological bias, and the doctrine lost its credibility. The implications were far-reaching. In the language of John Stuart Mill, the "optional" and "necessary" functions of government were no longer distinguishable.[8] In terms of legal reasoning, the burden of justification—of demonstrating constitutionality—was transformed into the burden of demonstrating unconstitutionality. This burden was then placed on those opposing the regulation. To invalidate legislation now required proving a negative, "[a] burden" the Supreme Court has held "virtually impossible to discharge."[9] In the area of property rights, the mechanism for challenging the regulatory process was dealt a near-fatal blow.

Recent Appeals to Substantive Due Process

In holding unconstitutional a Connecticut statute forbidding the use of contraceptives, Justice William O. Douglas, writing for the Court in *Griswold* v. *Connecticut*, attempted to make perfectly clear that his opinion was in no way based on notions of substantive due process.

> [W]e are met with a wide range of questions that implicate the Due Process Clause of the Fourteenth Amendment. Overtones of some arguments suggest that *Lochner* v. *New York* should be our guide. . . . But we decline that invitation as we did in *West Coast Hotel Co.* v. *Parrish.* . . . We do not sit as a superlegislature to determine the wisdom, need and propriety of laws that touch economic problems, business affairs, or social conditions.[10]

Justice Harry Blackmun made a similar effort in *Roe* v. *Wade*, as he prepared to hold unconstitutional the Texas criminal abortion laws.

> We bear in mind, too, Mr. Justice Holmes' admonition in his now vindicated dissent in *Lochner* v. *New York.*

8. John Stuart Mill, *Principles of Political Economy*, ed. J. M. Robson (Toronto: University of Toronto Press, 1965), pp. 799–804.
9. Miller v. California, 413 U.S. 15, 22 (1973).
10. 381 U.S. 479, 480–81 (1965).

"[The Constitution] is made for people of fundamentally differing views, and the accident of our finding certain opinions natural and familiar or novel and even shocking ought not to conclude our judgment upon the question whether statutes embodying them conflict with the Constitution of the United States."[11]

However, in spite of these attempts at disassociation, others on the Court and in the legal community were not convinced.[12] In *Griswold*, Justice Hugo Black read the decision as a return to *Lochnerism*;[13] in *Roe* v. *Wade*, Justice Potter Stewart was equally certain.

[I]n *Griswold* v. *Connecticut*, the Court held a Connecticut birth control law unconstitutional. In view of what had been so recently said in [*Ferguson* v.] *Skrupa*, the Court's opinion in *Griswold* understandably did its best to avoid reliance on the Due Process Clause of the Fourteenth Amendment as the ground for decision. Yet, the Connecticut law did not violate any provision of the Bill of Rights, nor any other specific provision of the Constitution. So it was clear to me then, and it is equally clear to me now, that the *Griswold* decision can be rationally understood only as a holding that the Connecticut statute substantively invaded the "liberty" that is protected by the Due Process Clause of the Fourteenth Amendment. As so understood, *Griswold* stands as one in a long line of [*pre-Skrupa*] cases decided under the doctrine of substantive due process, and I now accept it as such.[14]

If these cases did, in fact, mark the return of substantive due process, at least it could be argued, if justification were needed, that the laws held unconstitutional operated directly on intimate, personal rights. More recently, however, in *Moore* v. *City of East Cleveland*, a case in which an ordinance regulating inhabitants of a household was held invalid, the Court, speaking through Justice Lewis Powell, readily acknowledged that its decision was founded on notions of substantive due process.[15] The opinion counseled "caution and restraint" in the use of the doctrine, but rejected abandonment.[16]

11. 410, U.S. 113, 117 (1973).
12. See Richard Epstein, "Substantive Due Process by Any Other Name: The Abortion Cases," *Supreme Court Review* 159 (1973); John Ely, "The Wages of Crying Wolf: A Comment on Roe v. Wade," *Yale Law Journal* 82 (1975): 920; Laurence Tribe, "The Supreme Court, 1972 Term—Foreward: Toward a Model of Roles in the Due Process of Life and Law, *Harvard Law Review* 87 (1973): 1.
13. 381 U.S., 524.
14. 410 U.S., 167–68.
15. 431 U.S. 494 (1977).
16. Ibid., p. 502.

Justice John Stevens, in a strong concurring opinion, found the ordinance constituted a taking of property without due process of law and without compensation: clearly a return to language of a bygone day.[17]

Again, it could be argued that the *Moore* case could or ought to be restricted to its facts. After all, the housing ordinance had the incongruous effect of making it a crime for a grandmother to live with her grandson. However, four justices dissented and would have upheld the ordinance.[18] Three dissenting opinions were filed, and the tone of the opinions, especially Justice Byron White's, makes clear the case is not to be limited to its facts.[19]

Following the decision in *Moore*, it could certainly be argued that substantive due process had been restored as a viable doctrine in constitutional law decision making. What could not be said is the extent to which the doctrine would be used: whether its use would be confined to cases extreme on their facts—such as *Moore*—or extended to the status it occupied during its heyday.

The doctrine of substantive due process, ostensibly put to rest in 1937, never did, in fact, pass from the constitutional scene. In the area of so-called individual rights, the doctrine was retained, but under different labels—fundamental rights, the new equal protection, irrebuttable presumptions.[20]

17. Ibid., p. 521. Justice Stevens also resurrected *Nectow* v. *City of Cambridge*, 277 U.S. 183 (1928), which can be read as a limitation on *Euclid* v. *Ambler Realty Co.*, 272 U.S. 365 (1926). As to this, see Karlin, "Land Use Controls: The Power to Exclude," *Environmental Law* 5 (1975): 529, 550–52.

18. Justices Warren Burger, Potter Stewart, William Rehnquist and Byron White.

19. Justice White used the occasion to head off what he saw as an attempt to again broaden the doctrine of substantive due process.

20. In *Griswold* v. *Connecticut* and *Roe* v. *Wade*, footnotes 11, 13, and 14 (fundamental rights), the majority opinions were labeled as returns to substantive due process. In *Shapiro* v. *Thompson*, 394 U.S. 618 (1969) (equal protection), Justice John Harlan in dissenting read the majority opinion as " . . . making this court a 'super legislature,' " 394 U.S., 662. See also, Ralph Winter, "Poverty, Economic Equality, and the Equal Protection Clause," *Supreme Court Review* 41 (1972): 100. In *Vlandis* v. *Kline*, 412 U.S. 411 (1973) (irrebuttable presumption), Justice Rehnquist read the majority opinion as masking a substantive due-process rationale. "The [majority] opinion . . . relies heavily on notions of substantive due process that have been authoritatively repudiated by subsequent decisions of the Court." 412 U.S., 463.

Assignment of Rights

The fundamental problem, nicely exposed by use of the doctrine, is the inability of the law to fully assign rights. For example, in *Roe* v. *Wade*, the right of the fetus, which would certainly trigger a legitimate and, conceivably, a compelling state interest during the first trimester, must be ignored or rejected for the opinion to be logically persuasive. But certainly the woman does not have an exclusive right to her body. There are shared rights; not equally shared, of course. Indeed, the law recognizes such minority rights not only in the fetus, but also in the husband and the family. The right of the fetus eventually becomes an equally shared right. The real problem is that any of the described rights can never be exclusive because at crucial moments in time they coexist and are incompatible. As yet, the legal process has devised no satisfactory way of fully and exclusively assigning such rights.[21]

In *Moore*, a similar situation exists. Mrs. Moore owns her home, and ownership carries with it certain rights. But again, these rights are not exclusive. The incidence of nuisance, which the zoning ordinance attempted to anticipate and then abate, implicitly assumed rights in others and, accordingly, limited exclusivity. The housing ordinance, enacted under the police power, expressed the competing interests of others in society. And, the point is, whichever way a decision is rendered, in *Roe* v. *Wade* or in *Moore* v. *East Cleveland*, someone will be harmed. The purpose of the law "is to avoid the more serious harm."[22] In ignoring the interest of the fetus, the Court leaves itself open to the charge that it is deciding in a nonprincipled manner, substituting its beliefs for that of the legislative body. What tends to further destroy credibility in the Court and the governing principle of substantive due process is the notion that the Court could just as well have decided to protect the interest of the fetus. After all, the fetus, when compared to the woman, belongs to a class even more discrete and insular. If it is simply a matter of second-guessing the legislature, then the Court is, in fact, acting as a super-

---

21. Using an economic and Coasian analysis, Posner possibly has. Richard Posner, *Economic Analysis of Law* (Boston: Little, Brown and Co., 1972), pp. 16–18.
22. Coase, "The Problem of Social Cost," *Journal of Law and Economics* 3, no. 1 (1960): 2.

legislature, and it ought to recognize that the legislative judgment has the stronger claim to legitimacy.[23]

To reiterate, the fundamental problem is the inability of the law to fully assign rights and, therefore, entitlements. This inability flaws the reasoning process and is what led disquietingly to the judicially created distinction between property rights and individual rights. The distinction was necessary in order to permit the Court to protect individual rights under the Constitution, while sustaining legislation and regulation limiting property rights under the police power. To be analytically coherent, the distinction required a severely weakened due process clause – one that would yield to the police power. In 1937, in the case of *West Coast Hotel Co.* v. *Parrish*, the due process clause was given, vis-à-vis the police power, such an attenuated status. The effect, when done, left property rights exposed and constitutionally unprotected. However, today, as the cases become more complex, involving regulations that significantly and simultaneously affect both property and individual rights, the distinction is becoming more difficult to sustain.[24] Perhaps the weakening of the distinction helps explain why the doctrine of substantive due process is reemerging as a means for invalidating legislation. At the same time, economic analysis is providing additional insights into the regulatory process, thus necessitating a reexamination of the doctrine.

23. It is probably misleading to think along these lines. The question is not which branch can or ought to be able to trump the other, but rather whether the regulation or legislation is necessary. The preferable structure, suggested here, is one that places the issue on necessity or justification. Judicial review is then simply a matter of determining whether the burden of justification has been discharged. It is not now, nor was it previously, a proxy for judicial preference based on ideology.

24. Examples of such cases are: Village of Belle Terre v. Boraas, 416 U.S. 1, 14-15 (1974) (Marshall, dissenting); Young v. American Mini Theatres, 427-50 (1976); Friedman v. Rogers, 440 U.S. 1, 19-28 (Blackmun, dissenting). As to the distinction itself, in *Lynch* v. *Household Finance*, 405 U.S. 538 (1971), the court said, "[The] dichotomy between personal liberties and property rights is a false one. People have rights. The right to enjoy property without unlawful deprivation, no less than the right to speak or the right to travel, is in truth a 'personal' right. . . . In fact, a fundamental interdependence exists between the personal right to liberty and the personal right in property. Neither could have meaning without the other. That rights in property are basic civil rights has long been recognized." 405 U.S., 552. M. Jensen and W. Meckling put it this way: "Understanding the nature of private rights and the role of government in the system of rights is crucial to understanding why private rights are being gradually whittled away, . . . [I]t is worth pointing out another brilliant fallacy, namely, the false distinction between so-called 'human rights' and 'property rights.' All rights are, of course, human rights; there can be no other kind. Those who use this distinction are simply resorting to a clever semantic ploy. They are fabricating a conflict between one kind of rights ('human') which are 'good' and another kind of rights

Professor R. W. Coase set forth the problem facing the courts.

> The traditional approach has tended to obscure the nature of the choice that has to be made. The question is commonly thought of as one in which *A* inflicts harm on *B* and what has to be decided is: How should we restrain *A*? But this is wrong. To avoid the harm to *B* would inflict harm on *A*. The real question that has to be decided is: Should *A* be allowed to harm *B* or should *B* be allowed to harm *A*? The problem is to avoid the more serious harm.[25]

Thus, the courts reach for a "balancing of harm" test, and then a method for implementing their decisions "to avoid the more serious harm." The Court ought to understand well that property rights have not been fully assigned, nor is the extent of exclusive ownership known. It is insufficient, therefore, to look only at what, in the *Moore* case, for example, Mrs. Moore had lost because of the ordinance, and then to conclude that a taking had resulted. Instead, in *Moore*, the Court implicitly recognized that property rights are not absolute, and the extent of ownership not precisely known. Others have rights in the same property and these rights would be interfered with and harm done to these owners if Mrs. Moore were permitted to use the property as if it were exclusively hers. Mrs. Moore, of course, has been harmed by the ordinance, which seriously interfered with her exclusive use of the property. In *Moore*, as well as in so many other cases, the Court accurately saw the problem as one having reciprocally, although not equally, harmful effects.

Rights in the Marketplace

Ordinarily, in a market situation, where the parties to a transaction are known to each other, the parties to the transaction are free to bargain with one another in their own self-interest until terms are

---

('property') which are 'bad.' Since all rights are human rights, the only possible conflict is between individuals, i.e., conflict over which individual will have what rights." Michael Jensen and William Meckling, *Can the Corporation Survive?* Public Policy Working Paper Series (Rochester, N.Y.: Graduate School of Management, University of Rochester, 1976), p. 17. See also, Director, "The Parity of the Economic Marketplace," *Journal of Law and Economics* 7 (1964): 1; and Coase, "The Market for Ideas," *National Review* 26, no. 39 (Sept. 27, 1974): 1095.

25. Coase, "The Problem of Social Cost," *Journal of Law and Economics* 3, no. 1 (1960): 2.

reached at which a mutually beneficial trade is possible. Such a procedure underlies the law of contracts. In the bargaining process, through the pricing system, the conflict between "nonabsolute" rights and incompatible uses is resolved.

In addition, the pricing system will have already accounted for the interests of others—those not involved in the immediate transaction but who lay claim to rights in it. A promisor who must unavoidably abridge the rights of third parties in fulfilling a promise, must ordinarily contract for the privilege of abridging those rights. That the pricing system takes into account the rights of third parties can be demonstrated by considering the example of a promisor who promises to produce and deliver widgets to a promisee. In order to do this, the promisor may require the labor services of a third party. Yet, the promisor cannot interfere with the third party's right to alternative employment or leisure time, unless the third party voluntarily agrees to exchange that right for pecuniary or nonpecuniary rewards. If the promisor requires the use of a machine owned by a third party, it is not possible (ordinarily) to limit the owner's right to use the machine for other purposes, unless the owner consents to give up that right in exchange for compensation. Thus, the promisor is forced to consider the rights of third parties through the prices charged for entitlements to those rights. This will influence the minimum price the promisor is willing to offer the promisee for fulfillment of the primary contract. Similarly, the promisee, through the offer price of the promisor, is also forced to consider the rights of third parties, although the promisee may have no knowledge of the third parties in question. If, under these circumstances, the first two parties can still strike a bargain, fulfillment of the contract will result in a coherent allocation of resources and property rights, including those rights initially owned by third parties.

A coherent allocation of resources and property rights means that the resources and rights are put to their more highly valued use as *subjectively* set by the parties. If, in the example above, the third party had a use for the machine more profitable than its use to the promisor, the promisor would not have been willing to pay a price high enough to bid the services for the machine away from its alternative use. Under such circumstances, even if the promisor owned the machine, the services of the machine would still have ended up being allocated to the third party. This is because, by virtue of the third party having the more highly valued use, that individual would have been willing to bid more for the services of the machine than they were worth to the promisor. The coherent allocation of a resource or right, therefore, does not depend upon who owns it, but only on whether it is owned.

Thus, problems with conflicting uses of a resource arise only when ownership rights are not and cannot be fully assigned, or when the enormity of transaction costs prevents parties with more highly valued uses for a resource or right from bidding for it. Those seeking to resolve the conflict of competing uses through the regulatory process rather than through the market argue that, because of problems regarding the assignment of rights and transaction costs, market prices inaccurately reflect the rights and interests of third parties. That such problems exist may be true, but those opting for regulation make no attempt to determine the extent of the inaccuracy, and more importantly, to determine whether a right is already in the hands of the party who can benefit most from its use. The benefits accruing to third parties by assigning them rights through the regulatory process (and/or the courts) may be small compared to the harm that primary contractors suffer because third party rights are unavoidably abridged. Yet, to justify regulation, it is sufficient to show that there are rights in the transaction, however small and ill defined, that have not been fully assigned. In *Moore*, the state, in effect, stepped in as trustee for those having such ill-defined rights and was given "standing" to pursue their interests. First, the state noted there was harm against which those interests should be protected. Second, it passed an ordinance that would protect against the harm. Finally, the ordinance was upheld in the lower court through a principle that gives to such ordinances, under the police power, an overwhelming presumption of validity. In effect, the government had allocated to itself property rights in a particular resource, and then, by way of the regulation, had arbitrarily valued those rights as superior.

In *Moore*, the Supreme Court correctly identified the implicit issue as that of avoiding the more serious harm. It then correctly resolved that issue by refusing to accept as conclusive the legislative decision as to the value of the harm to be protected against. The legislative determination, it was understood, was limited to a finding that property rights of some dimension existed in others but had not been assigned. The lower court, on the other hand, in upholding the ordinance, as is customary in such cases, decided that it was sufficient that the legislature had passed the act, and that to disregard its provisions constituted, in effect, an enjoinable offense. What is obvious and disturbing in the lower court's decision and in courts that follow such reasoning is that neither competing uses, nor what constituted the more serious harm, had been considered or adjudicated.

Property Rights and the Police Power

Such judicial behavior, under an attenuated due-process rationale, essentially permits state interference by way of regulation in any situation, merely on a showing that property rights have not been fully assigned and that some rights exist in others. Thus, in property rights cases, as well as in individual rights cases that do not fit into protected molds, no conceptual tool other than substantive due process is capable of forcing first a balancing of harmful effects, and then a decision to avoid the more serious harm. Without a due-process rationale, the only inhibiting strategem is to show the legislation to be irrational. However, this test is so rigorous and so difficult to fulfill, that it cannot provide any serious limitation on police-power enactments.

Under the attenuated due-process rationale, property rights, as we have traditionally known them, have been made subservient to what is presumed to be the public interest or general welfare. The public interest is defined by the legislature, meaning that the strong interests in the community, either the majority or a powerful minority acting as if it were a majority, is able to impose its will through the police power.[26] The restraining influence of the Constitution has been removed.

In yielding to the police power, the Court accepts the legislative (political) assignment of "worth," and then renders a decision that protects that worth. In so doing, the Court redistributes property rights and awards entitlements much as a legislature does. In legal consequence, the police power has been extended so as to undermine many Fifth and Fourteenth Amendment guarantees.

---

26. "Government has coercive power, which allows it to engage in acts (above all, the taking of resources) which could not be performed by voluntary agreement of the members of a society. Any portion of the society which can secure control of the state's machinery will employ the machinery to improve its own position." George Stigler, "Director's Law of Public Income Redistribution," *Journal of Law and Economics* 13, no. 1 (1970): 1.

It is the Constitution that protects property rights, not the police power, which limits them. Thus, the Constitution and the police power are antagonistic toward each other. As the latter is extended, the former is diminished. In this connection, it is instructive to see how the legal process works when constitutional limitations are given priority over the police power.

The Due-Process–Police-Power Relationship

In areas falling within the First Amendment, interference is tolerated only upon a strong showing of necessity.

> Free speech, free press, free exercise of religion are placed separate and apart; they are above and beyond the police power; they are not subject to regulations in the manner of factories, slums, apartment houses, production of oil, and the like.[27]

Nonetheless, speech and forms of speech may and often do produce harmful effects on others. It has, of course, been argued that the state has an interest in protecting those who are harmed by such forms of speech. An analysis seeking to consider the reciprocal effects of speech would have to show the interests of each in the speech of the other, so that a balance could be struck and the more serious harm avoided. Parallel to the property rights cases, interests in speech have not been fully assigned. In fact, in this area, rights are more difficult to assign, and arguably present an a fortiori case for regulation. Nevertheless, unlike property rights cases in which the Court allows the state to exercise its police power by stepping in and protecting those with ill-defined rights, the Court, in deciding speech cases, usually denies such recourse to those claiming harm or injury from the speech. If the language qualifies as speech in the traditional communicative sense, interference is virtually impermissible.[28] Police-power interests are not a sufficient justification for regulation. If the subject matter qualifies as speech, there is virtually no balancing. If the speech carries with it political implications or the exposition of ideas, the presumption is that the speaker's interest so outweighs the interests of those who have been harmed that no balancing is neces-

27. Beauharnais v. Illinois, 343 U.S. 350, 286 (1951), (Douglas, dissenting).
28. See Laurence Tribe, *American Constitutional Law* (Mineola, New York: Foundation Press, 1978), sec. 12–2, pp. 580–84.

sary. The level of scrutiny is always strict.[29] In cases involving fundamental rights, the analysis is much the same. Indeed, in the entire area of individual rights, the reciprocal effects of any transaction are largely ignored. Without a demonstration of a compelling interest, police-power enactments fall before the constitutional limitations. On the other hand, in the area of property rights, police-power enactments, if not irrational, are sustained and protected from the constitutional constraints of due process.

Analysis under the First and Fourteenth Amendments is today exactly opposite.[30] Under the First Amendment, a police-power enactment is rarely allowed to interfere with the constitutional limitation. Under the Fourteenth, if property rights are involved, it almost always is permitted such interference.

In an earlier day, the police power could not shield legislative enactments from the constitutional limitations having to do with "taking" and due process. The same protective tests provided today under the First Amendment were similarly in effect under the Fifth and Fourteenth, with the Constitution operating as a limiting and reactive device.[31] The need for this was stated by Justice Oliver Wendell Holmes.

> When this seemingly absolute protection [the protection of private property under the Fifth and Fourteenth Amendments] is . . . qualified by the police power, the natural tendency of human nature is to extend the qualification more and more until at last private property disappears.[32]

In *Two Concepts of the Rule of Law*, Gottfried Dietze informs us that the origin of the police power is the police state.[33] Through the police state, by means of state law, the state invoked its own concept of justice and defined the limits of its powers. The obvious weakness in such a government is that "good police" could, and, empirically, do become "bad police."[34] A democratic state, based wholly on majoritarianism, suffers from such weakness. There are areas that involve the taking of life, liberty, and property in which the majority

29. Ibid., p. 582.
30. The Fifth Amendment is included along with the Fourteenth Amendment and the statement refers to cases involving what are considered to be economic regulations.
31. See Karlin, "Land Use Controls: The Power to Exclude," beginning on p. 532.
32. Pennsylvania Coal Co. v. Mahon, 260 U.S. 393, 416 (1922).
33. Gottfried Dietze, *Two Concepts of the Rule of Law* (Indianapolis: Liberty Fund, Inc., 1973).
34. Ibid., p. 25.

decision is not or ought not be controlling. Unless institutionally restrained, the majority faction may—indeed, does—impose its will on minorities, and proceed to such takings.[35]

The transition from the police state to a just state required an end to arbitrary majority decision making, and reflected a further understanding that a just state could not simply focus on ways to provide for the "happiness and welfare" of the individual. Not only are such notions too easily corrupted, but they are impossible to be provided for evenly. Happiness and welfare for one individual or group might well mean the opposite for another individual or group. What was attempted instead, under the Constitution, was to secure legal freedom. Advocates of constitutional government, such as Locke, Montesquieu, and the authors of the *Federalist*, saw in the Constitution an institutional structure for securing liberty. "It [would have] the tendency of limiting the activities of the state [via the police power] to the most necessary functions. . . . Constitutional government primarily was a reaction against [individual] infringements by the police state" acting through what today we call the police power.[36]

In the constitutional structure, due process was a crucial element. Its purpose was to ensure access to the marketplace of both property and ideas to all persons constitutionally qualified. The guiding principle was liberty. Operationally, due process meant the absence of restraint, and functioned to protect minorities from oppression by the majority.[37]

In the *due-process–police-power* relationship, the latter occupied a position ancillary to the former. Interference in the form of enactments or regulations was sustained only on a showing of necessity, unless this interference was designed to abate a nuisance, in which case it was permitted, provided it was evenly applied. In such a legal construct, individual liberty and the common good were equated.[38]

35. In *The Federalist Papers* (New York: Mentor Books, 1961), both Hamilton (no. 9, pp. 71–72) and Madison (no. 10, pp. 80–81) make the empirical observation.

36. Dietze, *Two Concepts of the Rule of Law*, p. 21.

37. Yick Wo v. Hopkins, 118 U.S. 356 (1886). See discussion of the case in Karlin, "Land Use Controls: The Power to Exclude," p. 536.

38. In an opinion holding invalid a minimum-wage law for women, Justice Sutherland stated: "If, in the face of the guaranties of the Fifth Amendment, this form of legislation shall be legally justified, the field for the operation of the police power will have been widened to a great and dangerous degree. . . . To sustain the individual freedom of the action contemplated by the Constitution, is not to strike down the common good but to

The way in which a concept is used defines its meaning and suggests the structure within which decision making will take place. The due-process clause in its substantive mode is a legislative-limiting doctrine, and is invoked to invalidate legislation that is viewed as a deprivation of life, liberty, or property. There is a clear bias against legislation.[39] Within the constitutional framework, the due-process clause is placed at the uppermost level and its tenets require satisfaction before legislation is held valid. The conceptual problem results from the fact that any act has discriminatory effects and thus imposes some form of deprivation or taking. This means that all laws within a substantive due-process framework are subject to invalidation, even acts which, presumably because of high transaction costs, could not be voluntarily performed by the people in the society.

In the political context, majoritarian values and minority interests are placed in conflict, with the former impinging on the latter. According to Madison, it was the majority faction that constituted the greater threat or evil.[40] The Founding Fathers forged a compromise between majority and minority interests requiring that legislation and regulation be justified and their need demonstrated. Justification and necessity would discharge the burden imposed by the due-process clause. In spite of Holmes's dictum in *Lochner* to the contrary, classical economic theory viewed regulation and legislation as interfering with (or, in today's jargon, "chilling") voluntary exchange and access to the market, and this classical theory was a necessary presupposition of a Constitution intended to be a charter of liberty. Martin Diamond described this rationale, noting that "for the founding generation it was liberty that was the comprehensive good, the end against which political things had to be measured; and democracy was only a form of government which, like any other form of government, had to prove itself adequately instrumental to the securing of liberty."[41]

---

exalt it; for surely the good of society as a whole cannot be better served than by the preservation against arbitrary restraint of the liberties of its constituent members." Adkins v. Children's Hospital, 261 U.S. 525, 560–61 (1923).

39. The Court would talk of the strong presumption of validity that attaches to a piece of legislation. It would then limit the presumption by requiring the legislation to satisfy due process.

40. Madison, *The Federalist Papers*, no. 10.

41. Martin Diamond, "The Declaration and the Constitution: Liberty, Democracy, and the Founders," *The Public Interest* 41 (Fall 1976): 39.

Against this form of reasoning were the police-power adherents, who exerted enormous pressures directed at undermining the constitutional limitations. The exigencies of the day, they believed, required enactments and regulations that would redress wrongs and produce greater equality.[42] In such an analytical structure, legislation and regulation were identified with the common good, and hence, considered to be in the public interest.

At first, the undermining of the constitutional limitations was accomplished by enlarging the notion of nuisance.[43] A doctrine with an elastic pull, it could be easily widened and then conveniently abated under the police power. A regulation or enactment, nevertheless, was still subjected to close scrutiny by the Court in order to determine whether its enactment violated the due-process clause of the Constitution. Since such scrutiny hampered the progress of those favoring more government intervention, such advocates required and sought a more expedient method to pave the way for easier passage of legislation. The method that would accomplish this aim took the form of an enlarged and more powerful "police power."[44]

Economic Effects of Regulation

How is it to be decided which ought to be the governing theory? In the process of deciding, the courts have perhaps not taken a close enough look at the economic effects of legislation that impose restraints on the market. This might be done, in part, by viewing legislation in terms of its effects on the gross national product. Other things remaining equal, does the legislation lead to an increase in production and a rise in per capita real income? Certainly, the current regulations with which we are mainly concerned do not produce such results. Rather, they cause the economic pie to shrink. Such regulations include, among others, wage-and-hour legislation, price and rent controls, land-use controls, restrictions on production and restrictions as to who may have access to the market and under what

42. Ibid. Diamond provides an excellent description of these early egalitarians. Justice Brandeis spoke for them on the Court.

43. See, for example, Brandeis, dissenting in Pennsylvania Coal Co. v. Mahon, 260 U.S. 393.

44. See Brandeis, dissenting in New State Ice v. Liebmann, 285 U.S. 262, 280–311 (1932).

conditions. Legislation and regulation of such a nature result in a reduced supply of the product involved because of the increase in the real marginal cost of producing such goods and services. Whether the product is jobs, housing, drugs, education, food, or gasoline, such laws or regulations act as a tax. As a tax they usually operate regressively, which means the heavier burden will be borne by the poor. Moreover, these laws or regulations have distributive effects. In terms of welfare, only the special-interest group that promoted the legislation gains. The rest pay for that gain in reduced real income.[45]

A second consequence of the legislation is its effect on inflation. Inflation is essentially a monetary phenomenon. However, to the extent that the police-power enactment shrinks the pie, the law operates as if the money supply had been increased. If the money supply and the productive output of the country increase at the same rate, there is approximate price stability. Inflation is produced when the money supply increases at a rate faster than production. If output is lessened as a result of the enactment, then even if the money supply remains constant, the same imbalance between money and production occurs, with inflationary results. Moreover, if the regulation requires a policing body, a regulatory agency, for example, then the government will require additional resources to support its establishment and operation.[46] These resources must be drawn from one of three sources:

1. The government can increase taxes, a politically undesirable procedure.
2. The government can borrow. If it does, it will then compete for resources with the private sector, with the result that interest rates will rise. Again, for the less advantaged, the effect takes the form of a regressive tax and, for the economy as a whole, the effect is to restrict production.
3. If the law is an enactment of the federal government or is a state regulation in part financed by the federal government, the most

45. This is because there is no organized objection to particular legislative schemes. Each scheme requires money to implement it. Spread over all, it takes a little from each, but not enough to provide the incentive for an organized protest. The special-interest group gets its regulation, and each of us pays a little. In the end, we have paid quite a lot.

46. A recent example is the late Department of Energy. In just a few short years it had grown to where it employed better than twenty thousand.

likely method of obtaining resources is through an increase in the money supply.[47] If so, the effect clearly will be inflationary.

These results will occur although the extent of the impact may not be easily measurable.

Finally, economic analysis demonstrates that most laws, although neutral on the surface, have discriminatory consequences. In his article, "Minorities in the Market Place," Harold Demsetz makes clear "that most legal infringements on the operation of the free market imply that they will work to the disadvantage of non-preferred persons."[48] When the market is operating without restraint, a person who wants to discriminate must pay for the right because the one who is discriminated against has the ability, through the market, to pay money or its equivalent to the discriminator as an inducement to stop discriminating. If the discriminator still chooses to discriminate, and in doing so must accept a lesser sum than that offered by the one discriminated against, then the difference in price is the cost of discrimination. From this point on, in fact, it becomes costly to discriminate.

However, if some law is passed prohibiting the use of wealth incentives to bid for goods or services (rent control, for example), other incentives will be substituted for money to allocate the resource. These incentives will take the form of personal characteristics – race, religion, size of family, or political favoritism.[49] Those who benefit least are the ones least preferred. Where the market, through the pricing system, is not allowed to operate, individual personal characteristics substitute for money as the rationing device.

Today, if an owner of a ball team decides to exercise a taste for discrimination against blacks, that owner will go broke. The team will win very few games; attendance will drop. No law is necessary to tell or direct the owner to stop discriminating because it soon becomes very costly to discriminate. The law of demand tells us that, other things being equal, the higher the price, the less the quantity demanded. As the cost of discrimination rises, the less discrimination

47. This takes the form of borrowing in the first instance since the Treasury does not "print" money. But the Federal Reserve Bank does, and then "lends" it to the Treasury indirectly by purchasing government bonds. So the Treasury acquires cash from a printing press that is operated by the Federal Reserve Bank.

48. Harold Demsetz, "Minorities in the Market Place," *North Carolina Law Review* 43 (1965): 290.

49. Ibid., p. 273.

there will be, because with each increase fewer people will be willing to pay the cost. In the example given, discrimination is virtually gone. Notice, too, how the process began. In the beginning, blacks worked for relatively small salaries. By working for less, in effect, they bribed the owners; and owners were given an incentive to sort out people as individuals without regard to color.

What does a zoning law or land-use control law do? It eliminates wealth compensation as a way of allocating land use. By artificially limiting the number of units to be constructed and increasing the cost of such units, government officials establish a price barrier, whose effect is to arbitrarily deny large numbers of people access to the housing market. Those responsible for the regulations then are able to exercise their taste for discrimination at almost no cost to themselves. Thus, the regulation results in government-sponsored discrimination. Through legislation and regulation, discrimination is made cheap. Inevitably, there is more of it. Economic analysis is a powerful tool in helping to expose the exclusionary effect regulation has on access.

Legislation and the Presumption of Validity

Once it becomes clear that legislation and regulation that impose restraints on the market produce the harmful effects just described, it becomes unclear why such legislation carries with it a presumption of validity. At the very least, those who propose the legislation ought to be required to overcome the burden of such harmful effects as a prerequisite to validation. The legislation would then address the issue of necessity. This is precisely what the due-process clause is intended to do, and, if allowed to function, does. If the showing can be made, the burden is overcome and the law is sustained. In this connection, it is absolutely crucial to note and understand that the process is not affirmative in nature and parallels precisely what is today required in cases involving speech, fundamental rights, and suspect classifications. Legislative interferences having to do with speech, fundamental rights, and suspect classifications are strictly construed, which means that unless some compelling interest is demonstrated by the state, the legislation is declared unconstitutional.

Viewed from this perspective, the Court, in its use of substantive due process, does not sit as a superlegislature, nor is it acting in an

unprincipled manner. Instead, the Court recognizes the initial harmful effects of the legislation and then assigns the state the burden of
justifying those effects. This process places obstacles in the way of
the popular will, or what is presumed to be the popular will, when
the initial effect produces harmful consequences.[50]

Viewed from another perspective, the doctrine of substantive due
process encourages market solutions to problems. In economic terms,
the result is more production and higher real income. For those in
society who are disadvantaged, it means a larger pie and easier access
to it. The price of entry to the market is reduced. To those who
would respond by saying, "What if even that price cannot be paid by
some?" the answer is that there is at least a price that will permit
entry. Compare that price with the price of entry in such places as
Arlington Heights, where zoning laws prohibited a construction firm
from building townhouses for low- and moderate-income tenants.
The legislation—the zoning ordinance—simply prohibited entry.[51]

As long as property rights cannot be fully assigned, in whichever
way the Court holds, someone will be harmed. The problem is to
avoid the more serious harm. The legislative response is a political
response. The nonpreferred will gain only by sufferance. An entitlement by sufferance is worth little and is unreliable.

Since 1937, legislation and regulation having to do with property
rights are minimally scrutinized by the courts. If the Court finds that
a police-power enactment reflects a legitimate state interest, and that
the means provided for in the enactment are rationally related to
such an interest, the judicial inquiry is at an end. Only a showing of
irrationality or arbitrariness will interfere with what is tantamount
to an automatic finding of constitutionality. The practical effect is
that legislation is now produced at a very low cost, and consequently,
is a product very much in demand. Under the circumstances it is not
surprising that legislation is being produced in enormous quantities.

---

50. "But plainly, I think, this Court must have regard to the wisdom of the enactment.
At least, we must inquire concerning its purpose and decide whether the means proposed
have reasonable relation to something within legislative power—whether the end is legitimate, and the means appropriate. If a statute to prevent conflagrations should require
householders to pour oil on their roofs as a means of curbing the spread of fire when discovered in the neighborhood, we could hardly uphold it." Nebbia v. New York, 291 U.S.
at 556 (McReynolds, dissenting).

51. See, Arlington Heights v. Metropolitan Housing Co., 429 U.S. 252 (1977). Most of
Arlington Heights is zoned for detached single-family houses. Metropolitan sought a zoning
change that would have permitted construction of townhouses for low- and moderate-
income tenants. The rezoning was denied.

For all practical purposes, the Court has abdicated its authority as a legislative-limiting body, thus permitting the legislature to function without restraint. It is now the legislature that can roam at will, at least in those areas in which it is directed by special-interest groups.[52]

THE IMPACT OF THE DEPRESSION ON DECISION MAKING

What caused this change in judicial attitude and its near-total acceptance in the legal community was, of course, the depression. It was a time of incredible and widespread suffering, and any effort at mitigation was welcomed. If blame could be placed, a direction for relief could be suggested.

Laurence Tribe described the situation as it appears to have been understood—and as it continues to be understood.

> Particularly after the ravages of the depression, it was difficult to argue with any conviction that the invisible hand of economics was functioning either to produce a social optimum or to protect individual rights. The legal "freedom" of contract and property accordingly came to be seen by many as illusory, and the suffering of underpaid or overworked laborers came to be perceived not as an inescapable corollary of personal liberty but as a foreseeable product of conscious governmental decisions—decisions to take some steps affecting the affairs of economic life—punishing some people as thieves, awarding others damages as victims of trespass or breach of contract, immunizing still others through corporate fictions—while not taking other steps that might have rescued people from conditions of intolerable deprivation.[53]

The Supreme Court as Scapegoat

The Roosevelt administration responded to the depression with a series of laws establishing programs whose main design was to raise prices and wages.[54] Prior to 1937, these programs were for the most

52. See footnote 8.

53. Laurence Tribe, "Unraveling National League of Cities: The New Federalism and Affirmative Rights to Essential Government Services," *Harvard Law Review* 90 (1977): 1065, 1085.

54. The National Industrial Recovery Act, (NIRA), the Railway Pension Act, Agriculture Adjustment Act (AAA), and the Guffy Coal Act, are among the most notable.

part held unconstitutional by the Supreme Court.[55] In doing so, the Court reinforced popular beliefs that the system of free enterprise had failed, and that the Court, as an institution, was responsible for standing in the way of relief. The Court was looked upon as favoring the rich and powerful, and the feeling was strong that to continue following its precepts would only lead to further damage of the economy. The enormity of the suffering gave credence to the view expressed by Tribe. It was a powerful argument and finally forced the Court to yield. Beginning in 1937, the Court began holding the administration's programs constitutional.[56] But in yielding to political expediency, the Court committed a momentous error.

The Effects of a Money Contraction

The fact is that the Federal Reserve Board, for reasons we need not examine here, had allowed, if not actually forced, the money supply to fall by more than one-third between 1929 and 1932, thus producing a disastrous deflation that reduced the price level by 50 percent in just four years.[57] By permitting (indeed, forcing) this deflation, the Federal Reserve Board, in effect, had rewritten all contractual undertakings to require a doubling of real payments. People with fixed obligations were hard put to meet these obligations. Indeed, a significant number could not; consequently, foreclosures and bankruptcies abounded. Businesses were faced with salary obligations that could not be met. Accordingly, salaries were reduced and workers laid off.

Almost overnight, the economy turned from one of prosperity and plenty to one of scarcity and poverty. Prices and incomes fell. Twenty-five percent of the labor force was unemployed. Sales declined; little was produced and inventories sat undiminished. We

55. Schechter Poultry Corp. v. United States, 295 U.S. 495 (1935); Retirement Board v. Alton Realty Co., 295 U.S. 330 (1935); United States v. Butler, 297 U.S. 1, (1936); Carter v. Carter Coal Co., 298 U.S. 238 (1936); Morehead v. New York ex rel. Tipaldo, 298 U.S. 587 (1936) (New York's minimum-wage law).

56. Prior to West Coast Hotel v. Parrish, 300 U.S. 379 (1937) there were others, including Nebbia v. New York, 291 U.S. 502 (1934); Home Building and Loan Assn. v. Blaisdell, 290 U.S. 398 (1934); and Ashwander v. T.V.A., 297 U.S. 288 (1936).

57. See Milton Friedman and Rose Friedman, *Free to Choose* (New York, N.Y.: Harcourt Brace Jovanovich, 1979), pp. 70–90; and Milton Friedman and Anna Schwartz, *A Monetary History of the United States, 1867–1960* (Princeton, N.J.: Princeton University Press, 1963), pp. 299–420 for a complete analysis of the period.

know today that an increase in the supply of money and an easing of reserve requirements would have provided a simple solution. But such a solution was not then available because the Federal Reserve Board did not recognize the problem as one requiring an easing of money. Another consequence was the relatively small amount of investment in new plants and equipment and in housing—as a result, interest rates fell and remained very low. The Federal Reserve Board took the low interest rates as a signal that credit was too easy in the economy. It responded by opposing any increase in the stock of money on the ground that such action might spark severe inflation. Without any interference and in due course, the market would have reacted appropriately by forcing a reduction of all prices and wages. Then, for the most part, the economy would have righted itself. It should be pointed out that contracts voluntarily undertaken relied on, as a basic assumption, the relative stability of the money supply.

The welfare programs of the Roosevelt administration (the National Industrial Recovery Act and the Agriculture Adjustment Act, for example) were designed to produce higher prices, higher wages, and a reduction in production. The effect on an economy in the throes of a contraction would have been totally perverse. With a reduced money supply, what was needed were lower prices, lower wages, and increased production. Whatever the characterization, the administration's programs were not in the public's interest.

The Supreme Court Capitulation

The inability of certain members of the Court to understand the economic forces at work was particularly evident in Justice Louis Brandeis's dissenting opinion in *New State Ice* v. *Liebmann*.[58] Apparently looking for any way out, Brandeis openly advocated the grant of a monopoly to New State Ice.[59] If New State Ice were then to act in characteristic monopoly fashion, it would lower production and increase price—again, the precise opposite of what an economy in a serious contraction required. Such monopoly effects would, of course, have exacerbated the intensity of the depression.

58. New State Ice v. Liebmann, 285 U.S. 262, 280–311 (Brandeis, dissenting).
59. Ibid., pp. 291–300. See Posner's analysis of the case in "Economic Analysis of Law," p. 267.

It was not the free enterprise system that broke down. It was the colossal blunder of a government agency, the Federal Reserve Board, that converted a minor recession into a major depression. The government programs, cartellike in structure, would only have compounded the error. The "old men" of the Supreme Court were correct in their decision to invalidate legislation such as the NIRA and the AAA. When they finally submitted to political pressure, they ignored the economic consequences that would result; and, moreover, they surrendered the right to force the legislative and executive branches to thereafter justify any of their proposed enactments. Before examining the economic and political consequences of the Court's decision to abdicate its role of limiting legislation it is worth noting the rationale the Court employed in holding the legislation constitutional.

In *Adkins* v. *Childrens Hospital*, decided in 1923, the Court struck down a minimum-wage law for women.[60] Justice George Sutherland, writing for the Court, identified the common good with the notion of individual freedom. It followed, therefore, that legislation interfering with individual freedom was automatically outside the public interest, and that the side wishing to sustain the legislation had the burden of justification. Moreover, the law was passed presumably to help women. Suppose the law had been sustained. A minimum-wage law for women would have increased the cost of hiring women. The result would have meant a decrease in the number of women employed.[61] Thus, given the economic realities, the state was unable to discharge the burden imposed upon it.

Fourteen years later, in *West Coast Hotel* v. *Parrish*, the Court overruled *Adkins.* In so doing, Chief Justice Charles Evans Hughes wrote for the majority as follows:

> The liberty safeguarded is liberty in a social organization which requires the protection of law against the evils which menace the health, safety, morals and welfare of the people. *Liberty under the Constitution is thus necessarily subject to the restraints of due process, and regulation which is reasonable in relation to its subject and is adopted in the interest of the community is due process.*[62]

60. Adkins v. Children's Hospital, 261 U.S. 525 (1923).
61. See Posner, "Economic Analysis of Law," p. 272.
62. 300 U.S. at 391 (emphasis added). Compare with Justice Sutherland's position in *Adkins* v. *Children's Hospital*, see footnote 38.

Justice Sutherland's concern was for the individual. He had identified the common good with individual liberty. Any law that constituted an infringement on an individual's life, liberty, or property required a clear showing of necessity. Otherwise, due process was not satisfied. Due process, as he perceived it, was designed to encourage individual liberty, not to restrain it. Hughes turned the notion around by identifying the common good with the "social organization." Henceforth, individual freedom would have to yield to "the interest of the community." Legislation is, of course, an expression of the social organization. As a manifestation of the police power, legislation traditionally and necessarily operates as a restraint on the individual. Thus, in what can only be described as an Orwellian *tour de force* in reasoning, "liberty" became "subject to the restraints of due process, and regulation . . . [became] due process." Since legislation was now an expression of due process, the state's burden of justification simply ceased to exist. In its place was a strong presumption of validity that could only be overturned by a showing of irrationality. Moreover, since irrationality could not be tied to economic principles, the burden on those resisting the legislation was virtually insurmountable.[63] The majority faction that the Court had for so long held in check was now free.

Justice Sutherland clearly understood what the Court had done and the transposition it had made, and urged in his dissent that

> [T]he meaning of the constitution does not change with the ebb and flow of economic events. . . . The judicial function is that of interpretation. To miss the point of difference between the two is to miss all that the phrase "supreme law of the land" stands for and to convert what was intended as inescapable and enduring mandates into mere moral reflections.
>
> If the Constitution, intelligently and reasonably construed in the light of these principles, stands in the way of desirable legislation, the blame must rest upon that instrument, and not upon the court for enforcing it according to its terms The remedy—is to amend the Constitution. . . . [M]uch of the benefit expected from written constitutions would be lost if their provisions were to be bent to circumstances or modified by public opinion. . . . [T]he meaning of the Constitution is fixed when it is adopted and it is not different at any subsequent time when a court has occasion to pass upon it.[64]

63. In Nebbia v. New York, 291 U.S. 502 quoting from Northern Securities Co. v. United States, 193 U.S. 197, 337, the Court stated, "Whether the free operation of the normal laws of competition is a wise and wholesome rule for trade and commerce is an economic question which this court need not consider or determine." 291 U.S. at 537.

64. 300 U.S. 402–4.

Sutherland's dissent constituted a warning that unless the doctrine of substantive due process was retained, the Court would no longer be able to function as a restraining force against the regulatory process.

The new Court was quick to see a danger. To follow *Parrish* would mean that legislative enactments governing the area of individual rights would also have been insulated from judicial review. Accordingly, in order to limit the effect of *Parrish* to matters involving economic regulation, Justice Harlan Stone in *United States* v. *Carolene Products* noted that where "fundamental rights" and "suspect classifications" were involved, the Court, as before, would continue to scrutinize such legislation carefully, and unless the state were able to show a compelling interest in the legislation, the legislation would not be upheld as constitutional.[65] In this way the distinction between property rights and individual rights was firmly established.

CONCLUSION

Today there is a growing fear that the regulatory process has run amok. It is now commonplace to view the situation with genuine foreboding. Irreparable harm is predicted for the economy, and the political structure is seen as being seriously threatened. None of this appears to be exaggerated. Even worse, no solution that is both satisfactory and feasible is being offered.

The powerful police-power model, out of which much of the current crisis emerged, was not that envisioned by the framers. Indeed, the structure they established was specifically designed to guard against the incredible expansion of government control over the economy.[66] They saw and understood the counterproductive effects that would inevitably accompany such control. The regulatory process, as we should now know and understand, even when well intentioned, mainly chokes off production, thus creating a situation that produces shortages and influences prices upward. The effect is as if the money supply had been increased. Whereas the official money supply can be reasonably controlled if the Federal Reserve Board

65. 304 U.S., 152–53, see footnote 4.
66. Had the court retained the substantive due-process structure, the increase in regulation would have been dramatically slowed.

wishes, the de facto increase in money produced as a consequence of regulation cannot be, at least not within the constitutional framework under which we are now being governed. The situation is made worse because there is no precise way to measure the lowering of productivity and the relationship it bears to the stock of money. If the imbalance is as small as 2-3 percent, this imbalance is still sufficient to sabotage efforts of the Federal Reserve Board to keep the money supply and inflation under control. In terms of welfare, within the space of five years, production can and will lag 10-15 percent.

To expect the legislature to engage in self-restraint is to believe the fox can be trusted to guard the hen house. The situation is such that concern over regulation rather than production is predominant in the minds of those making business decisions.

What is difficult to measure is the percentage decrease in productivity relative to the money supply. If decreased productivity caused by regulation is not being offset in terms of new opportunities, then the effect is a significant increase in the money supply, an increase the Federal Reserve Board will find difficult to measure and one that will interfere with its ability to control inflation.[67] It is not likely that a constitutional amendment limiting spending will take place. Legislators pursue their own immediate self-interest. They legislate to get reelected. It is futile to believe that the practice of providing special interest groups with the legislation they seek will be significantly abated.

This is precisely the kind of situation the doctrine of substantive due process was designed to confront. Its function was that of limiting legislation, not superlegislating. The application of economic

---

67. It used to be that the rate of inflation and the percentage increase in the money supply (the old M1 designation) were about the same. Within recent years, however, there has been a growing disparity between the two figures. The spread in early 1980 was approximately five points – the rate of inflation being approximately five points higher than the rate of increase in the money supply. This disparity represents lowered productivity and some anticipation of growing inflation. How much is attributable to each is hard to say. But if the lowered rate of increase in production due to regulation continues, then even if the Federal Reserve Board is able to keep the growth of the money supply within its stated goals, it will not have succeeded in controlling inflation. It will be possible to have so-called monetary control and double-digit inflation at the same time. The Federal Reserve Board will either have to severely contract the growth of money to a point that will compensate for the negative impact regulation is having on productivity or there will have to be a severe cutback in regulation. As this paper suggests, the latter prospect, under current constitutional interpretation, is unlikely. Because the effect of a severe contraction is today well understood, the former prospect is also unlikely.

principles to legal analysis suggests that the Court did not overreach in striking down much of the New Deal legislation. However, in causing the demise of substantive due process in the area of property rights, the Court locked itself into a framework that denied it a method for examining the costs and the reciprocal effects of legislation and regulation. The results are a built-in inflation that is now constitutionalized, and discriminatory practices that are de facto government sponsored. Moreover, to the extent that the Court fails to employ economic principles in its reasoning process, it continues to deny itself the opportunity of judging whether or not a regulation is rationally related to a legitimate governmental interest.

The matter deserves fresh consideration. That the distinction enabling property rights to be separated from individual rights is losing its credibility may force the Court to grant this consideration. More and more, we see, in cases before the Court, police-power enactments encroaching on property rights as they simultaneously impinge on individual rights. In an earlier day, Alexander Hamilton wrote that "a power over a man's subsistence amounts to a power over his will."[68] Economic analysis helps us make the connection. Once understood, presumed ideological preferences will be obscured by cost-benefit considerations that more accurately describe the incentive structure triggering behavior. It should then be easier to see that as government regulation grows, the effects on the economy are necessarily less than promised, and individual freedom is seriously diminished.

68. Alexander Hamilton, James Madison, and John Jay, *The Federalist Papers* (New York: New American Library, Inc., 1961), p. 472.

Chapter 3

THE PROCESSES OF ADJUDICATION AND REGULATION, A COMPARISON

J. C. Smith

INTRODUCTION

Individuals are protected by the law from the harmful effects of the conduct of others in a variety of ways, but in particular by adjudication consisting of the criminal and civil systems of justice, and by statutory regulation. The protection of individuals may not always, however, be the commonly recognized goal of these legal mechanisms. The criminal justice system is more often justified in relationship to the maintenance of public order, or in terms of protection of the community. The system of civil justice is usually viewed as existing to settle claims and allocate upon whom the inevitable losses arising from social action should fall. Statutory or governmental regulatory schemes, on the other hand, are commonly rationalized in terms of achieving or maintaining the public good. Nevertheless, so long as it is recognized that communities should exist for the benefit of the members rather than the community being an end in and of itself, and so long as the civil side of the law is conceived of as a system of justice based on the recognition of individual rights, the protection of individuals must be seen as a major, if not the major function of these three kinds of legal institutions.

A good many regulatory schemes exist for the precise purpose of protecting individuals from harm, and are generally justified in these terms. Safety regulations in the workplace, safety standards for the manufacture of products, the regulation of the sale and distribution of drugs, the control and licensing of professionals furnishing services to the public, and the regulation of and imposition of safety standards on enterprises providing transportation are but a few examples. The proliferation of such programs in recent years might lead one to believe that regulation is a more effective way of protecting people from harm than is adjudication, or that regulation, at least, can further diminish harm-causing behavior.

If in fact it does, we must still ask at what cost. Some kind of cost-benefit analysis cannot be avoided in evaluating and comparing these institutions as methods of furnishing individuals' protection from harm. Any system which imposes a greater cost than it furnishes benefits should clearly be suspect. Yet this appears to be the case for regulation, but not for adjudication. Ronald H. Coase, in summarizing the conclusions of studies of governmental regulation of industry up to 1974, stated that: "There have been more serious studies made of government regulation of industry in the last fifteen years or so, particularly in the United States, than in the whole proceeding period. These studies have been both quantitative and nonquantitative. . . . The main lesson to be drawn from these studies is clear: they all tend to suggest that the regulation is either ineffective or that when it has a noticeable impact, on balance the effect is bad, so that consumers obtain a worse product or a higher-priced product or both as a result of the regulation. Indeed, this result is found so uniformly as to create a puzzle: one would expect to find, in all these studies, at least some government programs that do more good than harm." [1] Bernard H. Siegan, in his book, *Economic Liberties and the Constitution*, after citing the above passage concludes that the studies carried out since 1974 confirm Coase's findings. [2]

The limitations of a cost-benefit analysis approach to the question of the merits and demerits of regulation is recognized by proponents of both sides of the argument. Tibor Machan, for example, has set out the moral argument to be made against regulation on the grounds that regulation inevitably entails the infringement of human

---

1. Ronald H. Coase, "Economists and Public Policy," in J. F. Weston, ed., *Large Corporations in a Changing Society* (New York: New York University Press, 1974), ch. 8, pp. 183–84.
2. Bernard H. Siegan, *Economic Liberties and the Constitution* (Chicago: University of Chicago Press, 1980), pp. 301–3.

rights.[3] Steven Kelman, on the other hand, argues in the defense of regulatory schemes, that in certain areas such as the protection of the environment, safety, and health, "there may be many instances where a certain decision must be right even though its benefits do not outweigh its costs."[4] A useful comparison of the processes of adjudication and regulation must take into account moral considerations of the kinds which are of concern to both Professors Machan and Kelman, and which cannot be given a monetary value, and therefore cannot be made the subject matter of a comparison in which all benefits and costs are reduced to a common denominator.[5] A comparison of costs and benefits, therefore, can be made only in a very broad and general sense, more by way of a systematic comparison of alternatives rather than an economic measure of differences.[6]

In making such a comparison one is faced at the outset with several conceptual problems. For example, the term 'law' is generally used to refer to both legislative enactments and the regulations often created thereunder, as well as to that body of nonstatutory law that we have inherited from classical Roman law, the English common law, and the set of legal precedents and principles which judicial decision and legal scholarship has constructed thereon, including reforms to that body of law made by statutory enactment. The basic assumptions entailed by legislation or law made by legislative fiat can be and often are quite different than those entailed in judge-made law, or law derived by reason from prior existing rules, precedents, and principles. Legislation entails concepts of validity, jurisdiction, sovereignty, democracy or general will, and public good. The law which has evolved through the system of the courts is based on concepts of rationality, universality, rights, obligations, action, responsibility, and agency.[7]

3. Tibor R. Machan, "Some Normative Considerations of Deregulations," *Journal of Social and Political Studies* 3 (1978): 363; "Should Business be Regulated?" in T. Regan, ed., *Just Business* (New York: Random House, 1983); "Human Dignity and the Law," *DePaul Law Review* 26 (1977): 807; "Liberty: Economic vs. Moral Benefits," *The Occasional Review* (Autumn 1974): 33.

4. Steven Kelman, "Cost-Benefit Analysis: An Ethical Critique," *Regulation* (January/February 1981): 33.

5. For a balanced discussion of the limitations of a cost-benefit analysis approach in the context of environmental issues, see Richard N. Langlois, "Cost-Benefit Analysis, Environmentalism, and Rights," *The Cato Journal* 2 (1982): 279.

6. "At the broadest and vaguest level, cost-benefit analysis may be regarded simply as systematic thinking about decision-making." Kelman, "Cost-Benefit Analysis."

7. J.C. Smith, *Legal Obligation* (London: Athlone Press of the University of London, 1976). See in particular chs. 3-6. S. Coval, J.C. Smith, P. Burns, "The Concept of Action and Its Juridical Significance," *University of Toronto Law Journal* 30 (1980): 199.

Judge-made law is the method whereby the parameters of rights are determined, while the determining factor of statutory law is the furthering of the public interest, however defined. This view of judge-made law would preclude the function of a judge as a balancer of interests, even though many judges, especially in the United States, perceive judicial decision making in this way.[8] It does not follow, on the other hand, that the view of judge-made law as a system of rights and obligations precludes judges making changes in the law, providing those changes can be shown go be deducible from the body of the law by well recognized patterns of inference. What I wish to compare are two institutional paradigms, the judicial or juridical, and the legislative-regulative, as methods of protecting people from the harmful consequences of action.

I hope to reveal through a comparison of adjudication with government regulation as legal processes for the protection of the public, why one should not be puzzled or surprised to find that there are almost no studies that show a particular governmental program doing more good than harm, and why this will be found to be the case not just for government regulation of industry, but for governmental regulation of noncriminal behavior in general. I will argue that the mechanism of social control of behavior through regulatory schemes is, itself, inappropriate for the uses to which it is put, and the point of making a comparison with adjudication, an alternative method of social control, will be to reveal the institutional inadequacies of regulation and the advantages of adjudication.

THE CRIMINAL JUSTICE SYSTEM

The criminal law functions to protect persons from the harmful effects of the conduct of others by prohibiting certain kinds of harmful actions, thus making them crimes, and providing a penalty, generally either a fine or imprisonment, or both, when a crime has been committed. A crime consists in the concurrence of a prohibited pattern of behavior often called the *actus reus*, and a culpable state of mind generally referred to as the *mens rea*. The criminal law tends to focus on the nature of the action, irrespective of its consequences. It is not necessary to prove that any harm has been caused, but only

8. J.C. Smith, *Legal Obligation*, chs. 9 and 10.

that the criminal act has been performed as criminal acts are generally harm causing by nature. In order for people to be able to avoid committing crimes, and to be held responsible for their criminal actions, they must know precisely which kind of acts are forbidden. Only those actions which are clearly definable and are generally known by common experience to be harm causing to others are really suitable for prohibition by the criminal legal process.

THE CIVIL JUSTICE SYSTEM

The civil law, rather than specifically prohibiting a long list of harm causing acts as does the criminal law, functions to regulate human behavior by minimizing the harmful consequences of action, by imposing a duty to compensate for the harm caused. The area of the civil law most concerned with the protection of members of the public through the enforcement of obligations by awards of damages is the law of torts. The subject matter of the law of torts consists of the rights we have regarding our own person, rights regarding our chattels, rights regarding our land or realty, and rights regarding certain of our economic interests or relations. These rights are protected through a variety of causes of actions or specific torts, each of which protects one or more sets of interests.

The law of torts has evolved over the centuries to maximize freedom of action while at the same time minimize risks of harm. The law of torts represents the product of generations of legal minds applied to hundreds of thousands of actual experiences of people drawn from the crucible of life, to find rational solutions to the conflicting claims of right arising out of human interaction. The result is a refined set of conceptual tools, each designed in the context of specific rights and specific kinds of conduct.

A COMPARISON OF THE SYSTEMS
OF CRIMINAL AND CIVIL JUSTICE

The criminal law doesn't settle conflicting claims of right. The criminal law defines patterns of behavior as crime, which practically always result in harm to someone else, and for which no reasonable claim of right can possibly be made. Murderers seldom can make a reasonable claim that they had a right to kill their victim, or robbers to steal property, or a rapist to rape someone. Where claim of right might arise as in the case of a killing in self-defense, or where there is a dispute as to ownership of property in a theft case, the rights in issue are taken into account in the definition of the elements of the crime, and in the legally recognized defenses. The issues, therefore, with which a criminal court generally deals are factual ones where the existence of the right is not questioned in the abstract, but only whether under the facts of the particular case the accused had the right to do what he did.[9] In a civil action, on the other hand, courts often have to decide whether, assuming the facts are as they are claimed to be by the plaintiff, the right claimed by the plaintiff in fact does exist in the law.

By its very nature the criminal process is not designed to resolve conflicting claims of right. The victim of a crime is not even a party to the criminal action. If a particular kind of criminal offense does give rise to conflicting claims of right, then it probably is the kind of action which should not be criminalized in the first place. Because the breach of rights is clear in criminal acts, and thus there are no legitimate grounds for even a conflicting claim of right on the part of the actor, we can on both a societal and an individual basis take positive action, whenever possible, to prevent crimes from being committed.

Unless the breach of a right is clear, the civil law generally functions only after the damage has already happened. If there are legitimate conflicting claims of right in issue, a person should not be prevented from acting until it has been proven that he has no right to act in that way.

The criminal justice system is designed and suitable for prohibiting and thus preventing actions which have an extremely high probability of resulting in harm to others, and which involve no conflicting claims of rights. The civil justice system is designed for resolving conflicting claims of right and for providing for compensation when rights have been violated. The criminal and civil systems of justice, therefore, are not mutually exclusive. Generally, if a person has been harmed by a criminal action, he or she will also have a civil cause of

---

9. Conflicting claims of right as between the state and the person charged with a criminal offense, can arise during the course of criminal proceedings, but these relate more to matters of due process and legal procedures, rather than to the action which is the subject of the charge.

action because punishing and awarding compensation are quite different functions.[10] The distinctive feature of the criminal law is that it prohibits certain kinds of harmful acts, providing us with fairly clear definitions of what will constitute an offense. The civil law, on the other hand, functions more to regulate human conduct by minimizing harmful consequences by imposing a duty to compensate, rather than furnishing us with a list of forbidden acts. The criminal law tends to focus on the nature of the action, because the harmful effects can be taken for granted, while the civil law tends to concentrate on the results or effects of actions, and if an act proves not to be harmful, seldom will it be considered contrary to the civil law. Nearly all criminal acts give rise to a civil cause of action because in general they do result in damage to other people. We can, consequently, divide actions into two kinds, those actions which nearly always result in harm to others and involve no conflicting claims of right, and those actions which are in general not harm causing unless carried out without skill and care. The first kind of action gives rise to both criminal and civil liability, while the latter kind of actions results in only civil liability.

STATUTORY SYSTEMS OF REGULATION

A wide variety of systems of governmental regulation exist to regulate a vast number of different kinds of activities to protect the public from possible harmful consequences that might result as those activities are being carried out. The regulations themselves might be set out specifically in the statute, the statute might set up a public administrative tribunal to set the regulations on an ongoing basis, the drafting of regulations might be the responsibility of a bureaucratic department of government, or the right to draft and enforce regulations might be given to a private body such as the governing body of a profession.

Statutory regulations function to protect the public by setting conditions as to whom is allowed to do certain kinds of actions, and conditions as to how those actions are to be carried out. Thus the two principal functions of governmental regulatory schemes are

10. George P. Fletcher, "Punishment and Compensation," *Creighton Law Review* 14 (1981): 691.

licensing and standard setting. Regulatory bodies decide who can do what, and how it is to be done. All action contrary to the set of regulations, or in conflict with the standards set is prohibited, and is made punishable by fine or imprisonment. Enforcement may be carried out through the courts, or by statutory bodies acting quasi-judicially.

A COMPARISON OF CIVIL ADJUDICATION AND REGULATION

Generality and Specificity of Standards

Both the civil and criminal law use generic terms to define classes of behavior. The criminal law specifies the necessary elements which make up the particular offense, while the civil law defines the necessary conditions or elements for each particular tort. Thus we have criminal offenses such as theft, murder, or burglary, and torts such as false imprisonment, trespass, nuisance, or negligence. Adjudication can thus deal with broad classes of behavior. Whenever a class of behavior is directly or indirectly prohibited, we can clearly predict that situations will arise, the specific circumstances of which we cannot predict, when it would be counterproductive or wrong to enforce the prohibition. Because these specific circumstances cannot be predicted ahead of time, they cannot be written into the law as exceptions. Rather we exclude these situations by sets of general and more specific defenses. The law thus can define behavior in terms of general classes, but handle it with a high degree of specificity.

Regulations, however, directly specify the prohibited pattern of behavior in much more specific terms.[11] Thus a regulation, for example, would prohibit driving a car unless the car had gone through a testing station and received a windshield sticker of approval. The tort of negligence, on the other hand, requires the existence of a reasonably foreseeable risk of harm as a necessary condition for liability. The law of negligence thus deters only those people from driving who know or ought to know that their car is unsafe, while the statutory regulation requires all drivers to take their cars through the

11. For a general discussion of the problems in setting standards through the regulatory process, see Stephen Breyer, *Regulation and its Reform* (Cambridge, Mass.: Harvard University Press, 1982), ch. 5, pp. 96–119.

test even though they know they are perfectly safe, and prohibits the driving of safe cars merely because they don't have a safety sticker.

Thus adjudication, by defining behavior in general generic terms which specify elements or conditions causally related to harmful events, is able to differentiate between behavior which will likely produce harm, and behavior which will likely not result in injury. Particular defenses then can isolate out situations having special circumstances, thus giving us the advantage of both generality and specificity. Even if, for example, the brakes of the car are not safe, a driver would be legally justified in risking an accident while rushing a child who had swallowed poison, to an emergency center.

This interrelationship between generality and specificity is best exemplified in the laws of negligence. The law of negligence places a general duty on all actors, "that whenever one person is by circumstances placed in such a position with regard to another that everyone of ordinary sense who did think would at once recognize that if he did not use ordinary care and skill in his own conduct with regard to those circumstances he would cause danger of injury to the person or property of the other, a duty arises to use ordinary care and skill to avoid such danger. . . ."[12] This is often referred to as the standard of care of the reasonable person.

This general principle is applied in each individual case to produce a specific standard of care for the particular set of circumstances. Regulatory systems which prescribe standards for specific kinds of activities, in making the standard sufficiently general to cover the kind of behavior to be regulated, cannot take into account all or any of the unique features of each individual instance of the activity, whereas under the civil law, each actor is self-regulating and establishes his own standard of care in the light of the unique particular circumstances. Where an issue of the adequacy of the standard arises in the contest of a civil action, the court will itself decide what the proper standard of care ought to have been, but always only in the context of the particular case.

When standards are established by regulations in general terms, they will inevitably be too high for some of the situations to which the regulations apply, and too low for others. Particularity is just not possible through regulation. Often where an adequate standard, in

12. Heaven v. Pender (1883) 11 Q.B.D. 503 at 509.

general, is too low for a particular situation, and a tragic accident takes place, the ensuing adverse publicity leads to the standard then being raised substantially higher than needs be for most of the situations to which the regulations apply in order to prevent a similar accident from again happening. In an unregulated situation where a serious accident has occurred, each individual actor or enterprise or industry will examine itself in the light of the particular circumstances, and in only those cases of a similar nature will corrective action need to be taken. One of the principal advantages of self-regulation is that the actor who is present and involved is the best person to know what is the most reasonable standard of care for each particular case.

The difficulties involved in setting standards a priori by fiat can be illustrated by an examination of the ways standards are set for the sale and marketing of drugs.[13] The Kefauver–Harris Amendment to the 1938 Food, Drug, and Cosmetic Act effectively places the onus on the drug company to prove by substantial evidence that the drug is both safe and effective, and according to rules and procedures set out by the Food and Drug Administration.[14] Thus a general standard of 'substantially proven safety' has to be met in regard to a wide range of different kinds of products, at a substantial cost, with the inevitable result that perfectly safe products and beneficial products carrying some risks, are kept off the market for years. The natural protein sweetener aspartame, for example, which is the safest of all artificial sweeteners, and which has been widely used for some time in other countries, has still not been approved for use in the United States, even though there is not even a prima facie case that it might be harm causing. The strict liability imposed by the law of torts on manufacturers furnishes in an economic fashion all the incentives that are needed for drug producers to take the necessary steps to ensure the safety of their products.

13. Paul J. Quirk, "Food and Drug Administration," in James Q. Wilson, ed., *The Politics of Regulation* (New York: Basic Books, 1980), ch. 6, pp. 191–235; David L. Weimer, "Safe-and-Available Drugs," in Robert W. Poole, Jr., ed., *Instead of Regulation* (Lexington: Lexington Books, 1982), ch. 8, pp. 239–83.

14. U.S., *Statutes at Large*, vol. 76 (Washington, D.C.: U.S. Government Printing Office, 1963), p. 781.

Impartiality and Rationality

Every governmental regulation of any human behavior which is implemented for the protection of any person or group will entail limitations upon the freedom of action of the persons whose conduct is the subject of the regulations. Where a claim of a right of freedom of action comes into conflict with the claim of a right to freedom from harm, the system of civil justice is able to resolve such disputes though due process of law. Each party to the dispute has the opportunity to be heard and to make its case. Rules of discovery require that relevant information held by each side is made available to the other. All evidence is brought forth in open court and all witnesses are subject to cross examination. The court has the duty to be scrupulously impartial. The decision settling the dispute must be reached through the application of legal rules and principles, and the reasons for the decision must be set out by the judge and made available to the parties. If the losing party feels that the judgment was made in error, there is an opportunity to appeal to a higher court.

Governmental regulations, on the other hand, are made as a part of a political rather than a judicial process. Affected parties may or may not be allowed to be heard. Parties whose interests are adversely affected by regulations often not only have no opportunity to present relevant evidence, but have no knowledge of the information upon which the regulators act in drafting the prohibitions and standards which are to be imposed. Reasons are generally not given and there is usually no appeal. Thus regulatory systems deprive people of rights without the due process of law.

Governmental regulatory schemes do not function impartially. They are subject to the political process, and through that process to the influence of special interest groups, lobbying, and the pressure of public opinion as manipulated through the media.[15] Regulatory agencies develop their own special interests as bureaucracies, which interests are often inconsistent with their statutory responsibilities. These agencies often develop special relationships with the industries they are to regulate. Robert Poole writes that, "As Ralph Nader and others are painfully discovering, there seems to be a regular pattern in the history of such agencies, they invariably come to represent and

15. James Q. Wilson, "The Politics of Regulation," in Wilson, *The Politics of Regulation*, ch. 10, pp. 357-94.

serve the special interests of the established companies in the industry being regulated. The ICC (Interstate Commerce Commission), the FTC (Federal Trade Commission), the FDA (Food and Drug Administration)—all have been investigated by Nader's Raiders over the last few years and the same pattern has appeared in each. The main function of the agency has turned out to be protecting the regulated industry from competition, while giving the government the appearance of protecting the consumer from the industry."[16] There is no corrective mechanism as in the common law where bad judgments can be overruled, distinguished on the facts, disagreed with, or ignored. Rather, agencies become self-protective, defending rather than correcting errors of judgment. Conflicts of interest are common such as where the Atomic Energy Commission is given the responsibility of both promoting nuclear power and setting the safety standards. Sometimes the government itself is directly involved as a participant with its own vested interests, as where some form of public ownership is involved.

Regulatory schemes, because they have no adequate method of resolving conflicting claims of rights, must inevitably end up with regulations that deprive people of what would be recognized as their rights within an adjudicative system of justice. If educational standards are made a necessary condition for the practice of a profession, then highly qualified persons who fail to meet those particular requirements or who achieve their qualifications by a different method, will have lost the right to practice the profession. Marketing boards deprive people of the right to produce if they are unable to acquire a license or a quota. Regulations prohibiting the sale of a particular drug such as laetrile deprive people of the choice of a particular form of chemotherapy. Human rights or affirmative action programs deprive employers of the right to hire whosoever they wish or landlords to select their tenants.

The greater the absence of impartiality and rationality in a regulative process, the wider will be the range of nonharm-causing acts which will be prohibited, ostensibly for the purpose of protecting the public. The wider the range of beneficial behavior that is prohibited, the greater will be the interference with fundamental rights.

16. Robert Poole, Jr., "Reason and Ecology," in Dorothy B. James, ed., *Outside Looking In: Critiques of American Policies and Institutions, Left and Right* (New York: Harper & Row, 1972).

Deterrence and Effectiveness

The principal function of the criminal process is the deterrence of harm-causing behavior, and this holds equally true when the criminal process is used in the context of governmental regulation as it does for the law of crimes. Although deterrence is not the prime consideration for the law of torts, making people financially responsible by requiring them to pay compensation for the harm they cause has a definite deterrent effect in reducing negligent behavior.

In general, statutory regulations enforced through criminal sanctions have little deterrence value. They, in fact, do not generally reduce accidents or prevent harm-causing activities. This is the case because the criminal process provided for in the regulatory legislation is seldom invoked, and for good reason. It is difficult to set standards with sufficient generality and clarity to function as guidelines and rules, and at the same time give them the specificity necessary to be able to state when an offense has been committed. Consequently standards are either set in such broad terms that it is difficult to prove that an offense has been committed, or there is such a mass of detailed regulations that enforcement becomes impractical.

The federal law of Canada alone contains about 20,000 regulatory offenses, and it is likely that the number in the United States is even higher given the larger population, greater complexity of industry, and wider federal jurisdiction in a number of critical areas.[17] If these were *effectively* enforced, the costs would be astronomical. Problems of proof are often complex, and the criminal standard of proof beyond a reasonable doubt is difficult to meet. Not only are successful prosecutions seldom achieved under statutory regulation, but even when a conviction is obtained, the fines tend to be relatively small. This fact is explainable, at least in part, because the conduct is generally noncriminal by its very nature, therefore questions of guilt and innocence, while critical in regard to punishment, have little relevance in much of the context of statutory regulation.

By far, the majority of conflicts of interest and disputes of a civil as contrasted with a criminal nature are settled by negotiations rather than adjudication. Solutions reached by mutual consensus will inevitably be found to be superior for the parties to those imposed against

17. H. Eddy, *Sanctions, Compliance Policy and Administrative Law* (Ottawa: Law Reform Commission of Canada, July 1981).

their will by legal or political authority. The system of civil justice is consistent with and encourages solutions based on achieving a consensus, by clarifying what the rights of the parties are, providing a mechanism for the enforcement of the negotiated agreements, and by providing a dispute-settling mechanism should a consensus and agreement not be reached.

The argument can be made, however, that the protection from harm furnished by the civil and criminal systems of justice is insufficient or incomplete.[18] The criminal law stops at the limits of criminal negligence. The civil law works retrospectively by awarding damages after harm has taken place. The payment of damages, so the argument would go, cannot remedy the death of a child or the loss of several hundred lives in a single airplane accident. Such terrible tragedies should be prevented at all costs. Hence the need for regulatory systems which act prospectively by preventing the harm from happening.

We must not, however, lose sight of the relationship between cost and benefit.[19] No one would die in an airplane accident if air travel were prohibited altogether. There might well be fewer children killed if there were stop lights at the corner of every block. The problem is to find the proper delimitation between the right of freedom of action, and the right not be caused harm. This, as I have argued, can be better discovered in the particular than the general, and through a rational, rule-governed, and impartial decision process than one which requires no reasons to be publicly given and which are subject to political and other forms of influence.

In fact, the regulatory process tends not so much to diminish the amount of harm, but rather to change the persons and situations where harm is suffered. The prohibition of thalidomide by the Federal Drug Administration is often cited as an example of the overwhelming benefits which can be gained through the regulation of drugs.[20] The victims of the affects of this drug are pitiful and obvious. It is much more difficult to measure and vividly portray the loss

18. U.S. National Commission on Product Safety, *Final Report* (Washington, D.C.: U.S. Government Printing Office, 1970), pp. 1–3.

19. Roger E. Meiners, "What to Do About Hazardous Products," in Poole, *Instead of Regulation*, p. 302.

20. Both Great Britain and Canada, which permitted the sale of thalidomide, apply the law of negligence to products liability so that a manufacturer need only show that a reasonable standard of care was followed in testing the safety of the company's products. It is

of life or physical well-being which could have been prevented if certain drugs had not been excluded or accepted more promptly, or by drugs which might have been discovered or marketed in a less regulated market.

As far as deterrence is concerned, the threat of damages should be a much greater deterrence than would fines, as the amounts of awards of damages generally far exceed the amounts of fines generally levied. In those situations where an actor has few assets or is in some way judgmentproof, both fines and awards of damages have equally little deterrent value. One might conclude that regulatory schemes could have an advantage in terms of deterrence by having the potential use of terms of imprisonment, a sanction not generally available in civil litigation. Such, however, is not the case. The prescription and imposition of a term of imprisonment for a failure to pay a fine is politically unacceptable since it would affect the poor more frequently and dramatically than it would the rich. It is equally politically unacceptable to imprison people for noncriminal behavior; consequently, legislatures are reluctant to prescribe, and courts to impose, imprisonment in lieu of fines. The power of legislatures to prescribe imprisonment for nonpayment of, or in lieu of, fines gives the regulatory process little, if any, advantage over the process of adjudication since it is very seldom used in regard to noncriminal behavior.

REPRESENTATIVE EXAMPLES

I have argued that the mechanism of the system of criminal justice is designed and suitable only for dealing with criminal behavior, and consequently its use to regulate noncriminal activity is costly, unjust, and inefficient. While this can be demonstrated in almost any area of governmental regulation for the prevention of harm, I will use three particular areas of experience as representative of the problems involved and typical of the results to be achieved: the regulation of professions to prevent incompetency, pollution control, and regulation for safety in the workplace.

---

quite likely that if the doctrine of strict liability had been applied by the courts in those countries as it is in the United States, manufacturers would have been even more thorough in their testing procedures, and thalidomide might not have been marketed.

The Regulation of Professions

The widest range of benign behavior prohibited in the name of the protection of the public occurs where the regulative body, rather than merely establishing standards for whomsoever chooses to act, prohibits people from acting altogether unless certain conditions are met. The effect of such regulations is to grant certain persons the privilege of acting while denying others the right to act.

One of the most fundamental of human rights is the right to earn a living by selling one's skills or services. The rationale for regulating the practice of a vocation or profession by licensing those who will be permitted to offer services and prohibiting by criminal penalties those who are not approved by the regulatory body, is to prevent the unqualified from causing harm to the public. It is in this area of regulation where we find the least amount of impartiality and rationality, and some of the most, if not the most serious infringements of people's rights by use of regulatory processes.

The regulations which govern the licensing of people to practice a trade or profession are invariably drawn up by the members of the trade or profession already in practice who therefore have a vested interest in keeping the numbers of the trade or profession as small as possible. They do this by making the educational requirements as expensive and onerous as they can, by excluding persons who have received their training at institutions outside the jurisdiction, or by requiring immigrants to retake all or a part of a training program within the jurisdiction, or write and pass a vigorous set of exams, and by barring altogether people from practicing a trade or profession who have trained themselves or who have learned by practical experience, as such a method of entry cannot easily be controlled. In some jurisdictions the governing body of a profession is empowered by statute to control the conditions of entry into the profession, while in others, the statutes furnish the requirements for the body statutorily empowered to enforce them. Even where the requirements are set entirely by a bureaucratic body, the members generally will be drawn from the profession regulated, and nearly always will act only after consultation with the governing body of the profession. Thus people who are qualified to offer skills or services will be deprived of the right to do so without due process of law, without reasons being furnished, and by a body which has a vested interest in limiting entry into the market.

One of the most blatant examples of a profession limiting entry in order to reduce the competition for jobs is the profession of school teaching. Nearly every jurisdiction requires at least a year of teacher training in a department of education or a teacher training school, along with whatever other academic requirements may be set. This stipulation excludes a vast number of persons who have university degrees with both minors and majors in subjects taught within the school system, but who have had no formal teacher training. Very few, if any at all, universities or community colleges require any formal teacher training for members of its faculties. All that is required is a good understanding and knowledge of the subject matter to be taught. Good teaching is a skill acquired through practice, and can't be taught in a formal program. Yet this simple single requirement bars thousands of highly educated and qualified people from a chance to practice the teaching profession.

Each trade or profession attempts to monopolize as many different tasks or kinds of services offered as it possibly can bring within the parameters of its control, thereby excluding people with less skill and training from doing the kinds of things that are clearly within their competence. Thus the division of any area of services is prevented from being broken down into specific kinds of tasks which could be easily performed by persons with less skills who could thus afford to offer the services more cheaply. To find examples, one need only examine how the legal profession has attempted to do away with notaries-public, or how the medical profession has attempted to destroy the practice of midwifery,[21] limited the range of services that nurses can offer, opposed the development of a profession of paramedics having skills between those of the doctor and the nurse, excluded pharmacists from prescribing drugs, and limited the role of psychologists without medical degrees in the treatment of mental illness, and the exclusion of alternative methods of dealing with disease and illness such as the use of nutrition or herbal remedies. Where the medical profession has finally been forced by sheer demand, as in the case of acupuncture, to accept alternatives to standard and conventional medical treatment, then the profession has insisted that the various alternatives be administered under the direction and in the presence of a medical doctor.[22]

21. Sarah E. Foster, "Up Against the Birth Monopoly," *Reason* 14 (September 1982): 23.
22. Ronald Hamowy, "The Early Development of Medical Licensing Laws in the United States, 1875–1900," *The Journal of Libertarian Studies* 3 (1979): 73. See also, Hamowy,

While the loss to the public in terms of increased costs for services by the exclusion of qualified people from a profession or trade, the prevention of persons from offering a more limited range of services at a lesser price, and the limitation on the freedom of individuals to choose alternative forms of services are extensive and obvious, it is not clear that there are even minimal benefits to be gained by licensing. Formal education is no substitute for judgment and practice, nor does it in any way limit factors such as alcoholism or dishonesty which truly do affect the quality of services. In this field the common law remedies of breach of contract, fraud, and negligence are sufficient and far more effective deterrents of malpractice than is licensing, and they deprive no one of the right to offer services. The licensing of trades and professions is one of the clearest examples of regulatory schemes doing far more harm than good.

Pollution Controls and Protection of the Environment

The difficulty of setting *enforceable* standards for the regulation of noncriminal, but potentially harm-causing behavior, is particularly evident in the area of environmental pollution.[23] The first problem is that of proving which substances will cause harm and how much harm. The Soviet Union has designated over 400 substances as harmful when in drinking water, and over 60 that adversely affect fish life.[24] K. G. Janardan and D. J. Schaeffer estimate that over 60,000 organic compounds are produced and used by various industries in the United States.[25] Robert T. Franson estimates that between 500 to 2000 new ones are being added each year.[26] There exist literally

---

Licensing and Restrictions on Entry into the Medical Profession in Canada: Its Historical Development (forthcoming).

23. Alfred Marcus, "Environmental Protection Agency," in Wilson, *The Politics of Regulation*, ch. 8, pp. 267–303; Peter H. Aranson, "Pollution Control: The Case for Competition," in Poole, *Instead of Regulation*, ch. 11, pp. 339–393.

24. D. P. Loucks, "Water Quality Management in the Soviet Union," *Journal of Water Pollution Control Federation* 49 (1977): 1751.

25. K. G. Janardan and D. J. Schaeffer, "Methods for Estimating the Number of Identifiable Organic Pollutants in the Aquatic Environment," *Water Resource Research* 17 (1981): 426.

26. Robert T. Franson, "How Environmental Standards are Made and Enforced" (Paper for University of British Columbia Student Pugwash Society, 1982–83 Public Lecture Series, Science and Society: The Setting of Standards, Oct. 12, 1982).

thousands of standards in regards to these chemicals but thousands of the chemicals are still not subject to standards. Add to these the further problem that these standards are made by a variety of agencies and exist in a wide range of legislation and regulations, how can manufacturers hope to comply with and officials enforce the body of regulations?

Given that it is possible to state a clear set of standards for a particular set of pollutants, a great deal of extra cost and inefficiency will be involved if the standards are not modified for each particular plant or situation. General industry wide standards are often inappropriate for particular areas. Thus the general requirement of the Environmental Protection Agency that all new coal burning power plants must install gas-scrubbers, equipment costing on an average of $56 million dollars, to reduce the amount of sulfur dioxide (SO_2) emitted into the air, may be justified in the Eastern United States which is rich in high-sulfur coal, but makes no sense west of the Mississippi where low-sulfur coal predominates and a simple and cheap process of crushing and washing will achieve the same levels of sulfur dioxide as will burning high-sulfur coal and using an expensive gas-scrubber.[27] The Kewaunee Plant on Lake Michigan, according to P. A. Krenkel, was required to equip itself with cooling towers to protect an estimated 1.4 to 10.4 kilograms of fish (mostly alewives) caught daily, that would be threatened if only once through cooling was used.[28] The total cost of this protection works out to between $1,729 and $5,572 per kilogram of fish actually caught. F. D. Brill and his colleagues estimate that the costs of adherence to a common standard of pollution discharge into a common river is three times the amount they would be were the regulating body free to vary the standard for each particular source.[29]

A particular pollution standard might be quite viable for a new plant but financially disastrous for an old one. Yet, on the other hand, the common practice of having lower standards for old plants, while requiring new facilities to purchase expensive equipment to meet a higher standard, usually results in old plants and equipment

27. Bruce A. Ackerman and William T. Hassler, *Clean Coal/Dirty Air* (New Haven: Yale University Press, 1981).

28. P. A. Krenkel, "Problems in the Establishment of Water Quality Criteria," *Journal of Water Pollution Control Federation* 51 (1979): 2168.

29. F. D. Brill, Jr., J. C. Tiebman, and C. S. ReVelle, "Equity Measures for Exploring Water Quality Management Alternatives," *Water Resources Research* 12 (1976): 845.

being maintained longer than they would otherwise be used, thus increasing the levels of pollution over what they would have been with a single higher standard.

Andrew Thompson and Robert Franson, after extensive study of environmental regulation in Canada, have reached the conclusion that the regulatory process for the protection of the environment simply doesn't work because it entails using the criminal process in situations where it is completely inapplicable. Thompson, who in his book *Environmental Regulation in Canada* analyzes six extensive case studies, concludes that " . . . bargaining is the essence of environmental regulation in Canada," and the criminal process entailed in statutory regulation merely makes the negotiation process more difficult to carry out.[30] Franson points out that a recent British Columbia task-force established to detect and deal with violations in the lower reaches of the Fraser River found that approximately half of the discharges were in violation of the terms of their permits, and that in many cases the violations had been going on for some time. He concludes that, "the criminal process has a number of serious disadvantages from the point of view of enforcing environmental standards. . . . The criminal law process is simply not a very good one for dealing with environmental problems."[31] Franson writes that,

"Industry and government bargain concerning pollution levels and abatement actions because of uncertainty about the causes of environmental degradation and the most effective means of abatement . . . this is the only way the system can work. If that is so, the principles of the criminal law can have no useful application. The problem is that the model we are using does not comport with reality. The command/penalty model that is the basis for the criminal law simply does not describe the process by which we establish and attempt to achieve environmental goals. It should not surprise us that judicial decisions, based on the essential principles of the criminal law, make it difficult or impossible for prosecutors to deal effectively with pollution offences."[32]

30. Andrew R. Thompson, *Environmental Regulation in Canada* (Vancouver: Westwater Research Centre, 1980), p. 30.

31. Franson, "How Environmental Standards are Made and Enforced."

32. Robert T. Franson, *Commentary in Proceedings: Environmental Law in the 1980s: A New Beginning* (Canadian Institute of Resource Law, University of Calgary, 1981), pp. 121–24.

Thompson and Franson argue that the contractual model of bargain and negotiation would be far superior to regulation through the criminal law.[33] While I would agree with this conclusion, I do not believe bargaining between industry and government furnishes adequate protection for the rights of the individual members of the public, nor is it superior to, nor an adequate substitute for, the process of civil adjudication. Regulations, even though reached through negotiations, in effect become limited licenses to pollute, or licenses to pollute up to a specified level. With the political influence that large corporations are able to wield, backed by the political power of large trade unions, industries are often able to have standards of pollution set which are far from onerous for the industry.

The only way that individual rights can be fully protected is through the system of civil justice. Even so, the legal doctrines and causes of action available to furnish compensation for harm caused by pollution are in certain respects inadequate to deal with the problems created for the environment by modern industry.[34] An action lies in the law of private nuisance for interference with the use and enjoyment of land, but it is limited in its availability to only those who have a possessory interest in the land. The law of trespass will lie where substances actually come onto and remain on the land such that it can be deemed to be a continuing trespass. An action in negligence is available where there is a creation of an unreasonable risk of harm which results in an actual loss or injury. Strict liability can be imposed by the courts where damage is caused by an ultrahazardous activity. Where there is an unreasonable interference with a right common to the public, an action in public nuisance can be brought providing the plaintiff or plaintiffs can show that they have suffered harm of a kind different from that suffered by other members of the public. Each of the above causes of action have been successfully brought in regard to some instances of pollution, while in many other situations none of the above would lie.

The most serious difficulties which face the courts in developing an adequate adjudicative response to the problems of pollution relate to questions of proof.[35] How does one prove the causal relationship

33. Robert T. Franson, Barry J. Barton, and Andrew R. Thompson, "A Contract Model for Pollution Control" (a study prepared for the Law Reform Commission of Canada, 1982).
34. Robert K. Best and James I. Collins, "Legal Issues in Pollution-Engendered Torts," *The Cato Journal* 2 (1982): 101.
35. Ibid., pp. 114–32.

between noxious emissions and disease where the pollution may be only one of a number of possible causes, or where there are also other contributing factors? Or how does one establish the identity of the defendant where there are a number of industries in a particular area, all contributing to the pollution of the environment? There are some legal techniques available which have been used with varying results. One is the use of class actions and another is the technique of shifting the onus onto a defendant to prove the absence of a causal link.

What is needed is an integrated set of legal principles to deal with environmental problems, grounded on the general assumption that industries ought to shoulder the financial responsibilities for the harm which they cause.[36] Government regulation has so preempted the field of environmental protection that judges are likely to feel that they would be encroaching on the legislative sphere if they attempted any far-reaching judicial reformation of the law in that field. Rather, courts are likely to accept standards of pollution established by regulative agencies as prima facie reasonable. Certainly both industry and labor would strongly oppose a shift from the legislative arena where political pressure can be brought to bear, to the rule governed, justice oriented, impartiality for which the adjudicative system of civil justice must constantly strive.

Regulation for Safety in the Workplace

The system of statutory regulation functions no more effectively in regard to the prevention of industrial accidents, than it does in controlling pollution of the environment. The problems are somewhat similar and stem from the same source, the use of the system of criminal justice through statutory regulation for the control of human behavior best regulated through the system of the civil law. Standards of safety in general terms are unworkable and inefficient in regard to particular plants. Consequently a mass of more specific regulations are generated, which then become so large as to be inaccessible and unmanageable. The report of the Robens Committee on Safety and Health at Work, concluded that in Great Britain, "The

---

36. Poole, "Reason and Ecology," pp. 239–59. See also, Cato Symposium on Pollution, *The Cato Journal* 2 (1982).

first and perhaps most fundamental defect in the statutory system is simply that there is too much law."[37] Nine groups of statutes, supported by nearly 500 subordinate statutory instruments containing detailed provisions of varying length and complexity, are being added to every year. Between 1960 and 1970, 107 statutory instruments were added to the Factories Act alone. "The Legislation," according to the report, "is badly structured, and the attempt to cover contingency after contingency has resulted in a degree of elaboration, detail and complexity that deters even the most determined reader."[38] The accelerating rate of technological changes coupled with the difficulties experienced in amending or revoking old regulations, creates a situation in which the maintenance of up-dating of a corpus of legislation of this type, size and complexity is an endless and increasingly hopeless task.[39]

The Robens Committee found that, "despite the existence of voluminous legal requirements, only a very small proportion of offences ever lead to prosecutions," and even when a conviction is achieved, more often than not the only penalty imposed is a small fine.[40] The English experience is not atypical. Between 1970 to 1975 although over 1000 workers died in British Columbia from industrially related causes, together with hundreds of thousands of injuries and permanent partial and total disabilities, fewer than 40 successful summary convictions of employers were obtained by the Workers Compensation Board, with an average fine of less than $250.[41] In light of the fact that the worker's compensation legislation of British Columbia, like most such schemes, gives the employer immunity from a civil cause of action by an injured employee, it is obvious that there is little incentive for the employer to adopt safety measures which carry a cost.

In a study of the impact of economic deterrence on the prevention of industrial accidents, Jenny Phillips concludes that, "In spite of current trends in both theory and practice, there seems to be evi-

---

37. Parliamentary Papers, House of Commons and Command, *Safety and Health at Work, Report of the Committee 1970-72* (1972, Cmnd. 5034), p. 6.

38. Ibid., p. 7.

39. Ibid.

40. Ibid., p. 81.

41. International Woodworkers of America, Regional Council No. 1, "Submission of Worker's Compensation in British Columbia," presented to the Minister of Labour, November 1976, p. 20. (Unpublished.)

dence that safety improvements have depended primarily on assessment of the economic costs and benefits involved. There is little evidence that regulations or safety inspections are effective. . . ."[42] "The most obvious method of self-regulation," she writes, "is one that operates through costs."[43] "The imposition of the full costs of accidents on dangerous industries would no doubt be unpopular, but the consequences of not doing so are serious."[44]

One of the most effective methods of achieving proper and effective safety standards in the workplace is through the process of free collective bargaining between the employer and the union. Statutory regulations are not only ineffective in fact, but interfere with the bargaining process. The employer is reluctant to go beyond any statutory minimum, and is unable to make a private agreement with his employees where the statutory regulation is excessive or not applicable because of unique circumstances. A study carried out by Paul Sands in which he compared accident rates in the construction industry between Ohio and Michigan, the former highly regulated and the latter not, showed, contrary to what he expected to find, no significant difference.[45] He did, however, find a more positive attitude toward safety on the part of management and labor in the state which was least regulated as the parties themselves assumed more of the responsibility for safety. "When one point was given for each of a number of safety activities and precautions, the Michigan firms received a total of 287 to only 201 for Ohio companies."[46]

Sands's findings support the conclusions and the principal recommendation of the Robens Report. The report states that, "The most fundamental conclusion to which our investigations have led us is this. There are severe practical limits on the extent to which progressively better standards of safety and health at work can be brought about through negative regulation by external agencies. We need a more effective self-regulating system."[47] The principal recommendation was that reform should be aimed at creating the conditions

---

42. Jenny Phillips, "Economic Deterrence and the Prevention of Industrial Accidents," *Industrial Law Journal* 5 (1976): 148–59.

43. Ibid., p. 152.

44. Ibid., p. 159.

45. Paul E. Sands, "How Effective is Safety Legislation," *Journal of Law and Economics* 11 (1968): 165.

46. Ibid., p. 175.

47. Parliamentary Papers, *Safety and Health at Work*, p. 12.

for more effective self-regulation by employers and workpeople jointly.

CONCLUSION

1. The distinguishing feature of the process of regulation is that, like the system of civil justice, it establishes standards of care for the prevention of harm for human conduct which in general becomes harm causing only in particular circumstances, but like the criminal law, it prohibits a wide variety of acts by providing for fines, imprisonment, or both, irrespective of whether harm will in fact result. Governmental regulatory schemes thus function to criminalize what is basically benign behavior.[48] The criminal justice system functions to prohibit those actions we know with a very high degree of probability will cause harm. The civil law functions not only in regard to criminal behavior, but also deals with a wide range of human conduct generally not likely to result in damage if carried out with care. The system of civil justice functions to deter only that conduct which actually does cause harm to others. Statutory or governmental regulations, in prohibiting behavior in order to decrease the possibility of harm, must inevitably prohibit a good deal of action which clearly will not result in harm, and will, in fact, often achieve beneficial results.

2. Under the system of civil justice people are responsible for regulating their own activities. Systems of governmental regulation require expensive bureaucracies to set, administer, and enforce standards.

3. Under a system of civil justice standards are set for each specific situation, generally by the people who are the most knowledgeable, while under a system of governmental regulation standards are either too general to be effective, or if specific, too numerous and complex to be operable.

48. For discussions of some of the problems which are entailed by using criminal processes to enforce statutory regulations of noncriminal-like behavior, see Sanford H. Kadish, "Some Observations on the Use of Criminal Sanctions in Enforcing Economic Regulation," *The University of Chicago Law Review* 30 (1963): 423; Harry V. Ball and Lawrence M. Friedman, "The Use of Criminal Sanctions in the Enforcement of Economic Legislation: A Sociological View," *Stanford Law Review* 17 (1965): 197; Francis A. Allen, "The Criminal Law as an Instrument of Economic Regulation," Paper 2, International Institute for Economic Research, June 1976.

4. Under the system of civil justice conflicts of interest tend to be worked out by the affected parties through bargaining and negotiation, while under a system of governmental regulation vested interests through the political process can often affect the outcome of conflicts of interest.

5. Under the system of civil justice rights are clarified and protected, and conflicting claims of rights are resolved in an objective and impartial arena. Under governmental regulation rights are infringed or extinguished by legislation.

6. Under a system of civil justice financial responsibility for harm is placed on the shoulders of those who are responsible for causing it, thus there is a powerful motive for people to take care. Under a governmental regulatory system on the other hand, given the problems of setting standards, problems of enforcement, problems of proof, the standard of proof for criminal actions, plus the low fines imposed when convictions actually are obtained, the fear of criminal sanctions seldom acts as an efficient deterrent when extensive costs are involved in maintaining a proper standard of care.

When the costs of governmental regulation are weighed against the benefits actually achieved, and when we compare them with the costs and benefits of an efficiently running system of civil justice, it should not puzzle or surprise us to learn that the studies show that nearly all the regulatory programs do more harm than good.

PART II
POLITICAL ECONOMY OF REGULATION

Chapter 4

IS THERE A BIAS TOWARD OVERREGULATION?

Leland B. Yeager

WHAT IS "TOO MUCH" GOVERNMENT?

Often it is appropriate to consider the question of government regulation industry by industry or problem by problem, focusing on specific facts. Heaven knows there has been enough of the opposite: adopting regulations lightheartedly, as if good intentions were justification enough. On the other hand, sometimes it is appropriate to step back from a narrowly factual focus and consider a broader question. Preoccupation with the immediate and specific is part of the problem with government action.[1]

A broader view suggests that our political system harbors a bias toward overactivity. Regulation is just one of several things that government does probably too much of. Such a bias, if it does exist, argues for seeking—or restoring—constitutional restraints on regulatory activity and for not letting each particular issue be decided on

---

1. As F. A. Hayek notes, "we are not fully free to pick and choose whatever combination of features we wish our society to possess, or to . . . build a desirable social order like a mosaic by selecting whatever particular parts we like best. . . . " Yet this idea "seems to be intolerable to modern man." The suggestion draws scorn that unwanted developments may necessarily stem from earlier decisions. "I am myself now old enough," Hayek continued, "to have been told more than once by my elders that certain consequences of their policy which I foresaw would never occur, and later, when they did appear, to have been told by younger men that these had been inevitable and quite independent of what in fact was done." *Rules and Order*. vol. 1 of *Law, Legislation and Liberty* (Chicago: University of Chicago Press, 1973), pp. 59–60.

its own narrow apparent merits. Despite the scorn of hard-nosed positivists, human rights belong in the discussion.

Strictly speaking, perhaps, what argues for restraint is not an incontestable bias toward too much regulation but a structure of government decisionmaking in which prospective costs and benefits escape accurate confrontation. The result may be too much regulation in some directions and, in some sense, too little in others. Errors of omission do not cancel out errors of hyperactivity, though, and a case for restraint remains.

What might the ideal amount of government mean? Even without being able to say (and without facing the anarchists' challenge to any government at all), one can still recognize aspects of decision-making processes that tilt the outcome toward too much government. Some utterly familiar facts suggest this conclusion. Admittedly, I may have overlooked some powerful and even overriding biases working in the opposite direction. As a contribution to discussion, though, I report the biases I see and challenge the reader to explain any opposite ones that might override them.

FRAGMENTED DECISIONS AND AGGLOMERATED ACTIVITIES

Almost everyone who plays a part in governmental decisionmaking, from the average citizen on up, has a fragmentary view. No one has, or has reason to seek, a full view of the prospective costs and benefits of a contemplated activity. (Just one kind of relatively specific and obvious example concerns federal sharing in the costs of many state and local projects, with the result that the local authorities are deciding on expenditure of what, from their points of view, are "ten-cent dollars" or "fifty-cent dollars.") Nothing in government corresponds to the market process of spontaneous coordination of decentralized decisions; nothing corresponds to its way of bringing even remote considerations to the attention of each decentralized decisionmaker in the form of prices.[2] Knowledge, authority, incentives, and respon-

2. Obviously, I have in mind F. A. Hayek, "The Use of Knowledge in Society," *American Economic Review* 35 (September 1945): 519–530.

Of course, externalities, transactions costs, and all that keep the price system from operating with all imaginable perfection. But what is a fringe "imperfection" of the market economy is a central characteristic of governmental decisionmaking.

sibility are largely fragmented and uncoordinated in the political and governmental process. Far-reaching and long-run consequences of decisions receive skimpy attention.

One aspect of this fragmentation, noted by Samuel Brittan, is that "the cost of a political decision is borne by people other than the voter. A customer buying a suit or a washing machine has to bear the cost himself." Someone voting for a candidate who makes some attractive promise, however, usually—and realistically—assumes "that others will bear the cost."[3]

Any number of government activities might each seem desirable by itself in the absence of most of the others, but it does not necessarily follow that the whole agglomeration of them is also desirable. To suppose so would be to commit the fallacy of composition, of supposing that anything true of the part or individual must also be true of the whole or group. Adding any particular government function to all the others complicates the tasks of choosing, operating, and supervising those others.[4] The more functions the government takes on and the more complicated they are, the more they must be left to the "experts"; and the people's elected representatives, let alone the people themselves, are less able to exercise close and informed control. The elected representatives, who supposedly should monitor the experts, must largely depend on them for information; and the experts have their own special views about their work.

Particular government programs, and especially agglomerations of them, have remote, unforeseen consequences. The current inflation is one example. Burgeoning programs—including, ironically, ones intended to help make the citizens economically secure—have led to federal deficits, government borrowing, upward pressures on interest rates, Federal Reserve actions to restrain their rise, consequent excessive expansion of the monetary base and money supply, price inflation, further allowance for inflation in interest rates, further short-run efforts to restrain their rise by monetary expansion, establishment of a momentum in prices and wages such that an antiinflationary turn in monetary policy would not bring quick success but would bring a recession, monetary accommodation of the rising

3. Samuel Brittan, in *The Political Economy of Inflation*, ed. Fred Hirsch and John H. Goldthorpe, (Cambridge: Harvard University Press, 1978), pp. 165–166.

4. See, in part, Milton Friedman, *Capitalism and Freedom* (Chicago: University of Chicago Press, 1962), p. 32. In the technical jargon, government activities have external diseconomies.

wages and prices, and so on. The result is all the *in*security that inflation brings, and all the disruption of economic calculation. A still
more pervasive example—so one might argue—is that the accumulation of government activities and their repercussions brings a drift
in the whole character of our social, political, and economic system;
yet that drift was never squarely faced and decided on as a political
issue.

THE "FLAW" AND THE CASE FOR LIMITS

Overregulation stems from a "basic flaw" in our political system
closely related to the flaw noted in current arguments for a constitutional limit to government taxing or spending.[5] Because of its close
relation to the present topic, the central argument is worth reviewing. The alternative to such a limit—letting total spending emerge as
the sum of individually enacted appropriations—is biased upward.
Some people are especially interested in government spending on
rivers and harbors and military installations, others in spending for
schools and teachers, others in housing subsidies, and still others in
energy research contracts. Because of its special interest, each group
is well informed about the government action it wants and has arguments for it readily at hand. Furthermore, since the benefits of its
favorite program will be relatively concentrated on itself rather than
diluted over the entire population, its members have incentives to
incur the trouble and expense of pressing the group's views on the
legislators. A candidate or legislator, for his part, knows that each
special interest cares intensely about what concerns it and fears that
losing the support of only a few such interests could cost him election or reelection; so he tends to be responsive.[6]

The links between particular government expenditures and particular tax collections are loose. No one really knows who will ultimately pay for a government program. The voter can drift into thinking that someone else, perhaps "the rich" or the big corporations,

5. One presentation of the diagnosis appears in William F. Rickenbacker and Lewis K.
Uhler, *A Taxpayer's Guide to Survival: Constitutional Tax-Limitation* (Briarcliff Manor,
N.Y.: National Tax-Limitation Committee, 1977), chap. 1.

6. See "Single-Issue Politics," *Newsweek*, 6 November 1978, pp. 48-60, and, on con-
gressmen's feelings of insecurity, see Thomas E. Mann, *Unsafe at Any Margin* (Washington:
American Enterprise Institute, 1978).

will pay or ought to pay. (Not even economists know who ultimately pays the corporate income tax.) It is easy to drift into thinking that the government gets resources out of some sort of fourth dimension. Politicians will not hasten to disabuse voters of this "fiscal illusion." Nowadays, with taxes and inflation being what they are, this illusion is evaporating; but the very fact that the present state of affairs could develop suggests that some such illusion has been at work until recently.

An art-loving journalist has unwittingly illustrated the sort of attitude that expands government activity—and thereby also illustrated the logic of the sort of limit he was complaining against.[7] State and local government actions taken after passage of Proposition 13 in California reveal, he complained, that many officials see the arts as an expendable elitist pursuit. The recent tremendous growth in public funding for the arts had suddenly been thrown into reverse. A 60 percent slash in the budget of a state agency making grants to art programs and individual artists had lowered California to 44th place among all states in per capita funding for the arts. Yet, he continued, the arts pay the wages of hundreds of thousands of people, directly and indirectly. How many restaurants near the Music Center in downtown Los Angeles would remain open without the audiences that the Center draws? The arts offer pleasure and entertainment and stimulation. State and local governments have made too much of a commitment to them to back out now without seriously retarding their progress. "A society that considers it a frill to nourish its soul is in deep trouble." In reply, a reader asked: "What kind of trouble can be expected by a society that depends on government to nourish its soul?"[8] The journalist tacitly accepts the notion that not to finance particular activities by taxes—by compulsion—is to be neglectful of them. Also noteworthy is his misuse, regarding downtown Los Angeles, of the overworked theoretical argument about externalities— here, spillover benefits.

Much the same points that apply to spending apply also to regulation. Some economic interest groups benefit from regulation (perhaps it protects them against competition) and automatically have the information and incentives to press candidates and legislators for

7. Stephen J. Sansweet, "Proposition 13's Impact on the Arts," *Wall Street Journal*, 14 July 1978, p. 11.

8. Roy A. Beaver, letter to *Wall Street Journal*, 26 July 1978, p. 12.

what they want. The latter, for their part, are rationally more responsive to special-interest pressures than to the general interest of the average voters, who are rationally ignorant and apathetic about the details of public policy. Furthermore, citizens who identify themselves with some cause — protecting the environment, cracking down on health and safety hazards, developing exotic energy sources, fostering the arts, remedying supposedly unjust inequalities, suppressing (or facilitating) abortion, improving the eating habits of school children, or whatever — take on the political characters of special interests and, like them, tend to have disproportionate influence with politicians or the relevant bureaucrats. The much discussed "new class" of activist intellectuals and publicists belongs in the story. Legislators, bureaucrats, and other members of the government themselves have personal stakes in government activism, though many of them are no doubt sincerely motivated to do good as they conceive of doing good in their own special niches in life.

METHODOLOGICAL INDIVIDUALISM
IN ANALYZING GOVERNMENT

None of this amounts to casting aspersions on the moral characters of the people who take part in deciding on government activities. I am simply drawing implications from the fact that these people decide and act within particular frameworks of information, incentives, tests of performance, and rewards.[9] Economists, long successful with methodological individualism in their own field, are now applying that approach to understanding how people behave in the governmental framework. We, the analysts, project ourselves into the role of businessman, consumer, bureaucrat, legislator, political candidate, or whoever it is whose decisions and actions we are trying to understand. We consider his motivations and incentives, perhaps even including the circumstances affecting his self-esteem, as well as the opportunities and constraints he faces. We can draw relevant infor-

---

9. Kenneth N. Waltz makes an analogous point, which illuminates this one, in his *Theory of International Politics* (Reading, Mass. and Menlo Park, Calif.: Addison-Wesley Publishing Company, 1979). Almost regardless of the internal character of its regime, we can say much about how a country behaves in the arena of international politics in view of the situation confronting it — in particular, according to whether or not it is a dominant power and, if it is, whether it is one of several or one of only two dominant powers.

mation from our own personal thoughts, actions, and experiences. Such an approach does not depend on the profundities of psychology. It draws inferences from familiar facts about human nature and about decision-making situations.

Circumstances and Ideas of the Average Voter

The "average voter" is the voter considered at random, otherwise than as a member of any special-interest group. (To take account of *non*voting, perhaps the term should be "average citizen.") He does not automatically possess the information needed to weigh the pros and cons of more or less spending on each special group's favorite project. Furthermore, obtaining such information would cost him money, time, and trouble better devoted to other purposes. He profits more from a day spent learning the strong and weak points of different makes of car or refrigerator, when he wants to buy a new one, than from a day spent trying to learn the advantages and disadvantages of increased government spending on aircraft carriers or urban renewal.

Acquiring and acting on information about public issues has a low payoff because it is a "public good." The standard rationale for having any government at all is that it is necessary to provide public goods, such as national defense, police protection, and the legal system. Their benefits cannot be confined to people who voluntarily contribute money or effort for them. Each person might as well sit back and enjoy a free ride on the expenditures or efforts of others. So government sells public goods compulsorily, for taxes. But no such solution, imperfect as it may be, has been found for the public good of monitoring the government itself.[10] If an average voter should go to the trouble of keeping informed and politically active, most of the benefits, in the form of sounder policy, would accrue to others. While reaping only a very minor share of these benefits, he would have to bear all of his own costs. He has about as little reason to incur them as he would have to stop driving his car to hold down air pollution. He has little incentive to work for what is in the general interest.[11]

10. The concept of monitoring as a public good is due, I believe, to Roland McKean.

11. The weakness of personal incentives to seek collective rather than individual benefits is a leading theme of Mancur Olson, Jr., *The Logic of Collective Action* (Cambridge: Har-

Exhorting citizens to study the issues and take an active role in politics largely ignores these facts. It tacitly regards concern with governmental affairs as a noble activity holding a special claim on each citizen's attention. Actually, badgering him to divert his money, time, and energy from work or recreation to political studies that perplex or bore him will contribute little to wise policymaking. It is an imposition, too, if holding down the range of government decisions in the first place could have held down these demands on his attention.

Even if, implausibly, the voter should become well informed and vote accordingly, he cannot express himself on each program separately. If he is voting on issues at all when choosing between candidates, he is voting on policy positions all jumbled together in vaguely specified packages, along with the candidates' actual or advertised personalities. Furthermore, his own monitoring of the government through informed voting (and lobbying) would do little good unless other voters joined him. He is only one out of many, and his own informed vote would hardly be decisive for the outcome of an election or for the decision on some program. It is rational for him to content himself with superficial notions about election issues, voting for a party label out of habit or for a well-packaged personality out of whim.[12] His position is different from that of people who would reap concentrated benefits from particular programs and have good prospects of promoting government *activism* in their favor. Average and special-interest voters alike, though, enjoy an apparent freedom from personal responsibility in the voting booth; each is acting anonymously along with many others.

It is doubtful that businessmen, as such, have any strong interest in working to limit government intervention. Just because they are the key actors in a free-market economy, it does not follow that the individual businessman finds it in his self-interest to work to preserve such an economy. Businessmen can cope with regulation. Its burdens

---

vard University Press, 1965). The free-ride motivation of the average voter also characterizes the individual member of a special-interest group. It operates, though, to a lesser degree. The group member belongs to a smaller group with a more intense and concentrated interest than the average voter does; his own interest is less diluted by being shared with others. Furthermore, as Olson notes, an organized interest group may be able to command the support of its members by supplying services of value to them individually, such as business information and other trade-association services, in addition to its collectively desired lobbying function.

12. "Rational ignorance" is a leading theme of Anthony Downs, *An Economic Theory of Democracy* (New York: Harper, 1957).

may not be much worse than those of competition, which, anyway, some kinds of regulation restrain. The prospects for businessmen of ordinary ability relative to the prospects of the most dynamic entrepreneurs may even be better in a highly regulated economy than under substantial laissez faire; enjoying the quiet life may be easier. Hence the pointlessness of businessmen exhorting each other to do a better job of communicating their case to the public. Businessmen as such, rather than simply as human beings, are not the main beneficiaries of a free economy.

With little personal incentive really to understand public affairs, the average voter tends to work with ideas that are in the air. The attitude does seem to prevail widely these days that if anything is bad—pornography, or small children's eating medicine that they shouldn't have, or junk food in the schools—then it is the government's job to suppress it. Similarly, if anything is good—housing, arts, effective drugs, good nutrition—then government ought to promote or subsidize it. This attitude parallels the doctrine of altruism, which receives wide lip service, the doctrine that one ought to be primarily concerned with the (supposed) interests of other people. It is wickedly selfish, then, to oppose a program for doing good, even if it does cost tax money. (Government programs in one's own special interest can readily be rationalized in altruistic terms, as good for other people also. It is a routine theoretical exercise for economists to concoct "externality" arguments for government interventions.) The altruist doctrine meshes well with the idea that it is slightly indecent to be a rightist and the presumption that the decent and humane position on any issue is at least a little left of center.[13]

The psychological roots[14] of interventionism include people's tendency to believe what they want to believe and the readiness of politicians to exploit this tendency. In political argumentation, plausibility counts. Mere slogans and name-calling sometimes work. The acceptance of merely plausible arguments is aided by a trait of contemporary thought roughly equivalent to what F. A. Hayek has called "scientism."[15] Just as Chanticleer thought his crowing made

---

13. Jacques Ellul, *A Critique of the New Commonplaces*, trans. Helen Weaver (New York: Knopf, 1968), pp. 215–219.

14. Here I am falling into temptation—into amateur psychologizing—and what follows should perhaps be discounted.

15. His articles on "Scientism and the Study of Society," *Economica* (August 1942, February 1943, and February 1944), are reprinted in *The Counter-Revolution of Science* (Glencoe: Free Press, 1952), pt. 1.

the sun rise, so voters and politicians seem to think that their laws are what make good things happen. People are unaccustomed to conceiving of how good results will occur unless they are explicitly sought; the invisible hand is not universally appreciated. When a problem has become politically fashionable, to suggest leaving its solution to private initiative seems callous.[16] Action is considered "positive" and therefore good, while opposition is "negative" and therefore bad.

Support for activism intertwines with the idea that democracy is a good thing. That idea slides into the belief that doing things democratically, that is, through democratic government, that is, through government, is a good thing.

Another reason for the widespread appeal of government intervention is disregard of the incompleteness of knowledge and the costs of information, transactions, and decisionmaking in the public sector while emphasizing such "imperfections" of the private sector. Tacitly, the government is regarded as a philosopher-king, totally benevolent, omniscient, efficient, and effective.[17] Handing over a problem to such an entity seems like solving it.

Special Interests and Synthetic Majorities

So far we have been considering the average voter, his circumstances and attitudes, and the appeals directed toward him. Next we turn to special interests and then to "hobbyists." Politicians are tempted to appease each clamoring interest by helping it get what it wants and to compensate the others by doing the same for them. Under these circumstances, logrolling (explicit in legislatures and implicit in political platforms) assembles majorities out of essentially unrelated minorities. "Minorities rule"[18] — not *the* minority, but an implicit

16. See below in the section on "crowding out."

17. George Stigler quotes a pair of rather typical passages on the defects of a private market economy that could readily be overcome by "a socialist economy" (Oskar Lange) or by "the State" (A. C. Pigou). Then he substitutes "Almighty Jehovah" and "his Serene Omnipotence" for the words here in quotation marks — with amusing and telling effect. See Stigler, *The Citizen and the State* (Chicago: University of Chicago Press, 1975), pp. 112–113. The assumption illustrated is now being undermined by the application of methodological individualism to the study of government.

18. "Minorities Rule" is the title of the reprinted version, in *American Democracy*, ed. Leonard J. Fein, (New York: Holt, Rinehart and Winston, 1964), pp. 125–130, of Robert A. Dahl, *A Preface to Democratic Theory*, (Chicago: University of Chicago Press, 1963), pp. 124–134.

coalition of several minorities. Suppose that for each of three programs, 25 percent of the voters favor it so intensely that they would vote for whichever candidate supports it, regardless of his position on other issues. Seventy-five percent of the voters oppose each program, but only mildly. Suppose, further, that the minority favoring each of the three programs is a distinct group. (To recognize that two or three of the groups have some members in common would complicate the example without affecting its point.) A candidate supporting all three programs would be elected overwhelmingly and be put in a position to work for their enactment, even though 75 percent of the electorate opposed each program. The same sort of implicit logrolling operates, though less clearly than in this example, in the growth of government budgets. As the example suggests, by the way, the political process affords scope for political entrepreneurship and not just for passive response to existing demands.

Particularly as the vote-trading process spreads out over time and over numerous separate ballots, spurious consensus becomes possible. Policy combinations get adopted that could not have commanded a majority if considered as a whole. The procedure of making decisions year by year leads to commitments to the future growth of spending that are not seen or not appreciated when made, yet are hard to reverse later. Furthermore, the automatic growth of revenue as the economy grows and as inflation proceeds, pushing taxpayers into higher brackets, allows the government to avoid an *explicit* decision to raise taxes to cover increased spending.[19]

The politics of abortion illustrates the influence of intensely concerned minorities. The California and Massachusetts legislatures were so embroiled in controversy over public funding of abortions in July 1978 that they failed to finish their budget work in time for the new fiscal year. A single issue fought over intensely by small but well-organized groups can distract politicians' attention from matters of broad but unfocused public concern. Similarly, a vast majority may grumble about high taxes, but its concern is so diffuse (or has been, until recently) that it can seldom counterbalance powerful minority pressures working for specific spending programs.[20]

19. Herbert Stein, "The Real Reasons for a Tax Cut," *Wall Street Journal*, 18 July 1978, p. 20.
20. *Wall Street Journal*, editorial, 12 July 1978, p. 20.

Hobbyists

Activists on all sides of the abortion issue are examples of what I call "hobbyists," who engage in political study and activity not so much for obvious material gain as because they have identified themselves with some mission or are seeking an outlet for their energies or a sense of participation in admirable causes. Hobbyists include people who want a federal crash program to cure a disease that killed a relative, or who have lost a child in a boating accident and therefore seek federal regulation, or want subsidies for art or music, or want preservation of the unspoiled wilderness. People acting out of disinterested public spirit count among the hobbyists; the term is not meant disparagingly. Stretched a bit, the term also covers "consumer advocates," who, for the publicity they thrive on, require "a constant supply of new charges against new villains . . . suitably printed in the hot ink of outrage."[21]

By the very nature of their "hobbies," just as by the very nature of special economic interests, most hobbyists are pressing for more government activity. A belief in laissez faire or limited government is itself a hobby for some people, to be sure; but it is just one among a great many hobbies, most of which do tend toward interventionism. It is no real embarrassment for this argument that some intellectuals do take an *anti*interventionist stand. Of course some are libertarians, but psychological factors and aspects of the democratic process make it difficult for their view to prevail in practice.

Hobbyists are charmed at having one central focus, Washington, for their persuasive efforts and charmed by the prospect of using the force of government to *impose* what they want. Success seems easier along that route than along the route of persuading myriads of individuals voluntarily to observe, for example, stricter standards of boating safety. Hobbyists seeking entertainment or a sense of participation are inclined to want to be in fashion. If altruist and interventionist doctrines prevail, they will go along.

The Politician

The politician, to thrive in his career, must recognize the voters as they are – the average voters with their susceptibilities, the special

21. Stigler, *The Citizen and the State*, p. 188.

interests and hobbyists with their particular concerns. Like most people, he wants to think well of himself; he wants to think he is accomplishing something. His particular mission in life is to perceive problems and get government programs enacted to solve them.[22] Even when out of office, the politician does not typically strive to limit the scope for doing good in the office he hopes to win at the next election.[23] In office, he wants to carry forth his uncompleted programs and continue serving the public better than his opponents could do.

Publicity is helpful in the quest for votes. (So is having patronage with which to reward supporters, and to which government expansion contributes.) One way to gain favorable publicity is to become identified with one or more problems and with proposals for their solution—pollution, unemployment, the urban crisis, the energy crisis, the expenses of medical care, poverty, inequality, or whatever. It may even count as a solution that the proposed legislation merely creates a new agency assigned to deal with the problem.[24] One reason for delegating work to regulatory agencies is that the legislature has too much to do to consider problems and solutions in detail; legislating, along with the bargaining necessary for it, is a high-cost activity with steeply rising marginal costs.[25] Furthermore, the vagueness inherent in handling a problem by turning it over to a new agency can itself be helpful in lulling possible opposition, just as vagueness in the wording of a proposed international agreement may be helpful in getting all parties to accept it.

The individual advocate of one particular bit of government expansion has little personal incentive to consider the external dis-

22. "... the people's representatives seem to be enchanted with the notion that they are not doing their job unless they are manufacturing laws." James McClellan, "The Tyranny of Legalism" (a review of Bruno Leoni, *Freedom and the Law),* *University Bookman* (Spring 1974), p. 66.

23. Benjamin Constant, *Cours de Politique Constitutionnelle* (1818-20), I, 10, as quoted in Bertrand de Jouvenel, *On Power*, (New York: Viking, 1949), p. 384, and also de Jouvenel himself, p. 10.

24. Relevant here is Amitai Etzioni, "The Grand Shaman," *Psychology Today* 6 (November 1972): pp. 88-92, 142-143. Headed "Got a problem ... ? ... call or write The Grand Shaman," the article notes people's propensity to look to the federal government for solutions to all sorts of problems. Its main concern, however, is the empty, symbolic character of many ostensible solutions. Speeches are made, conferences held, commissions appointed, bills passed, agencies established, funds appropriated, and programs launched, often doing little of substance to treat the problems involved.

25. Richard A. Posner, "Theories of Economic Regulation," *Bell Journal of Economics and Management Science* 5 (Autumn 1974): 339-340.

economies that may result in the form of the enhanced role of inadequately supervised experts and the worsened difficulties of monitoring government. Neither he nor the voters will recognize any responsibility of his for such long-run consequences. Later on, after such pseudosolutions have enhanced the power of administrators, reduced the relative power of the people and their elected representatives, increased the difficulties of monitoring the government, and expanded the scope for court cases, these unintended results will hardly be traced to and blamed on the original sponsors of the legislation. Meanwhile, they get credit for being *concerned* with problems.

Politicians and government officials tend to have short time horizons. Unlike corporation executives, who may hold stock or stock options of their companies and whose performance tends to be assessed and reported on the stock market anyway, government officials hold no shares of stock whose current prices might reflect assessments of the *long-run* consequences of their actions; hence, short-run electoral concerns tend to prevail. How much incentive, for example, do mayors have to mount strong resistance to the demands of unionized city employees? Mayor John Lindsay of New York "took the attitude that he would not be around in ten years. He thought he would be either in the White House or doing something else, so he decided to pay people off with promises of pensions that would come due when he was no longer mayor."[26]

The personal qualities useful in gaining favorable publicity and in political wheeling and dealing are not likely to coincide with the personal qualities of a competent, far-sighted, and courageous statesman. Neither are the qualities of a successful campaigner, which include adroitness in projecting an appealing personality and in cleverly stating or obscuring issues.[27] Similarly, a competent and de-

26. Robert Bork in *Taxpayers' Revolt: Are Constitutional Limits Desirable?* American Enterprise Institute Round Table, July 1978, (Washington: American Enterprise Institute, 1978), p. 13.

27. See Jacques Ellul, *The Political Illusion*, trans. Konrad Kellen (New York: Knopf, 1967), pp. 150–151: "The politician is generally not competent with regard to the problems that are his to solve, particularly if, as it is now inevitable, he has become a specialist in political affairs. . . . The political leader must be a politician by trade, which means to be a clever technician in the capture and defense of positions. . . . desire for power clearly has priority . . . because he cannot undertake just and desirable reforms or guard the common good unless he *first* obtains power and keeps it. . . . The two forms of politics . . . demand radically different personal qualities and contrary preoccupations. To be a clever maneuverer

voted public servant would have rather different qualities than a personally successful bureaucrat, whose abilities might run more toward cultivating superiors by promoting their personal ambitions.

Exceptions do occur. Why can't a politician see it as his mission in life to do good by resisting and reversing the trend toward ever more government? If that resistance really is in the interest of the average citizen, why can't the politician both serve his self-esteem and win votes by campaigning on such a platform?

Conceivably he might. But these questions, instead of refuting the argument about activist biases, merely note a possible offset. For several reasons, this offset is unlikely to be strong. (The exceptional politician to whom the following remarks do not apply stands at a disadvantage in winning elections and wielding influence.) First, a political career would generally have been less appealing in the first place to a skeptic about government than to a man who saw great opportunities in it for doing good. Opportunities for also gaining personal success in that endeavor are greater for a politician, as for a bureaucrat, if government is big and growing than if it is kept small. Secondly, winning elections on a platform of *restricting* government activities depends on a greater degree of sophisticated understanding among voters than they are likely to have (although hope on this score is now emerging). Even if a politician is concerned with enlightening the citizens over the long run, he must realize that his chances of providing enlightenment are poor if the voters remove him from political life. He directs his campaigning to the citizens as they are and as they think, not to the economists and political philosophers that they are not.

A third line of rebuttal denies the common idea that politicians try to sell their programs to voters for votes quite as businessmen try to sell their wares to consumers for dollars. The analogy is defective in many respects. For example, candidates go beyond direct appeals to the electorate. They also seek votes indirectly by appealing to influential opinionmakers and to other politicians. Alliances are essential for getting nominations, getting allocations of party funds and other help in campaigns, and logrolling the enactment of one's

in arriving at the summit is no qualification for perceiving the common good, making decisions, being politically enlightened, or mastering economic problems. Conversely, to have the moral qualities and intellectual competence to be capable of genuine thought and of eventually putting a genuine political program into operation in no way ensures having the equipment to reach the top."

favorite projects (and thereby gaining in personal status). The individual politician has to tailor his appeal partly to other politicians, most of whom incline toward an activist government for the reasons under discussion. Even the exceptional politician is restrained, then, from advocating as much limitation of government power as he might otherwise personally favor.

Our amateur psychologizing about politicians should pay some attention to the members of legislators' staffs. With government expansion and legislative burdens making increasing demands on their employers' time and ability to absorb information, staff members have growing influence. They further their own careers by helping their employers gain prominence. Bright ideas help. Although a few ideas may focus on repealing laws and abolishing agencies, activism generally offers more scope for brightness, as well as for maintaining political alliances, especially in an intellectual atmosphere predisposed to activism.

The Bureaucrat

The bureaucrat, like the politician, may well see his mission in life as doing good through the agency of government. He is likely, though, except at the highest levels, to be a specialist. (At the highest levels, he is likely to be mobile between government positions and to be judged more by his reputed abilities and performance in the short run than by the long-run consequences of how he runs any particular agency.) The specialist identifies with the mission of his bureau, appreciates the value of its services, but appreciates less clearly the alternative results obtainable from devoting the necessary money and resources to other purposes, public or private. Like most people, he wants to think that his job is important and demanding and that he is doing it well. With a bigger budget and a larger staff, he could serve the public still better. Fortunately for his ambitions, the legislators must depend largely on what he and his fellow experts tell them about the benefits and costs of his agency's activities. Because his job is specialized and complicated and because they have other tasks also, the legislators cannot monitor him closely. Furthermore, alliances tend to form among the agency, the members of the legislative committee monitoring it, and the constituency in the private sector that benefits from the agency's services or regulations.[28]

The Courts

Judges, like other government decisionmakers, are often in a position to take a narrow view, doing what seems good or benevolent in the particular case at hand without having to weigh costs against benefits carefully and without having to exercise adequate foresight about the long-run repercussions of a particular decision. Of course, judges are under an obligation to decide according to the law, including precedent; but when legislation, administrative decrees, lawsuits, and court decisions have vastly proliferated, the judge — cued by the litigants' attorneys — has all the more decisions to hunt among for the precedent that will rationalize the decision he wants to make.

Nathan Glazer describes several factors contributing to a tide of judicial activism. Powerful new interests are at work, including public-advocacy law centers supported by government or foundations. "Law — for the purpose of the correction of presumed evils, for changing government practices, for overruling legislatures, executives, and administrators, for the purpose indeed of replacing democratic procedures with the authoritarian decisions of judges — became enormously popular." Second, the courts must work out the logic of positions once taken and cannot easily withdraw from their implications. New decisions create precedents whose applications and extensions cannot be fully foreseen; case law evolves with a momentum of its own. Examples concern the concepts of "standing" to sue, of due process, and of equal protection. Third, expansion of government activity provides all the more subject matter for court cases. The "facts" relevant to court decisions become all the more numerous and complex. Social science becomes relevant; and as it changes, so may the law. The judges acquire all the more opportunities for second-guessing not only ordinary citizens but also the legislative

28. William A. Niskanen argues that bureaucrats strive to maximize their budgets. See *Bureaucracy and Representative Government* (Chicago: Aldine-Atherton, 1971). Years earlier, Ludwig von Mises had stressed the contrast between a profit-seeking firm and a bureau. In a firm, the higher executives can monitor the performance of their subordinates by financial accounting and the test of profit and loss. Monitoring is more complicated in a nonprofit organization. Especially in one that gets its funds from budget appropriations rather than by selling goods or services to willing customers, the financial tests are necessarily weakened, and detailed "bureaucratic" rules and regulations must take their place as best they can. *Bureaucracy* (London: Hodge, 1945).

and executive branches of government.[29] In short, the courts well illustrate the main theme of this paper: the fragmentation, on the governmental scene, of cost-benefit calculation, decisions, and responsibility.

A Possible Counterargument

Considering the circumstances and incentives of voters, politicians, bureaucrats, and judges does seem to reveal a bias toward hyperactive government. Yet Anthony Downs, who had lucidly explained the rationality of voter ignorance, went on to offer a supposed explanation of "why the government budget is too small in a democracy."[30] The core of his argument is that the rationally ignorant voter does not appreciate all the remote and problematical benefits that government programs would provide. As society becomes wealthier and more complex, the potential scope for remote and poorly understood but genuine government benefits expands. Public goods do not enjoy the advertising that private goods do. The average voter is highly aware, however, of the costs of government programs as reflected in his taxes. Catering to such voters, politicians hold taxing and spending down to levels at which the benefits of additional spending would still exceed the costs.

Several things are wrong with this argument. First, taxes are not all that evident to the individual voter. Excise taxes are concealed in the prices of products, and just which persons ultimately bear the burden of the corporation income tax is even more obscure. Even personal income taxes can be made less conspicuous by withholding. Downs does not take adequate account of these tax concealments. He does not adequately recognize the several distinct ways in which inflation can bring what amounts to hidden tax increases. He does not recognize how easy it is for government to spend the incremental tax revenues generated by economic growth. He does not take "fiscal illusion" seriously enough. Second, politicans have discovered the beauties of deficit spending; and working as they do with short time horizons, they do not agonize over an ultimate day of reckoning. Third, Downs

29. Nathan Glazer, "Towards an Imperial Judiciary?" *The Public Interest* 41 (Fall 1975): 104–123, quotation from p. 123. (I have rearranged and interpreted Glazer's points.) Glazer cites numerous specific examples of judicial activism.
30. Anthony Downs, "Why the Government Budget is Too Small in a Democracy," *World Politics* 3 (July 1960): 541–563.

gives only unconvincing examples of government activities that have thin but widespread benefits, or benefits that are great in the long run but unnoticed in the short run. In fact, his chief example seems to be foreign aid. Although he notes the coercive nature of dealings with government, he seems not to recognize that private activities carried out with resources not taxed away might themselves have remote benefits and that the coercive nature of the expansion of government activity makes that expansion less likely to leave a net excess of benefit over cost than the alternative of voluntary expansion of private activity. He does not recognize the differential incentives that special private interests have to press exaggerated claims about the benefits of the government programs that they are seeking.

Fourth, while Downs applies the approach of methodological individualism to the voter, he does not apply it consistently to bureaucrats, politicians, judges, and litigants. In some passages, he refers to "the governing party" or even "the government" as if it were a monolithic entity making coordinated choices rather than an assemblage of individual persons each working with his own drives, motives, opportunities, incentives, constraints, and special point of view. He does not take heed of how individual legislators or candidates can call for particular spending programs without calling for the taxes to pay for them. He supposes that each bureau would submit its budget requests to, in effect, "the directors of the governing party," who, anxious for votes, would develop suitable checks on the bureau's expansionism. He does not recognize, as William Niskanen later explained, that self-aggrandizing bureaus are in fact not supervised by a sufficiently authoritative central budgeting agency.[31] On the contrary, they are likely to develop cozy relations with the congressional committees that are supposed to monitor them. In short, Downs fails to grasp the full implications of fragmented government decision-making.

EFFECTS ON POLICY

Policy Drift

The fragmentation of decisions over time contributes to an unintended drift of the character of the whole economic and political

---

31. Niskanen, *Bureaucracy and Representative Government.*

system. Especially under a two-party system, platform-builders and campaigners often avoid drawing issues in a clear-cut way.[32] A candidate opposed to protective tariffs would not call for complete free trade for fear of losing some protectionist voters who would support him on other issues. He realizes that many a voter will choose the lesser evil rather than "waste his vote" on a third party even if one happened to mirror his own set of views more accurately. Political straddling, together with the jumbling together of unrelated issues (and even the candidates' personalities) in every election, water down the issue of interventionism versus the free market into an uninspiring choice between parties leaning just a little more one way or a little more the other. Incentives and prejudices favoring a middle-of-the-road position leave the direction of cumulative policy drift to whoever are most active in locating the two sides of the road, or even just one side. The kinds of choices that voters and politicians consider feasible (and, similarly, the positions they consider unrealistically extreme) are conditioned by how policy has been drifting. Resistance to drift weakens when not only politicians but even scholars make a fetish of recommending only policies they consider politically "realistic."[33] Under such circumstances, discussion does not adequately consider long-run repercussions and long-run compatibilities and clashes among various goals and measures. Major choices, such as ones affecting the general character of the economic and social system, may get made by default as the cumulative result of piecemeal decisions whose combined tendencies were not realized when they were made.

Fragmentation Bad and Good

Closely related to dispersion of decisionmaking among persons and over time is dispersion of responsibility. Things that would be considered morally reprehensible if done by a single decision maker escape moral condemnation when done by government, since it is

---

32. An early explanation was provided by Harold Hotelling in an article basically dealing with economic matters: "Stability in Competition," *Economic Journal* 39 (March 1929): 41–57.

33. On the harmfulness and even immorality of such "realism," see Clarence E. Philbrook, "'Realism' in Policy Espousal," *American Economic Review* 43 (December 1953): 846–859.

not apparent where the responsibility lies. Examples are our inflation mess, the quasi repudiation of government debt, the taxation of phantom earnings and phantom capital gains, even when the tax-payer has suffered a real loss and even when he has suffered it on bonds of the government itself, and the government's continued pushing of its savings bonds.

Fragmentation of decisionmaking is not to be condemned *tout court.* In many cases, keeping decisions close to the affected level will improve the cost-benefit confrontation. Furthermore, it helps preserve freedom. In fact, this is one of the chief arguments for the market as opposed to government control.[34]

Crowding Out

Another disadvantage of routine reliance on government to suppress all bad and promote all good is that it tends to freeze out alternative solutions to the problems tackled. It can hamper diverse initiatives and experimentation. It can crowd out private activity by taxing away funds that people would otherwise spend themselves on satisfy-ing their wants, by transferring real resources from the private to the public sector, by creating or threatening subsidized competition with private approaches, and by stifling imagination with the thought that the problem in question is already being taken care of. It is instruc-tive to ponder what the state of affairs in education, health and re-tirement programs, housing, transportation, the mails, and other fields would be today if government had not gotten so heavily involved as it has in fact. One frequent advantage of private over government financing is that it can take better account of how

34. "The system of direct regulation cannot allow flexibility in the application to indi-vidual cases because favoritism cannot be distinguished from flexibility and diversity of con-ditions cannot be distinguished from caprice. The price system, however, possesses this remarkable power: if we make an activity expensive in order to reduce its practice, those who are most attached to the practice may still continue it. It is the system which excludes from an industry not those who arrived last but those who prize least the right to work in that industry. It is the system which builds roads by hiring men with an aptitude for road-building, not by the corvée of compulsory labor." Stigler, *The Citizen and the State*, p. 36.

The recent gasoline shortage and proposals to deal with it by rationing or by making everybody forgo driving one day a week, or the nonsystem of rationing by inconvenience, all illustrate Stigler's points about regulation versus the market. Regulation cannot take into account the detailed personal knowledge that people have about their own needs and wants and circumstances.

strongly people desire an activity on the whole and in its various possible forms. Far from the importance of an activity arguing for its being taken over by the government, one should think that its importance argues against its being dominated by one big supplier. It is all the more regrettable when various monopolized activities are monopolized by the same monopolist and when economic and political power are combined, with all that implies about potentialities for coercion.

What crowding out means is illustrated in the field of energy. Proposals abound for government action and subsidies to develop nonconventional sources. Taxpayers would in effect have to pay the difference between the high cost and lower price of subsidized fuels; and they could not, acting individually, escape this burden by energy conservation. Production from conventional sources and potential production from unsubsidized new sources will suffer as producers find it easier and less risky to take government handouts. Not only money but also talent and ingenuity will be diverted from other types of production, exploration, and research into those favored by the government. Business firms and investors will shy away from risky, expensive, long-term-oriented projects not only for fear of future government-subsidized competition but also for fear of future infringements on property rights. The history of energy policy, together with current demogogy, provides ample grounds for the latter fear: firms and investors must recognize the prospect that even after risking heavy losses, they will not be allowed to collect exceptionally large profits from successful hunches and good luck.[35] Government reassurances, even if made, would nowadays not be credible. This example bears on a broader point about remote repercussions — remote in time and in sector affected. A violation of property rights — perhaps restrictions on use of property rather than outright public purchase — may seem the economical and expedient thing to do in the individual case. Yet in contributing to an atmosphere of uncertainty, it can have grave repercussions in the long run.

An advocate of limited government cannot specify just what nongovernmental solution to a problem might have been found if it had not been crowded out. An economist sympathetic to the market can explain how entrepreneurs have incentives to seek unfilled wants and

---

35. Paul L. Joskow and Robert S. Pindyck develop points like these in "Those Subsidized Energy Schemes," *Wall Street Journal*, 2 July 1979, p. 12.

ways of filling them, but he cannot predict what unfilled wants are going to be filled, and how and when.[36] Hence his position seems complacent; it reeks of the ivory tower. In contrast, the interventionist position looks concrete, active, practical, and down-to-earth.

Here I am in danger of being misunderstood. While I deplore regulating voluntary transactions that are not immoral and that adults are undertaking with their eyes open, the case is different with hidden safety or health hazards or with the imposition of costs onto innocent third parties. I have qualms about cold-turkey deregulation in such cases. Yet over the long run, phasing out government regulation could open the way for entrepreneurial discovery of alternatives that we can hardly imagine in advance. Such alternatives might, for example, include inspection and certification by specialist firms, as well as regulations imposed by insurance companies as a condition of insurance. My emphasis, however, is not on predicting alternative approaches but on their unpredictability and on how central control can forestall their discovery.[37]

Still Broader Costs of Regulation

Costs (and conceivably benefits) of regulatory measures include effects on the whole social, political, and economic climate and on people's attitudes. One example of what I have in mind concerns how even the vaguest hints about discriminatory enforcement of myriad regulations can be used to encourage "voluntary" compliance

36. See Hayek, *Rules and Order*, especially the section headed "Freedom can be preserved only by following principles and is destroyed by following expediency," pp. 56–59. Hayek reminds us that the benefits of civilization rest on using more knowledge than can be deployed in any deliberately concerted effort. "Since the value of freedom rests on opportunities it provides for unforeseen and unpredictable actions, we will rarely know what we lose through a particular restriction of freedom." Any restriction will aim at some foreseeable particular benefit, while what it forecloses will usually remain unknown and disregarded. Deciding each issue on its own apparent merits means overestimating the advantages of central direction.

37. Israel M. Kirzner explains how regulation can impede the process of discovery. His concern, however, is not so much with alternative solutions to problems taken under the government's wing as, rather, with discovery of new and better goods and services and production methods. Furthermore, regulation diverts entrepreneurs' energies from seeking discoveries of these constructive kinds into coping with or circumventing the regulations themselves. See *The Perils of Regulation: A Market-Process Approach*, Law and Economics Center Occasional Paper (Coral Gables: Law and Economics Center of the University of Miami, 1979), especially chap. 4.

with the wage and price controls decreed by the president, without legal authority, in October 1978.[38] Another hard-to-fathom cost is the danger (already alluded to in the section on "The Courts") of undermining the rule of law and the law's objectivity, predictability, and worthiness of respect.

My worries do not hinge on any particular one of the several theories of regulation that are in circulation.[39] I am not, for example, adopting as the central story the theory that regulated industries "capture" their regulatory authorities. No doubt some aspects even of the public-interest theory of regulation enter into the explanation of why we have so much of it. Numerous pressures, motivations, and governmental decisionmakers interact.[40]

The issue of regulation falls under the broader question of whether policy should serve principle or expediency, the latter meaning to act on the supposed merits of each individual case, narrowly considered. Elements of an answer to that question argue for framing policy with prime attention, instead, to the general framework of rules within which persons and companies can pursue their own goals. (In philosophical terminology, the argument favors rules-utilitarianism over act-utilitarianism.)

Some types of regulation are even open to objection on ethical grounds. Notions of human rights properly belong in the discussion, including rights of people to make open-and-above-board voluntary transactions with each other and to use and deal in their own property.[41] It is a questionable view to accord equal respect to people's

38. Referring to this program, one Federal Reserve economist has written as follows: "Violators are explicitly threatened with bad publicity and loss of government contracts. Implicitly, possible violators must be aware of potential retaliation by regulatory agencies not formally incorporated in the wage-price control program. . . . Due to the magnitude of discretionary authority possessed by the Internal Revenue Service, Environmental Protection Agency, Federal Trade Commission, Occupational Safety and Health Administration, etc., a large potential for retaliation confronts any business." Roy H. Webb, "Wage-Price Restraint and Macroeconomic Disequilibrium," Federal Reserve Bank of Richmond, *Economic Review* 65, no. 3, (May/June 1979): 14n.

39. See Stigler, *The Citizen and the State*; Richard A. Posner, "Theories of Economic Regulation," *Bell Journal* 5 (Autumn 1974): 335–358. Sam Peltzman, "Toward a More General Theory of Regulation," *Journal of Law and Economics* 19 (August 1976): 211–240.

40. "More generally, different types of constitutionally empowered agents on the political scene — bureaucrats, judges, legislators, and elected executives — each bring distinct motivations, authorities, and constraints into the process of political exchange that leads to the final regulatory outcome." Jack Hirschleifer, "Comment" [on Peltzman's article], *Journal of Law and Economics* 19 (August 1976): 242.

41. See Tibor R. Machan, "Some Normative Considerations of Deregulation," *Journal of Social and Political Studies* 3 (Winter 1979): 363–377.

use of their own property and forcible interference with that use. That view sets aside the question of who has a right to do what in favor of the question of which expected pattern of property use and resource allocation appeals more to politicians and other outside observers.

POLICY IMPLICATIONS

What implications follow from my argument, if it is broadly correct? Most generally, it recommends alertness to activist bias, and an appropriate constitutional attitude. Proposals have been made for a regulatory budget: included in the annual limit to each regulatory agency's expenses would be not only its own cash outlays but also the estimated costs that compliance with its regulations would impose on the private sector. Admittedly, implementing such a proposal would run into practical difficulties, but it is mainly its spirit that concerns us here.

It is instructive to review the rationale for the analogous proposal of placing a constitutional limit on federal government taxing or spending. The opportunity to enact such a limit would give the public at large the hitherto lacking means to vote on the total of the government budget. By voting for a limit, a majority could override the spending bias that arises from the accumulation of smaller special-interest decisions.[42] The people assign a budget to the legislature and require it spend the limited amount of money in the most effective way. (Supporters of a limit ask: if families have to operate within income ceilings, why shouldn't the government also?) Overall limitation would force choices among the many spending programs that might be separately desirable. To argue persuasively in the face of a given budget total, a group wanting a particular program would have to point out other budget items that could and should be cut. Special interests would then be forced to work for the general interest rather than against it.

Regulatory activity is not as quantifiable as taxing and spending. But it would be premature to give up on ingenuity. Perhaps a quantitative specification will prove impossible and procedural restraints will have to serve as a substitute. A constitutional amendment might

42. See *Wall Street Journal*, 12 July 1978, editorial, page 20, and, in particular, Milton Friedman, "The Limitations of Tax Limitation," *Policy Review* 5 (Summer 1978): 7–14.

require that enactment of new regulatory measures be coupled with repeal of others of comparable scope (perhaps as judged by numbers of regulators involved, or number of persons or dollar volume of activities in the private sector directly affected.) Perhaps it would be necessary to settle for some vaguer and more nearly only hortatory restraint. Anyway, good intentions would not be enough to justify a new regulation; the proposed measure would have to be shown to be not merely desirable but exceptionally so, desirable even against the background of an already overgrown government. The objective is a framework of constraints and opinion in which different government activities are seen to be in rivalry with one another, each costing the sacrifice of others. Ideally, advocates of each new regulatory measure would accept the obligation of showing it to be so desirable as to be worth the sacrifice of specified existing regulations.

Opponents sometimes charge that a budget limit would undemocratically tie the hands of democratic government, and a similar objection would no doubt be made to constitutional restrictions on regulation. Yet the purpose of either limit is not to undercut democracy but to make it more effective by remedying a flaw that has so far kept the people from controlling the overall consequences of piecemeal decisions. A budget limit or a regulatory limit no more subverts democracy than the First Amendment does by setting limits to what Congress may do. Without that amendment, popular majorities might have placed many particular restrictions on freedom of speech, but our Founding Fathers rolled all these issues up together instead of letting each one be decided by a separate majority vote.[43]

Just as proponents of tax cuts or budget limits face the supposedly embarrassing demand that they draw up lists of specific expenditure cuts, so proponents of limits to regulation might encounter a similar demand. This one might well be easier to comply with than the demand about spending cuts. Either demand, however, is unreasonable. It in effect invites the limitationists to shut up unless they exhibit detailed knowledge of government (and private) activities that they cannot realistically be expected to have. It tacitly denies that the principle of specialization and division of labor applies in public policymaking as in other areas of life. It tacitly supposes that general knowledge — namely, knowledge of bias in the current system — is

43. Milton Friedman, *Policy Review* 5 (Summer 1978): 8–10.

worthless unless accompanied by detailed further knowledge on the part of the same persons. Yet the very purpose of an overall limit is to bring the detailed knowledge of its possessors to bear in coping with that bias.

SUMMARY

The private sector is routinely made the target of regulation because of externalities, meaning cases in which the persons who decide on some activity or its scale decide wrongly because they do not themselves bear or take full account of all of its costs and benefits.[44] How ironic, then, routinely to expect a solution from government! Government is the prototypical sector in which decision makers do *not* take accurate account of all the costs as well as all the benefits of each activity. The fragmentation of decisionmaking and responsibility goes part way toward explaining this condition, along with the kinds of opportunities and incentives that bureaucrats, politicians, legislative staff members, judges, and citizens have.

It is difficult to compare even the relatively direct and obvious costs and benefits of an individual government policy action. It is practically impossible to assess the indirect and long-run consequences of individual actions and of their aggregate, including their effects on the drift of policy and on the character of the economic and social system. The aggregate of activities all appearing individually desirable may itself turn out quite undesirable. Hence the importance of frankly allowing considerations of political philosophy into policy discussions. Broad principles should count, including a principle of skepticism about government activity. Even when no strong and obvious disadvantages are apparent, there is presumption (though a defeasible one) against each new government function. The pragmatic, "realistic" approach of considering each individual function separately and narrowly, on its own supposed merits, is fatally flawed.

Our Founding Fathers accepted the concept of human rights that government should not violate. That concept need not be based on mysticism. It follows from a version of rules-utilitarianism (as dis-

---

44. Externalities are due, anyway, not to the very logic of the market system but to difficulties and costs of fully applying that system, including property rights, to the cases in question.

tinguished from act-utilitarianism). As John Stuart Mill argued (in *Utilitarianism*, Chapter 5, writing when the word "justice" had not yet been stretched into uselessness for all but emotive purposes), unswervingly to put respect for justice ahead of what might be called narrow expediency is a rule of topmost utility (or expediency in a broad and deep sense). I believe it can be shown that respect for and basing policy on certain rights and values, like justice, accords with human nature and with the sort of society in which people have good chances for cooperating effectively as they pursue happiness in their own specific ways. Ludwig von Mises and Henry Hazlitt, following David Hume, have persuasively argued that social cooperation is such an indispensible means to people's pursuit of their own diverse specific goals that it deserves recognition practically as a goal in its own right.[45] Considerations like these merit respect again in appraisals of government regulation.

45. See Ludwig von Mises, *Human Action* (New Haven: Yale University Press, 1949), and *Theory and History* (New Haven: Yale University Press, 1957), esp. pp. 57–58, and Henry Hazlitt, *The Foundations of Morality* (Princeton: Van Nostrand, 1964). An emphasis on social cooperation as a near-ultimate criterion, if not the use of the term, traces back at least as far as Thomas Hobbes.

Chapter 5

REGULATION AND JUSTICE
An Economist's Perspective

M. Bruce Johnson

The predominant contemporary theme in both academic and popular debate suggests that although some government regulations may be justified, the dynamic of our democratic institutions leads to unjustified overregulation. According to some contributors to the debate, the bias toward overactivity by government is caused by the purposeful, nonmarket, political behavior of consumers, producers, voters, legislators, judges, bureaucrats, and so forth, as they pursue their own perceived welfare in the context of these democratic institutions.

JUSTICE AND REGULATION

How "just" is the result of this apparently uncoordinated jockeying for preferred position by members of special interest groups? As loosely interpreted by economists, "unjustified" regulation is regulation that is inefficient. Thus, an economist condemns a particular piece of legislation when analysis shows that the costs of the activity are greater than its benefits. Consequently, on a proper accounting society's output and welfare are reduced by the regulation. Hence, the economist will condemn the specific regulation as being unjustified because it is inefficient—output and welfare would have been greater in the absence of regulation.

Noneconomists typically exhibit impatience with this approach because they place efficiency well down the list in their concerns—certainly far below their concern for the distribution of income and wealth. Thus, the noneconomist is quite prepared to pronounce one distribution of income and wealth as unjust and another just with only passing regard for the efficiency implications of redistribution. The economist, by contrast, understands that noneconomists hold such views but cannot, qua economist, take a position on the justness of redistribution per se.

As usually understood in the methodology of economics, justice is a normative concept, lying beyond the scope of economic analysis. To the pure economist, definitions of justice thus rest ultimately on individual value judgments not subject to scientific standards of confirmation or refutation. Everything considered, the economist rests his case on efficiency criteria because efficiency can in principle, and frequently in practice, be measured. Whether the income and wealth distribution should be changed or whether the institutions that lead to a particular distribution should be changed is almost universally thought to be a normative issue, the standards for which properly fall within the framework of moral philosophy (ethics in particular). On the other hand, whether the income and wealth distribution and the institutions *can* be changed is a legitimate task for positive economics.

In spite of these caveats, let me attempt to define a weak notion of justice for the sake of discussion. Let me suggest that we initially adopt two widely accepted premises as the foundation for a definition of justice: (1) individual preferences alone matter; and (2) the notion of Pareto optimality is valid.[1] Expanding, I suggest that justice is served when individuals are able to carry on voluntary, mutually advantageous trades and exchanges. The first assumption precludes both paternalistic and misanthropic behavior by which some individuals impose their preferences on others via coercion. Thus, if B objects, individual A cannot justly cause wealth to be taken from

---

1. The economy has reached a position of Pareto optimality when no further mutually advantageous exchanges or reorganizations are possible. The only possible actions or interventions remaining are those that will reduce the utility (injure) at least one member of society. The concept of Pareto optimality does not preclude government action; interventions that increase the utility of at least one individual without reducing the utility of any others are said to be "Pareto efficient." Finding interventions that unambiguously satisfy the Pareto criterion is, of course, another matter.

B and transferred to C. The second assumption suggests that justice is served when one individual's utility is increased, as long as no others suffer utility decreases.

A market economy meets this standard of justice under certain conditions: assume the existence of a general equilibrium system with appropriate shapes for production and utility functions. There will emerge from this system a unique general equilibrium price vector for every initial endowment of resources. With each initial endowment (i.e., distribution) of resource ownership, we expect one, and only one, Pareto optimal solution. Thus, for each initial endowment of resources, there is a unique point E on a utility possibility frontier represented by P(U) in Figure 5-1. At each and every point on the frontier, the utility of individual i cannot be increased except by reducing the utility of individual j. Hence, the slope of the utility frontier is negative.

Given that individual utilities are not cardinal and can not be compared in a meaningful way, we must conclude that points along the utility frontier cannot be ranked in terms of social desirability. Such a ranking would imply the existence of a social welfare function unanimously accepted by all parties. As a consequence, governmentally induced movements along the utility frontier involving either redistributions of endowments or ex post income and wealth are outside the purview of modern welfare economics. Redistributions leading to different distributions of final utility do *not* per se involve efficiency questions and thus can neither be supported nor condemned in the context of economic analysis. However, such redistri-

Figure 5-1.   Utility Possibility Frontier for Individuals i and j.

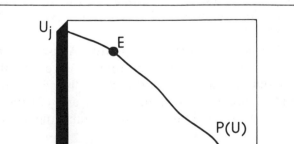

butions do violate the provisional definition of justice offered here. Movements *along* the utility frontier are *not* voluntary and must therefore involve coercion that reduces the utility of (and thereby does harm to) at least one individual.

TRADITIONAL EXPLANATIONS

Regulation in the abstract has been "explained" traditionally on three grounds: (1) by market failures caused by monopolies; (2) by market failures caused by externalities; and (3) by socially "undesirable" distributions of income and wealth. By implication, contributors to the welfare economics literature have tacitly assumed that the economy would achieve a Pareto optimal production and allocation of goods and services in the absence of the conditions described in (1) and (2), the two sources of market imperfections. The third rationale for government regulation listed above (income and wealth distribution) is, in fact, not an economic rationale. Under the assumed conditions of the model set forth here, all mutually advantageous exchanges have already taken place in the "process" of reaching the Pareto optimal general equilibrium position on the utility frontier.

The first two rationales for intervention (monopoly and externalities) are irrelevant in the context of the standard Arrow–Debreu model where information and transaction costs as well as all other frictions are assumed to be zero.[2] In such a case, private contracting will lead to the elimination of relevant monopolies and externalities since, with zero transaction costs, those consumers hurt by the output restrictions of the monopolists will pay the monopolists to increase their output. Similarly, externalities will be internalized as described in the Coase theorem. These points have been brilliantly illuminated by Carl J. Dahlman.[3]

I conclude that in the standard competitive Arrow–Debreu model with zero transaction costs, there is no role for government intervention and regulation if one adopts the generally accepted premises that (1) individual preferences alone matter, and (2) the notion of Pareto optimality is valid. Under these circumstances, no relevant

2. See K. Arrow and G. Debreu, "Existence of Equilibrium for a Competitive Society," *Econometrica* 22 (1954): 265–90.

3. Carl J. Dahlman, "The Problem of Externalities," *The Journal of Law and Economics* 22, no. 1, (April 1979): 141–62.

monopolies or externalities exist, and redistribution of income and wealth is inadmissible.

But the characteristics of any economy of record are not those of the competitive Arrow–Debreu model. Various types of transaction costs such as transfer, bargaining, decision, policing, setup, and so forth, are real and ubiquitous. Hence, a second theoretical model is relevant. Assume that we begin with the same endowment of re-sources as in Model I above but also introduce transaction costs into the system. A new and in general different vector of prices, quantities, and utilities will be generated in Model II. The existence of transaction costs thus implies that the particular Pareto optimum of the first model will not be attained.

The rationale for intervention can be described in this context: the observed equilibrium is now in the interior of the set of utility possibility points whose outer boundary is defined by the utility frontier associated with the Arrow–Debreu model. Call such a point E_o in Figure 5–2. The standard "market failure" argument in favor of intervention is based on the assumption that government intervention will move the system from E_o to a point on the utility frontier $P(U)$ in the quadrant northeast of E_o.

Figure 5–2. Utility Possibility Frontier for Individuals i and j.

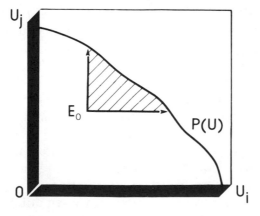

THE CASE AGAINST REGULATION

This case for government intervention rests on shaky ground. First, any movement from E_0 (the equilibrium associated with positive transaction costs) northeasterly to a point on the utility frontier $P(U)$ implies: (1) that such a point on the utility frontier $P(U)$ is attainable — that Model I, the world of *zero* transaction costs, is the relevant reference point for public policy; and (2) that government intervention can succeed in moving the system in a northeasterly direction when the market has failed to do so. This implies that government intervention eliminates or at least reduces transaction costs.

I argue that neither assumption can be justified a priori. The utility frontier of Model I is an idealized, utopian concept that is unattainable in any world of record. In addition, it appears to be an act of faith to assume that government intervention will move the system from E_0 in a northeasterly direction as opposed to a southwesterly direction further inside the frontier. It is for the latter reason that economists universally ask for cost-benefit studies of proposed government regulations. Imperfect as such studies may be, they offer at least a weak test of efficiency-enhancing as opposed to efficiency-reducing government intervention.

Yet time and time again we see governments proceed with interventions that fail cost-benefit tests and, hence, not only move the system in the southwesterly direction *away* from the idealized and unattainable utility frontier, but also move it *inside* the attainable frontier associated with laissez faire. How can these interventions and regulations be explained? Two answers are possible: (1) the intervention is a "mistake" occasioned by imperfect information, and so forth; or (2) the purpose of the intervention was to redistribute wealth from one group to another and had nothing directly to do with the elimination of transaction costs and a Pareto-preferred move in the direction of the utility frontier.

At minimum, interventions of the second variety move the system from E_0 in a north*westerly* or south*easterly* direction to E_0' or E_0'' in Figure 5–3. Superficially, these interventions are qualitatively indistinguishable from movements along any given utility frontier since they benefit some individuals and harm others. As such, the interventions are purely redistributional in nature and cannot be supported by standard economic analysis. However, to the extent that

Figure 5-3.   Utility Possibility Frontier for Individuals i and j.

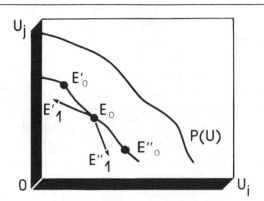

such interventions are also "inefficient," they also move the system from E_0 to a point *inside* the feasible utility frontier on which E_0 is located.

The point is simply that government interventions *must* involve the expenditure of resources. Referring to Paul Samuelson:

> The essential point now to be stressed is that we could move people to different points on the utility-possibility function only by an ideally perfect and unattainable system of absolutely lump-sum taxes or subsidies. In point of fact, suppose that, in the simplest case, competitive laissez faire puts us at one point on the utility-possibility function. Then we can only seek to change the distribution of income by a system of feasible legislation: e.g., progressive income tax, rationing, etc. All such policies involve a distortion of marginal decisions, some involving great distortions, but in every case, some distortion. They move us then *inside* the utility-possibility curve. We can pick policies which strive to minimize the harmful effects of redistribution, but in practice we cannot reduce these effects to zero. A "feasible-utility function" can conceptually be drawn up which lies more or less far inside the utility-possibility curve. We can pick policies which strive to minimize the harmful effects to zero. A "feasible-utility function" can conceptually be drawn up which lies more or less far inside the utility-possibility function, depending upon how utopian were our assumptions about legislation, public opinion, etc.[4]

4. Paul A. Samuelson, *Collected Scientific Papers*, vol. 3 (Cambridge, Mass.: MIT Press, 1972), p. 1061.

I interpret Samuelson to say that starting from a point E_0 on a feasible-utility frontier, any government intervention undertaken will involve a movement to a point, say E_1' (or E_1'') in Figure 5-3 that lies inside the utility-possibility curve.

The government interventions in our recent experience can be characterized as movements of this variety. For example, take the case of local governments constraining or prohibiting the conversion of apartments to condominiums. I would represent these interventions as a "mere" redistribution of wealth from apartment owners to tenants; in the short run, the quantity of rental housing (the total number of apartments and condominiums) is unaffected by the intervention. However, wealth is redistributed, transaction costs are increased, and the system moves from E_0 to E_1' or E_1''. In the long run, of course, other purposeful responses to the intervention will move the system to a point still farther inside the original utility frontier.

The typical behavior of various participants in the economic and political arena appears to fit the category of income and wealth redistribution activities. Individuals perceive that it is cheaper to use the political system than to redistribute wealth via the market. Politicians perceive that it is easier to remain in office by legislating redistributions of wealth from the large group to the concentrated special-interest group.

In sum, it would not do great violence to the facts to state that every government action has implications for wealth redistribution but few reduce transaction costs and increase efficiency. Economists might well recognize what politicians have known since the beginning of civilization: the average person is intensely interested in issues of wealth and income redistribution but cares not at all about efficiency. Many would think it just that they have more at the expense of less for everyone else. Although I am not optimistic about the prospects for success, I suspect that the only defense against this arbitrary view of justice and the myopic behavior it generates is a constitution that protects each individual against coerced redistribution of wealth through the political process.

PART III
RIGHTS AND HARMS

Chapter 6

SOME QUESTIONS ABOUT GOVERNMENT REGULATION OF BEHAVIOR

Judith Jarvis Thomson

INTRODUCTION

Government has always been, and must continue to be, in the business of regulating behavior. The question before us is not whether it should be in this business at all, but only which behavior it should, or even may, regulate.

For example, it is illegal in this, and in every other civilized society, for one private citizen to kill another for pleasure or profit. Government declares such behavior impermissible and attaches severe penalties to it. There is an interesting theoretical question *why* government may do this; but it is a datum *that* it may.

Killing someone is causing him a serious physical harm. And we may, more generally, accept as a given that government may make it illegal for one private citizen, A, to cause another, B, a serious physical harm, intending to cause that harm, and having no further intention in causing that harm than pleasure or profit. This formula is not without its difficulties, but its difficulties are not important for present purposes.[1]

What interests us here are the harms that A can cause B *without* intending to cause them. It is when one turns to unintentionally

---

1. What about harms to which one consents? For the most part I ignore them — but see concluding section.

harmful behavior that government regulation begins to seem problematic.

The issues are complex; I hope merely to sort out some considerations relevant to the settling of them.

Causing Harm

Suppose you manufacture bread, and that you sell me a loaf. I eat a piece, and am thereby caused a harm. You did not intend that harm; you did not intend to cause me any harm at all. Is it permissible for government to have had, in advance and already "on the books," a law under which your conduct was illegal? There obviously is no saying. Different answers are in place according as further details are filled in one way or another.

Let us attend first to the question why eating that bread caused me a harm. And let us suppose first that it caused me a harm because it was made in unsanitary or unsafe conditions—for example, it contained rat droppings. Here we are inclined to say "Yes." Government may make it illegal to cause harms by negligence as well as by intention.

But *may* it? Why not merely say that the manufacturer who does not wish to spend resources on keeping his factory clean and safe must print on his labels: "Eat at your own risk—we do not guarantee that the conditions under which this particular loaf of bread was made were both clean and safe"? I shall come back to printed warnings later.

Meanwhile, however, it does seem plain that government may make it illegal to cause harms by negligence in the absence of warnings of the possibility of those harms. If the tiles on my roof are loose, and I am too lazy to fix them, and if one falls off onto a passerby, I am, as things stand, legally liable for the harm caused that person, and rightly so.

Tort Law and Statute

It should go without saying that government regulates in other ways than by legislation and executive order—that it regulates also via the common law. When I spoke of government having had, in advance and already "on the books," law under which this or that conduct is illegal, I put the words "on the books" in scare-quotes, for I meant to include case-books as well as lists of statutes.

That government regulates via tort law is surely plain. Government regulates behavior primarily by attaching penalties. A statute (I shall use this term to cover both legislation and executive order) may say: "Penalty for letting it be the case that your roof tiles are loose: $50." Tort law, however, does not attach a penalty to anything so simple and straightforward as allowing your roof tiles to be loose. It says, for example: "If the tiles on your roof are loose due to your own negligence, and if one falls off onto a passerby, causing harm, then you must pay damages"; *that is*, it says: "Penalty for letting it be the case that your roof tiles are loose due to your own negligence, and that one falls off onto a passerby, causing harm: Payment of damages." So it too attaches penalties.

There is a morally important difference between these two samples of government regulation that I conceal by using the same term "penalty" in both cases. The statutory penalty of $50 that I invented is a fine, paid to the government; the tort penalty I invented is not a fine, and is paid, not to government, but to a private person, the victim of the harm.

This difference connects with another morally important difference, namely that the tort penalty is attached to actually causing a harm, whereas the statutory penalty is attached to imposing a risk of harm. We should examine all this more closely.

Suppose that the only law in a certain country concerning roof tiles is tort law, and that all tort law in that country says concerning them is this:

> (T) Penalty for letting it be the case that your roof tiles are loose due to your own negligence, and that one falls off onto a passerby and causes harm: Payment of damages.

Is there any injustice in there being such a law? I take it to be a datum that there is not. If one causes a harm by one's negligence, it is entirely just that one pay damages for it.

For quite some time (we may imagine) all goes well: homeowners in that country mostly keep their roof tiles tight, out of a moral concern to avoid causing harm, or out of fear of having to pay damages, or out of some mix of both.

But alas, all does not go well indefinitely. One after the other, there now begin to occur an increasing number of harms done by flying roof tiles, and the harms are increasingly serious. Many homeowners are no longer moved by the moral and prudential considerations that moved the earlier generation of homeowners. What should be done?

One possible answer is that nothing should be done because nothing will work on homeowners of the kind I am asking you to imagine.

What is of more interest is that there is in the wings an argument to the effect that nothing need be done. No doubt increasing numbers of people are being more seriously harmed by flying roof tiles; but as things stand, all victims of harm can sue for damages for the harm done them. Let us be clear: they can sue for reimbursement for *all* of their costs, including not merely medical and legal costs, but also the pay they forfeit while convalescing and even a sum in return for the pain they suffer. All of this is plausibly included under the heading of "damages." And if it is—if, that is, the tort law already in force does require the negligent homeowner to pay all of this to the victim—then the victim is reimbursed. Homeowner and victim have then squared their accounts. And who are we, or what is government, to ask homeowners that they do more than settle equitably with their victims?

One reply is that those who bring suit do not always win. Thus a passerby might in fact be harmed by a homeowner's negligence, and yet be unable to establish this fact to the court's satisfaction. This worry may be real, but I do not think it theoretically interesting. Whether a homeowner will have to pay the tort law penalty turns on whether the plaintiff wins the suit; but similarly, whether a homeowner would have to pay a statutory penalty would turn on whether the government "won *its* suit"—in other words, on whether the government's agents were able to establish that the statute was violated.

The theoretically interesting reply seems to me to come out as follows.

It may have been noticed that I have so far used only the term "damages"; I wanted (for the space of this paper) to reserve the term "compensation" for something special.

Let us say that A causes B a compensable harm if and only if A causes B a harm, and there exists a sum of money for which B did, or would have been willing to, sell A the right to cause B that harm for that sum of money. If you destroy some of my property, you cause me a harm. So suppose you smash my paperweight. The harm you thereby cause me is a compensable harm, for there is a sum of money for which you could have bought from me the right to cause me that harm—$50 would certainly do it. By contrast, if you cause me to go blind, then you cause me an *in*compensable harm, for there is no sum of money whatever for which I would have sold you the right to cause me to go blind.

If by your negligence you cause me to go blind, then I shall sue you for damages; some would say, "for compensation." Though I will certainly take what I can get, no sum of money would compensate me for the loss of my eyesight: I not only will not, I cannot, win in the courts a sum of money for which I would have sold you the right to cause me to go blind—for no such sum of money exists. I sue for damages all the same, but only because being blind and rich is preferable to being blind and poor.

My example of a compensable harm was a harm to me caused by a harm to my property; my example of an incompensable harm was a physical injury. But there are compensable harms that are physical injuries. Thus, for example, $100,000 would easily buy you the right to cause me a case of twenty-four-hour flu (if I can be sure that's the worst harm your injection will do me). And there are incompensable harms that are caused by harms to property. Thus it might be that there is no sum of money that would buy you the right to smash the teacups I inherited from my great-grandmother.

No doubt there are also borderline cases. No sum of money would buy you the right to cut off my little finger. Is there a sum of money for which I would sell you the right to break it under anaesthetic? I don't know.

Now if you cause me an incompensable harm, you cause me a harm for which (by definition) no amount of money in damages will compensate me. There is no way in which you can reimburse me, or make full restitution, for causing me an incompensable harm.

Let us even suppose, then, that the judicial system in the country I have envisioned is maximally fair and efficient. I said we are to suppose that increasing numbers of people are being caused increasingly serious harm by flying roof tiles; and let us suppose that these harms are not merely serious, but incompensable. Then the argument to the effect that nothing need be done—the argument whose premise is that the existing tort law ensures that negligent homeowners make full restitution to their victims—does not succeed. For however fair and efficient the judicial system may be, homeowners who cause incompensable harms by their negligence *cannot* square accounts with their victims.

Homeowners who cause compensable harms by their negligence *can* square accounts with their victims. But will they? In every case? There are a number of reasons for thinking that they will not.

If you cause me a harm so serious that it would have cost you a great deal of money to buy from me the right to cause me that harm, I will sue. And I *may* get what I sue for. But I may not. In the first place, the court may not assess my costs exactly as I do. (You have torn my autographed photograph of John Wayne; the court may not agree with me in valuing that photograph at $100,000.) In the second place, other considerations will weigh on a court in setting damages than simply the cost to the plaintiff of the defendant's act.

If you cause me a harm so superficial that it would have cost you only a small sum of money to buy from me the right to cause me that harm, I will not sue – the cost to me (in time and effort) is more than I will get back in damages. Even a maximally fair and efficient judicial system cannot (indeed, should not) be made costless to those who bring suit. And if it were imagined that a successful plaintiff is to get back, in damages, a sum that includes a fair assessment of the costs (in time and effort) of bringing suit (an inefficient policy, in that it encourages suits), even then, the court again may not value my loss (now in time and effort) exactly as I do, and has other considerations in mind when setting damages than simply my own costs.

So the argument claiming that nothing need be done – on the premise that the existing tort law in our imaginary country ensures that negligent homeowners square accounts with their victims – does not succeed. In the case of incompensable harms, they cannot square accounts with their victims; in the case of compensable harms, they very often will not.

What can be done? Well, what do the people in that country *want* to do? They want to get homeowners to keep their roof tiles tight, with a view to cutting down on the number of harms done by flying roof tiles. They can try to do this in one of two ways. In the first place, they can try to "indirectly coerce" homeowners into keeping their roof tiles tight by increasing the penalty for causing harms by flying roof tiles. In the second place, they can try to "directly coerce" homeowners into keeping their roof tiles tight by instituting a (new) penalty for allowing one's roof tiles to be loose.

INDIRECT COERCION

How might the attempt at indirect coercion proceed? The simplest way is for a statute to be passed that says:

> (S_1) Penalty for letting it be the case that your roof tiles are loose due to your own negligence, and that one falls off onto a passerby and causes harm: $1,000.

A more complicated statute might have attached different penalties according to whether the harm is compensable or incompensable — for example, $100 for a compensable harm, $5,000 for an incompensable harm. But I shall ignore this. Our concern is not the fairness of the particular penalty attached to the conduct described in the statute; our concern is only why it is permissible to adopt *any* increase in the penalty.

Again, they might have thought to attach a different penalty: not $1,000, but (as it might be) ten days in jail. Wiser legislators would have prevailed, however. People who are sitting in jail are not out on their roofs, tightening their roof tiles. I mention the possibility, not because I think it a good idea, but to stress that the additional penalty they contemplate attaching constitutes, not damages, but punishment. The $1,000 penalty (assuming they choose that) will be, not damages, not even "punitive damages" (which would be paid to the victim), but *mere* punishment — a fine, to be paid to government.

To avoid complaints of ex post facto law, we may imagine that people are given advance warning: the statute is to go into effect only six months after date of passage.

Let us suppose that the small print in the statute tells us that the rules of the game are to be as follows: If A's roof tiles are loose, and B is thereby caused a harm, B may proceed to bring civil suit against A. If B does so, and actually wins the case, B is awarded damages, under existing tort law (T). A then must pay damages to B. In addition, A must pay a fine of $1,000 to the Government Collector-of-Fines. Thus, the penalty for the conduct described in the statute is increased: from mere payment of damages to B, it is increased to payment of damages to B plus a fine to government.

I take it to be a datum that they may adopt this new policy. Why is it permissible for them to do so? It is not at all easy to say. Utilitarian arguments are notoriously overblunt: we know in advance that they permit, and may even prescribe, violations of rights. On the other hand, it is not at all plain that there is any natural right to punish, where punishing involves extracting more from an aggressor than fair damages to the victim.

I should think that the answer lies in the right to self-defense. But what the content of that right is, and how it is to be brought to bear here, are not at all easy to say.

Let us begin with harms. There is a kind of harm that, when inflicted by one person on another, does *not* infringe a right. I have in mind what might be called "market harms." Suppose, for example, that you make lace and now have a cupboardful ready to bring to market tomorrow. This afternoon, I invent a way of making lace cheaply, by machine, which only an expert can tell from handmade lace like yours. I thereby cause you a market harm: I cause a drop in the value of your lace. I do this without damaging your lace or dirtying it, without in any way touching it. It seems plain enough that I infringe no right of yours in doing so.

As we all know, it is not at all clear what precisely counts as a harm. So might it be argued that a market harm is not really a harm at all? I think not. Notice how we react when *government* causes what I am calling market harms. If I have (at considerable expense) turned parts of my house into rental units, and have done this compatibly with existing law, and if then, the local zoning board passes a new ordinance under which no more than one family unit may live in any one house, it will have caused me a serious market harm—and we shall all rightly feel that I am owed damages.

Market harms are compensable harms, of course. So what I think we may say is this: if A causes B an incompensable harm, then A infringes a right of B's; if A causes B a compensable harm that is not a market harm, then A infringes a right of B's.

Now the relevant thesis about self-defense seems to me to be this: no one has a right that we shall *let* him infringe our rights. No one has a right that we shall not prevent him from infringing our rights.

Let us distinguish between "direct prevention" and "indirect prevention." I directly prevent you from engaging in an activity if I prevent you from engaging in it by force—for example, I break your arm, or lock you up. I indirectly prevent you from engaging in an activity if I do so by attaching a penalty to your engaging in it—I make it be the case (and let you know I made it be the case) that if you engage in it, you will suffer this or that penalty.

It seems to me a plausible idea that if B *knows* that A will infringe a right of B's unless B prevents A from infringing that right, then B is at liberty as regards A to prevent A from doing so—even directly, in other words, by force. A has no right against B that B not do this.[2]

Such knowledge is rare, however. (This explains our views on "preventive detention.") And without such knowledge, B may not directly prevent A from infringing B's right—even if, in fact, A has every intention of infringing the right, and will do so unless prevented from doing so. B is at liberty to protect himself, however: B is at liberty as regards A to *indirectly* prevent A from infringing his right—by attaching a penalty to infringing it. A has no right against B that B not do this.

Each of us has this liberty in regard to *all* others. So we are all at liberty as regards all of ourselves to jointly attach penalties to right-infringing conduct.

Now to say that B is at liberty as regards A to do such and such is *not* to say that it is morally permissible for B to do it. Thus, B may be at liberty as regards A to defend his rights by force, and it may be morally impermissible for B to do this because too great a degree of force would be required, or the force would have to be used on an innocent bystander. If A proposes to smash B's favorite concrete garden gnome, B is at liberty as regards A to use force to prevent A from doing so—and it would be morally permissible for B to knock A down. But if preventing A requires killing A, or killing an innocent bystander, it would not be morally permissible for B to act.

I concluded, above, that we are all at liberty as regards all of ourselves to jointly attach penalties to right-infringing conduct. Is it morally permissible for us to do so? Presumably yes—so long as the penalties to be attached are not disproportionate to the stringency of the rights infringed.

This, in brief, and in very rough, is how I think the argument to the permissibility of punishing those who engage in right-infringing behavior should go. Something *like* it must surely be right.

If so, the citizens of our imaginary country may pass statute (S_1)—for we are supposing that increasing numbers of incompensable harms are being caused by flying roof tiles, and we may also suppose

---

2. Readers familiar with Hohfeldian terminology will recognize it here.

that none of the compensable harms so caused is a mere market harm.

But perhaps it will be thought that I have gone on too long about this, since increasing the penalty for actually causing harms does not trouble most opponents of government regulation. What they *really* find irksome is, rather, adopting (new) penalties for imposing risks of harms. It is that to which we must now turn.

Direct Coercion

Let us suppose that passing (S_1) turns out to be ineffective: homeowners who were not moved to keep their roof tiles tight by the fact that tort law (T) was in force are not moved to do so by the fact that statute (S_1) is in force. The lazy, who were prepared to risk having to pay damages for harms done, are equally prepared to risk having to pay damages, plus $1,000 for harms done.

Now "direct coercion" seems to be called for, and the legislature considers passing the following additional statute:

(S_2) Penalty for letting it be the case that your roof tiles are loose: $100.

How should (S_2) be administered? One way is to leave it to the citizenry to report seeing loose tiles on their neighbors' roofs—and to the Government-Collector-of-Fines to present an additional bill for $100 to a defendant homeowner who loses a suit under (T). But the legislators do not expect that to be particularly effective. So they consider declaring also that homeowners are to permit monthly inspection of their roof tiles by the Government's Roof-Tile Inspector, who is then to decide whether the penalty set out in (S_2) is to be imposed on a homeowner, ensuring that this inspection will be permitted by also passing:

(S_3) Penalty for refusing entry to Government Roof-Tile Inspector: $125.

We may (but need not) also imagine that the government's Roof-Tile Expert has found that there is only one way in which one can be absolutely certain of tight roof tiles; so the legislators consider prescribing it by passing also the following:

(S_4) Penalty for failing to keep roof tiles tight by use of two-inch stainless steel nails, hammered in three to a tile, in a triangular pattern, apex down, and so forth: $50.

It seems right to imagine the penalty in (S_2) to be smaller than the penalty in (S_1). Why this seems right is a good question, but I shall not pursue it. It is first cousin to the good question why it seems right that mere attempts at murder should be penalized less heavily than murder itself.

What we must consider, however, is why it would be permissible for the legislature to pass (S_2). I take it to be a datum *that* it may, and that our question is only why it may.

Permitting your roof tiles to be loose imposes a risk of harm—indeed, as we are supposing, incompensable harm—on the neighbors. All would be well if we could say that people have a right not to have imposed on them a risk of incompensable harm. An argument exactly like that of the preceding section would show it to be permissible to attach a penalty to permitting one's roof tiles to be loose. Unfortunately it does not seem obvious that people do have a right not to have a risk of incompensable harm imposed on them.

Suppose I play Russian roulette on you. (Gun with six chambers, one bullet.) And suppose that nothing happens: the bullet was not under the firing pin when I fired. Suppose that I did this without your knowledge, so that you were caused no fear. Did I infringe a right of yours? It does not seem obvious that I did.

There is an argument to the effect that I did which I think it worth our while to look at. If you break my little finger, you harm me; but if I have to choose, I would prefer your breaking my little finger to your playing Russian roulette on me. If you cut off my little finger, you harm me; but if I have to choose, I would prefer your cutting off my little finger to your playing Russian roulette on me. And does this not suggest that your playing Russian roulette on me *is* harming me—harming me more seriously in fact than your breaking my little finger, or even cutting it off? And do we not assume that to harm a person—where the harm is not a market harm—*is* to infringe a right of that person's?

This argument has *some* merit. Which would I prefer you to give ne, a plum or a ticket in the state lottery? Well, I like plums, but not all that much; I'd prefer the lottery ticket. If you give me the ticket, you give me something I'd like to have (indeed, I'd have paid a certain amount for it myself); and even if it turns out I lose, can't you later say that you gave me a benefit—that you benefited me? Why not similarly say, on similar grounds, that if you play Russian roulette on me then you harm me—even if no bullet is under the firing pin when you fire?

Some people think you *do* benefit me by giving me a lottery ticket, even if I do not win the lottery. If they are right, we have to make a choice. We can say (1) harm and benefit are asymmetrical. You benefit me by giving me a chance to win a lot of money, but do not harm me by giving me a chance at death. Or we can say (2) harm and benefit are symmetrical. You benefit me by giving me a chance to win a lot of money, and harm me by giving me a chance at death.

It seems to me that (1) is preferable.

If we choose (2), we must relinquish the link we assume exists between harm and rights. Suppose I like concrete garden gnomes, but *hate* plastic garden geese. I own a concrete garden gnome, and if you smash it, you harm me, for you destroy a piece of my property. The fact is, however, that if I have to choose, I would prefer your smashing my concrete garden gnome to your installing plastic garden geese on your lawn. If we take this to show that your installing plastic garden geese on your lawn is harming me — harming me more seriously in fact than your smashing my concrete garden gnome — then we can no longer say that if A causes B a (nonmarket) harm, then A infringes a right of B's. For your installing plastic garden geese on your lawn is no infringement of any right of mine.

Why not say that your installing plastic garden geese on your lawn *is* harming me, and therefore *is* an infringement of a right of mine? (I cannot imagine who would wish to say this, but let us see the argument through.) If we do say this, we must give up the link we assume exists between rights and damages. It is a very plausible idea that if A infringes a right of B's, then A owes damages to B. No doubt this is at best a rough-and-ready rule of thumb. (What if A kills B? To whom does A then owe damages? Again, suppose A breaks an appointment with B without warning; must A *pay* B something? Mightn't an apology be quite enough? I leave these worries aside. There is always a presumption that *something* is owing when a right is infringed.) But you plainly owe me nothing at all in damages (or anything else) if, loving plastic garden geese as you do, you install them on your lawn.

If we wish to retain both the link between harm and rights, and the link between rights and damages, we must choose (1) — in other words, we must say that harm and benefit are asymmetrical. If this makes the concept of harm seem puzzling, well and good — it *is* puzzling.

To return to Russian roulette. It is preferable to say (as I suggested) that if I play Russian roulette on you, and there is no bullet under the firing pin when I fire, then I do not harm you. So we do not have available the fact that my doing so is my harming you as ground for thinking that I infringe a right of yours when I do so—for there is no such fact.

Indeed, we have available to us now a ground for thinking that I do not infringe a right of yours when I do so. For consider that rule of thumb again: if A infringes a right of B's, then A owes damages to B. If I play Russian roulette on you, and there is no bullet under the firing pin when I fire, do I owe you damages? *No doubt* I ought not have done what I did; but do I *owe* you anything for doing it? I am inclined to think I do not.

So I think we do well to see if there is not some ground for thinking it permissible for our people to pass statute (S$_2$) that does *not* rest on the supposition that imposing a risk of harm on someone thereby infringes a right of that person's.

Imposing Risks

Considerations of self-defense help here too. If I am about to play Russian roulette on you, you do not have to sit back and accept my doing so, even if I will have infringed no right of yours if no bullet is under the firing pin when I fire. You may defend yourself. You may prevent me from going ahead—directly, if necessary. That is, if stopping me requires breaking my arm, it is morally permissible for you to break my arm. If stopping me requires killing me, it is morally permissible for you to kill me.

I don't say that it would be morally permissible for you to do absolutely anything necessary to prevent me from playing Russian roulette on you. It would not be permissible for you to kill three innocent bystanders in order to stop me. But I should think it permissible for you to use *on me* any degree of force whatever which is necessary to stop me.

If it would be permissible for you to use any degree of force on me whatever (direct prevention), if that were necessary, then I should think it would be permissible, *a fortiori*, for you to attach a penalty (indirect prevention), if that were necessary—for example, arrange that I will be charged $100 if I go ahead, and let me know that you have arranged for that.

But what if you don't *know* that I am about to play Russian roulette on you? What if you think I may be about to do this, but cannot be certain of it? Then it would not be permissible for you to kill me, even if in fact that were necessary to prevent me from doing so. Perhaps there is some degree of force that would be permissible for you to use on me, even if you were in doubt; but not just any degree at all.

What if you think—indeed, are fairly certain—that *somebody* is about to play Russian roulette on you, but haven't the least idea who? Then I should think it would not be permissible for you to use any degree of force on anyone to prevent that person from doing so. But you surely do not have to sit back and allow it to happen. You are entitled to try to protect yourself by trying indirect prevention.

So it seems to me we are not confronted with a quite general problem about risk imposition. There are cases of risk imposition in which it is plainly permissible (on grounds of self-defense) to arrange for later punishment of the risk imposer—even when it is not known who the risk imposer will be.

What we are confronted with is, rather, a narrower problem: *which* risk impositions fall into this category? This poses a narrower question.

Two things seem to come together in cases in which it is plainly permissible to arrange for later punishment of the risk imposer. First, the risk imposed is relatively high. (How high is relatively high? I cannot say. But I think we recognize the extremes when we meet them.) If A plays Russian roulette on B, then A imposes a one-in-six risk of death on B, and that is a relatively high risk of death.

I said "the risk imposed," and not "the risk A imposes." Consider people who play what I'll call Polish roulette. (Gun with thirty-six chambers, one bullet.) Each imposes only a one-in-thirty-six risk of death; but if six Polish-roulette players are planning to play *their* little game on B, they jointly impose the same risk of death on B as one Russion-roulette player does.

There is a second thing at work in these cases that I find considerably less clear. If I buy a gas lawn mower to mow my lawn with, I shall be imposing a risk of death on you—for that gas lawn mower just *might* explode, not only destroying you and me, but many others as well. Of course the risk of that is very small indeed. (Note that if it were relatively high—for example, one in six—you would do well to go to court to get an injunction; and you'd probably get one.) What's the risk? One in 50,000? One in 250,000? But is isn't just the fact that the risk is small that disinclines us to think you may prevent me, even indirectly, from using my new gas lawn mower. For however many chambers there are in my gun (50,000; 250,000), you may still, nevertheless, try indirect prevention on me, and probably use some degree of force as well, if that is necessary to prevent me from firing my gun at your head.

What is this additional feature that is present in the gun-roulette cases and absent in the lawn mower case? Though I have no clear idea, I *suspect* that it has to do with this: We think it morally bad to impose a risk of death on another for the sheer pleasure of doing so, however many chambers in one's gun; we do not think it morally bad to impose a (tiny) risk of death on another while using a gas lawn mower to mow one's lawn. But why we think this is not obvious.

In any case, both of these features are surely present in the case of the negligent homeowners. By hypothesis, there have been increasing numbers of incompensable harms caused by flying roof tiles; perhaps no one homeowner, alone, imposes a relatively high risk of an incompensable harm on anyone, but the risk they jointly impose is relatively high. And if it is morally bad to impose a risk of an incompensable harm for the sheer fun of doing so, it is also morally bad (not *as* bad, no doubt, but all the same morally bad) to impose such a risk out of negligence.

So I should imagine that something approximating the self-defense argument for the propriety of adopting (S_1) should be available to support the propriety of adopting (S_2); and (S_3), if policing is really required; and perhaps even (S_4), if *that* is really required.

Risk and Ignorance

The harms caused by flying roof tiles in our hypothetical country are harms caused, not by intention, but by negligence. Three further ways in which A can cause harms to B should be briefly mentioned.

Suppose that (1) eating your bread caused me to go blind, not because you were negligent in making it, but rather because you used a new preservative, not knowing (let us suppose that at the time of your using it, *nobody* knew) that the preservative would cause blindness.

Had the preservative been appropriately tested? And, on the basis of the tests had it been found to be harmless? Suppose that (1a) it had been. Under a system of strict product liability you would be found liable all the same. Is that fair? I should imagine that a variant of the self-defense argument would show that it is, though I shall not examine it.

Suppose instead that (1b) the preservative had not been tested at all, and this was why nobody knew it was harmful. What is regarded as negligence varies with information. (Compare the nineteenth-century doctor who thought his hands were sufficiently clean when he had merely brushed the mud off.) Nowadays the use of a new preservative, without appropriate testing, would be regarded as gross negligence, and therefore the risk imposed would be considered as similar to the risk imposed by the negligent homeowners of the preceding sections.

Suppose that (2) eating a pint of your ice cream caused my death, not because there was any negligence in your production of it, but rather because I am a diabetic. I should think it would be grossly unfair to hold you legally liable for my death, whether or not I knew I was a diabetic. If a product is labeled "ice cream," and is not also labeled "sugar-free." it is (quite properly) assumed that everyone knows it contains sugar. It is also assumed (equally properly, I think) that people have the responsibility of finding out for themselves the known risks to which they are especially susceptible (due to their own individual characteristics), and thereafter of avoiding activities that increase them. A child, of course, is not expected to know these things; but parents are.

By contrast, nobody is expected to know about the harmful effects of a preservative that has been tested and found harmless; and that, I think, explains the difference between cases (1a) and (2)—in other words in (2), but not in (1a), the consumer is thought to have accepted the risk.

Suppose that (3) drinking a can of your diet soda caused my death, not because there was anything faulty in your method of making it, but rather because it contained saccharin, and saccharin is (let us suppose) carcinogenic.

Is this just another case like (2)? Carcinogens do not cause cancer in everyone; and if B and C both eat saccharin, but only B gets cancer, there must be some physical difference between them to account for this. But we do not know what this difference is, and therefore, nobody is expected to know who is among the especially prone, and therefore, who must take special care to avoid saccharin.

If saccharin is known to be carcinogenic, and you do not print a warning on your labels, then your behavior is faulty, and it is right to hold you liable for any deaths you cause. But why not merely require that you print a warning (e.g., "Warning: The Surgeon General Has Determined That Saccharin is Dangerous to Your Health—and this product contains saccharin")? We shall turn to printed warnings in the following section.

OFFERING RISKS

If I let my roof tiles be loose, or play Russian roulette on you without your permission, I *impose* a risk on you. If I offer you, for purchase, products that are defective, or that for some other reason are dangerous, then I do not impose a risk—I merely *offer* one, for you do not have to buy what I offer for purchase.

Let us set aside cases in which the seller commits fraud—either by commission (explicitly denying known risks) or by omission (failing to mention known risks). Let us suppose the seller's labels plainly display what the known risks are.

The crucial distinction here is between products people merely want, as opposed to products people need. Having said that, I regret having to admit that (like everybody else) I have no very clear idea how to make this distinction. We do recognize extremes easily enough, however. For example, I *want* well-cut clothing, but do not need it; I *need* food. So what I propose we do is attend only to extremes. In the case of things needed, that will mean attending to a hypothetical, rather than a real case. (The real, in this area, is full of noise, foreground as well as background.) And that is unfortunate because the real, in this area, is very much more interesting.

In respect of products that people merely want (cigarettes, diet soda containing saccharin, gin, heavy cream), it is plain that there may not be an outright ban—people must be allowed to run whatever risks they think are worth the payoff in satisfaction. The two major problems here are familiar: on the one hand, there is the possibility of the seduction of children by advertising; on the other, is the fact that, as things stand, society will largely be responsible for paying the costs of medical care for those who are run down by their risks. It is plain, however, that these matters can be dealt with at lower cost in infringements of freedom than by an outright ban of the risky products. (Though I do not say that working out a formula here is easy.)

Of considerably more interest are the products that people need. Consider the following story: The people of a certain country need food; but the only food they need to eat is bread. Moreover, bread is the only food they want to, or even can, eat. So bread is the only food that is produced. Now they have discovered two ways of making bread: one yields safe bread, but is very expensive; the other is cheap, but it yields risky bread. They call the products Safe Bread and Risky Bread.

What are the risks you run when you eat Risky Bread? The main risk is twenty-four hours of very severe stomach cramps. That does not happen often; but it happens often enough to be worrisome. From time to time, the stomach cramps are accompanied by fever, which leaves blindness in its wake; this rarely happens, but it does happen. The country's chemists believe it quite possible that Risky Bread will one day cause death; but so far no one has died of it.

Who would eat Risky Bread, then? Well, Safe Bread is very expensive. Let us single out a class, which I'll call the Very Poor. You are a member of the Very Poor just in case, however hard you work, however carefully you manage your finances, you will starve unless you either (1) eat at least *some* Risky Bread, or (2) break the law (e.g., by stealing Safe Bread).

Indeed, we may make (2) into an unrealistic alternative: We may imagine that the police in that country are very efficient and that prison inmates are fed only Risky Bread.

We might imagine that some who are not members of the Very Poor also eat Risky Bread. For example, a man who could afford to live wholly on Safe Bread might prefer to eat a little (or a lot) of Risky Bread with a view to saving up for a four-speaker stereo set.

Here we are, the legislators of that country; and the question arises what, if anything, we should do about this state of affairs.

We can, (a), do nothing at all, in the hope that, technology being what it is, someone, someday, will invent a procedure for making safe bread cheaply.

Alternatively, we can, (b), ban the production and sale of Risky Bread and do nothing else. This would be outrageous. We would thereby cause the Very Poor to starve to death. (And all prison sentences would essentially be death sentences.)

A better option is (c), to ban the production and sale of Risky Bread, and provide a subsidy to the Very Poor sufficient to enable them to eat Safe Bread.

But a still better option is (d), to permit the production and sale of Risky Bread, while providing a subsidy to the Very Poor sufficient to enable them to eat Safe Bread. I think (d) is preferable to (c): the same end is reached in respect of the Very Poor (for they will be able to eat Safe Bread), and those who wish to eat Risky Bread for the sake of four-speaker stereo sets (compare cigarettes, saccharin, gin, and heavy cream) may continue to do so.

Now choosing (c), or better still, (d), would not be costless, obviously. That subsidy would have to be paid for, ultimately by taxation. If there are producers of Risky Bread with large supplies on their hands, or specialized equipment not easily converted to the production of Safe Bread, they would be caused a market harm; and if they are to be paid damages for it, or helped to convert to the production of Safe Bread, or both, that too would have to be paid for, ultimately by taxation.

On the other hand, choosing (a) would be unacceptable in even an only moderately well-off society.

I have no doubt that a beginning student of economics could easily give reason to think that the story I imagined could not, in fact, really, be true of any country. But I see no logical impossibility in it; and the question is, what if it *were* true?

I take a rather hard line, myself, on what people have a right to. For my part, if a stranger is starving, and I can easily give him food, he all the same does not have a right against me that I give it to him. (But I shall not even try to defend this here.) What does seem plain to me, however, is that if a stranger is starving, and I can easily provide food, I *ought* to. If we can, jointly, among ourselves, provide for the starving among us at no great cost to ourselves, then it is morally indecent to fail to do so — dividing the costs fairly among ourselves. These are matters of degree, of course. But even an only moderately well-off society can, at no very great cost to itself, provide for its starving.

And similarly for those who are faced with a choice between starving on the one hand, and running a risk of an incompensable harm on the other. It is morally indecent that anyone in a moderately well-off society should be faced with such a choice.

Where things really needed are concerned, then, printed warnings are by no means adequate. How government should regulate is presumably a matter for case-by-case consideration; but that it should regulate seems plain.

Conclusion

A man who offers to hire me to work in his plastics factory, or his coal mine, is in some ways like a man who offers to sell me Risky Bread. He does not impose any risks on me; he merely offers one.

How great are the risks? What kind of harm is risked? Is the pay higher than in safer employment, so that I get a return for the risks I run if I accept? (Compare construction work.) I need a job; do I need *that* job? What social cost would be imposed by this or that variety of regulation? How large an increment of safety would be bought by how much cost in safety-devices, and so on? (The noise of the real is deafening.)

I draw no conclusion whatever about government regulation of conditions of employment—other than this: to the extent to which we see the risks as both high and serious, and the prospective employee as having no realistic alternative to accepting the job, we shall, rightly, think that some form of government regulation is, not merely permissible, but required.

Chapter 7

CHOICE AND HARMS

J. Roger Lee

Should governments protect their citizens from harms? The proper answer to this question, so broadly put, is no. If governments ought to protect people from harms at all, a small range of harms ought to be prevented. The fact that something is harmful to someone does not, by itself, make it be the case that a government ought to take steps to prevent it from harming someone.

My position, of course, is contrary to popular sentiment. The fact that shooting guns in the city streets is potentially harmful to pedestrians is thought to be good reason for preventing that practice. Use of asbestos in ventilating systems, use of saccharin in diet sodas, and the use of frayed elevator cables in skyscraper elevators are each thought to be so harmful or potentially harmful that the practices have all been outlawed. And those who disagree with me about the connection between harms and just legislation will think that because each of those practices is either harmful or potentially harmful, a good reason exists for thinking that governments should outlaw the practice.

Now, in fact, though all of these practices are reprehensible, only one of the practices mentioned *ought to be outlawed* (shooting guns on city streets for sport) while the others should not. Some of the others may be proper subjects of civil suits, given appropriate circumstances, over and above the harmfulness of the practice. But that is a different matter than government regulation of these practices, through regulatory agencies, to prevent harm. Some harmful or potentially harmful acts ought to be outlawed while others should not. It's not the *harmfulness* of a practice that should attract the legislator's interest, but something else. What that something else is, I discuss later.

Before presenting a positive case about what justifies government prevention of *some* harms, I will first develop my case against the claim that government ought to prevent *all* harms.

OUTLAWING HARMS

First, it should be noted that some harms ought to be tolerated because they bring about good. Not all of these ought to be tolerated. We ought not tolerate a terrorist, for example, who arbitrarily selects and shoots innocent individuals in the kneecaps, thereby intending to bring about universal happiness as the conclusion of the apocalyptic battle of the class war that would result from the state's repressive policies toward kneecap terrorism. Clearly the lawmaker should not treat those harms as the sort that should be allowed by virtue of producing good.

On the other hand, suppose I undergo gallbladder surgery and I am thereby cured of gallbladder disease. I have been harmed because for some time I won't be able to indulge my passion for doing 500 situps before breakfast. That is an impairment and a harm. But health is a future benefit and one good enough to make us chary of laws forbidding such actions. No one, in fact, believes that all harms ought to be outlawed. There are some harms, like those incurred in surgery, that I think no one believes ought to be outlawed just because they are harms. Only theorists in the grip of a theory would ever articulate and defend the principle that I am attacking: the principle that all harms ought to be outlawed.

The contrast between the case of the terrorist and the surgeon is clear in terms of different consequences of their different practices. I do not think, however, that considerating good consequences is helpful in deciding less clear-cut cases. My point in citing consequences here is just to draw out the commonsense point that some harms cannot justifiably be outlawed, when considerations of consequence determine policy.

Defining Harms

But there's more that can be said against the principle that all harms ought to be outlawed than just an appeal to commonsense revulsion to certain consequences. First, we can clarify the meaning and the extension of the term *harm*. Then, with many types of harm in front of us, we can sort out which types are more or less justifiably to be proscribed by law. Toward that end I consult four senses of harm taken from the literature.

According to John Kleinig, we can distinguish four senses in which the term *harm* is actually used.[1] They are: (1) grief or sorrow, (obsolete); (2) a loss that, *if* known, would occasion grief or sorrow; (3) a moral notion that "only acts are harmful; only people do harm . . . I come to harm only at someone else's hands. Who harms me wrongs me."; (4) "In law, harm has come to be understood as the violation of a legally protected interest."

Now, in which sense(s) could someone argue cogently that government ought to regulate economic affairs because it ought to protect people from harms. Senses (1) and (4) would not be useful to such a proponent. If sense (1) were intended, then the statement, "Government ought to protect us from harms" would be implausible because of the unrestricted subjectivity of grief and sorrow.

In sense (4), the "ought" in the claim that government ought to prevent harms can be taken as either a legal or a moral ought. If it is read as a legal ought, then the claim is trivial. If, on the other hand, ought is read morally, then the truth or falsity of the statement, "Government may (ought) to protect us from harms (sense 4)" will depend (in part) on whether the law relating to the harm is a good or a bad law. If it is a good law, and if it is permissible or obligatory for government to enforce any law, then government may surely enforce this law (prevent this harm).

If, however, the law in question is a bad law, then the answer to the question of whether it ought to be enforced (the harm be prevented) is established from our discussion, for the harm shouldn't be forbidden—at least not in that way. That is, the regulation in question ought not to be on the books. So only circular arguments could

---

1. John Kleinig, "Crime and the Concept of Harm," *American Philosophical Quarterly* 15 (January, 1978): 27-28.

be offered for the claim that government ought to regulate economic affairs on the basis of the claim that it ought to protect people from harms (sense 4).

That leaves senses (2) and (3) from Kleinig's list. Sense (3), we should note, is put forth as a "narrowing of" sense (2).[2] All these wrongs at another's hands are losses. So I propose to treat such harms as losses and discuss losses, either at another's hands or in nature, together.

Before doing so, however, it is useful to look at a special class of wrongs at the hands of others. A proper subset of wrongs at the hands of others are those that violate rights. If a class of harms were made, having as members all and only those harms at the hands of others that were violations of rights (let us call these sense (3') harms), then government ought to protect us from sense (3') harms since government ought to defend our rights. *In this sense*, it would certainly be true that government ought to protect us from harms. But in this case, in order to identify something as a harm (sense 3'), we would first have to identify it as a violation of someone's rights, or we'd have to somehow show that to be harmed is to have one's rights violated. I don't think that the latter case can be substantiated. If it *could*, then all harms ought to be outlawed since all violations of rights ought to be outlawed. If a general identification of harms as violations of rights could be substantiated, then a universal harm-prevention mandate for government could be defended. Of course, this mandate would then just be a case of the standard maxim that the business of government is the protection of rights, and the proponents of regulation to prevent harms would have to show that *rights theory* and not simply our protection from harms calls for regulation.

Ought government to protect us from harms understood as losses (sense 2)? All of them? Suppose I lose my watch. Has the government failed to protect me? Surely not.

Suppose it turns out that Jones took my watch. Now that *sounds* like just the sort of loss from which government should protect us. But be careful here. Suppose Jones took the watch with my consent, or at my invitation and I am mentally competent. Should the government have protected me from that? No. Of course, it should have prevented Jones from taking the watch without my consent.

2. Ibid., p. 27.

Suppose I lose a tooth. It would *seem* that government's role is dictated by whether I lose it to an oral surgeon or to a bully. But consider the case in which I expressly forbade the oral surgeon to extract the tooth but it was removed anyway. Or consider the similar situation in which, in the grip of a perverse desire I asked the bully to knock the tooth out. If the government adopts a paternalistic attitude it might say that the oral surgeon is not prohibited from removing my tooth without my consent for there is, in fact, no loss, since the professional's judgment is better than my own. The government would also then undertake to stop my voluntary exchange with the bully.

But then have I not *lost* the freedom to decide for myself how my life is to proceed? And, if government ought to protect us from harms defined as losses, ought not the government have protected me from that loss? I don't think that the harm-preventing government can operate here.

So far, the issue of losing my tooth seems clear enough. But what if I lose it in the course of a football game that I am voluntarily playing? It's a harm, that is, a loss. Should the government have prevented it? No. Why? That's a question I'd like to reserve for later.

I want to tell one more story about loss. In this story I have a growth. It may be malignant. It certainly is unsightly, all discolored, growing on my forehead. My doctors are undecided about the wisdom of removing it. It may be that after removal there would be abnormal cells still on my forehead that would quickly replicate. Furthermore, I'm very uncertain about whether to have it removed, even for cosmetic reasons, for I am squeamish about the prospects of surgery. But I really am undecided.

One day, I'm walking the streets of the town when an insecurely fastened roof tile comes flying down off a building and strikes me in such a way that it completely amputates the growth at the very narrow spot where it joined my forehead. I'm a bit shaken, but a quick look at my reflection in a car window shows that I'm really all right. There's superficial bleeding, but otherwise I'm perfectly intact. In fact, my appearance is improved. I now have a smooth forehead again. Subsequent medical inspection shows that there's no sign of cancer in the remaining tissue, the wound heals and the scar disappears.

I have not been harmed. Oh, I was given a start, but that really doesn't count (see the discussion of serious harms below). Had I overcome my indecision, gone to a surgeon, contracted to have the growth removed and had all these results, all would have been ideal.

But not all is ideal. When I went strolling the streets of the town that day, I did not *want* roof-tile surgery. When I stepped in front of that house, I didn't want that to happen. Had someone made me an offer, saying something like this, "A large, sharp piece of slate falling at an accelerating rate of 32 ft/sec² will plunge toward you, etc.," I would have declined the procedure.

I am disturbed that this happened to me, and rightly so. I got much more than I would have consented to. Something should be done to those people (the owners of the house and sidewalk) who put me through that ordeal. And government ought to assume the role of ensuring that what ought to be done to them is done.

I'm glad that I wasn't harmed. But my moral indignation is just as strong as it would have been had I been harmed against my will. It's not *harm* that forms the basis of tort and negligence law and other law, but the imposition of *nonvoluntary* relations. And that is the central point I am urging here.

I am, of course, harmed by being thrust into a situation in which my choices don't count. But it's *not* because it is a harm that it is offensive. It is a fitting object for government prevention under the description, "imposition of nonvoluntary relations," *not* under the description "harm."

I urge this conclusion, which has been the common theme of these stories, in the last section of this paper. There, I have also added the necessary qualifications. In the next sections, however, I have more to say about harm.

What Counts as Harm

Not all losses are harms. I have nothing original to say on this point since it's well-traveled ground in the literature.[3] For Joel Feinberg:

> A person is harmed when someone invades (blocks or thwarts) one of his interests. [and] A person has an interest in Y when he has a *stake* in Y, that is when he stands to gain or lose depending on the condition or outcome of Y.[4]

3. See, for example, ibid., and Joel Feinberg, "Harm and Self-interest," in *Law, Morality and Society: Essays in Honor of H. L. A. Hart*, ed. P. M. S. Hacker and J. Raz (Oxford: Clarendon Press, 1977).

4. Feinberg, "Harm and Self-interest," p. 285.

But not just any frustration of desire will count as the invasion of an interest, a harm. This is so, according to Feinberg, because "no mere 'desire of the moment', like a desire to go to the cinema can generate an ulterior interest . . ." and "few persons can 'invest' enough in a wanted outcome to create a stake in it unless promoting that outcome becomes a personal goal or objective."[5]

Kleinig has a more restrictive notion of harm than Feinberg. Like Feinberg, he distinguishes between welfare interests and ulterior interests.[6] Unlike Feinberg, however, he maintains that only the impairment of a welfare interest counts as a harm.

For Kleinig, welfare interests are "those interests which are indispensable to the pursuit and fulfillment of characteristically human interests, . . . their satisfaction is not to be identified with a person's happiness or well-being so much as the conditions which make happiness and well-being possible."[7] They are interests in those things that are necessary for, but not sufficient to ensure, human happiness.

Some restriction on harms of the sort suggested by Kleinig and Feinberg is needed if we are to avoid labeling as harms innocuous events like a millionnaire being shortchanged a nickel, or a philatelist not being able to indulge in that hobby for two hours because of a visit from a boor.[8] For this paper I propose to adopt Kleinig's restriction of harms to impairments of welfare interests, since his definition is prima facie less supportive of my position than is Feinberg's. Generally, a violation of a right is a very serious business, and the more serious a loss must be before it can count as a harm, the more likely there will be a positive correlation between harms and violations of rights supporting the view that government ought to prevent harms. If my argument opposing that view works using Kleinig's interpretation of harms, it would certainly work using Feinberg's.

RIGHTS VERSUS HARMS

Consider how many different things we call harms:

1. Physical damage to myself caused by others.
2. Physical damage to myself caused by inanimate objects owned by others (flying roof tiles).

---

5. Ibid., p. 286.
6. Ibid., and Kleinig, "Crime and the Concept of Harm," pp. 31–33.
7. Ibid., p. 31.
8. Ibid., pp. 28–29.

3. In one sense of harm, if an unowned tree falls on my leg, breaking it, I am harmed.
4. "A man can harm his son's chances in life by the way in which he conducts his own. . . ."[9]
5. In a legal sense, I harm you if I trespass on your property, although I do not in any way alter it by so doing and neither you nor anyone else ever finds out.
6. I harm you by taking or destroying your property.
7. "Suppose that after my death, an enemy cleverly forges documents to 'prove' very convincingly that I was a philanderer, and communicates this 'information' to my widow, children, and former colleagues and friends. Can there be any doubt that I have been harmed by such libels?"[10]
8. I construct a tall building in the neighborhood ruining your television reception.
9. I invent a new, more efficient industrial process, thus lowering the market value of your inventory.
10. I insult you.
11. I fire you from your job.
12. I give you my cold.
13. I get your placement officer drunk at the American Philosophical Association Meeting smoker, thus ensuring that you won't get any job interviews.
14. I harm myself.
15. I place a tree behind my two-story house that blocks the magnificant view you had from your third-floor rooms.
16. By snubbing you on a particular occasion, I cause you to lose some business contacts.
17. I snub you and hurt your feelings.
18. I may be harmed by having my freedom of action curtailed.
19. As part of a budget cut, I lower your pay and thus reduce your income.
20. I file bankruptcy, thus leaving you with a lot of worthless IOU's.
21. I take my patented and unlicensed product off the market, thus harming its former users.

---

9. Ibid., p. 27.
10. Feinberg, "Harm and Self-interest," p. 306.

22. "Courage wanting good sense . . . is only a sort of confidence? When a man has no sense, he is harmed by such confidence. . . ."[11]

That was a long list. Some of the items are clearly such that nobody would even think of *outlawing* those harms. They are items (9), (10), (13), (17), and (22). Others are very much like those, but some people have succumbed to a temptation to consider outlawing them. Number (15) can evoke rights talk. Number (19) excites trade union talk of rights. And the risk posed by Typhoid Mary is an extension of (12).

Some items on the list, we might think are properly called harms only by a stretch of the sense of "harm." Numbers (5), and (22) fit this description.

Some items on the list, however, are paradigmatic cases of harms literally construed. Numbers (1), (2), (4), (7), and (14) are examples of this. Importantly, even on this smaller list of clear cases, it seems absolutely counter-intuitive to say that the business of government includes protecting me from such harms. It is absolutely counter-intuitive to say that the business of government involves protecting me from all such harms. And it is absolutely counter-intuitive to say that harming, in these cases, constitutes a violation of anybody's rights.

Take number (14). Suppose that, unwittingly, I harm myself by blurting out something indiscreet to my boss. As a result, I am fired. To simplify the story, I am a childless widower who has no one dependent on me for support. Whose rights have I infringed? I've done myself a harm. But I haven't transgressed anyone's rights.

It's appropriate to talk of rights violations only in at least two-party situations. Consider case (4). What should we say of the father harming his child's chances in life by the way he conducts his own life? In the case of, say, Thomas More, it can be argued that he harmed his children's chances in life by taking the stand of conscience that he did. In more contemporary cases, it can certainly be said that the present-day Soviet dissident who has children harms the chances that those children have living in that society. In the other direction we could speak of the effects famous parents have on their children. Johann Sebastian Bach, by being such an extraordinary

11. Plato, *Meno* 88b, trans. Jowett.

musician, set a parental ideal that his musician sons found either impossible or exceptionally difficult to attain, and thus harmed his children's chances for happiness in life. Nor is this just a philosopher's peculiar use of the term *harm*. According to the *Oxford English Dictionary*, if I injure you, I harm you, and if I "impair (you) in any way," I injure you. These are harms to welfare interests, in addition to being what common sense, as recorded in the *OED*, certifies as harm. But certainly our intuitions are clear that these harms should not be outlawed.

Now has the father violated a right of his progeny? Surely not. The fathers in these cases were under no obligation to go against conscience or to pursue mediocrity in order to provide the proper degree of opportunity for their children. Indeed, we may stress that the children of Soviet and Tudor-era dissidents do have their rights violated. But they are violated by those who impose unjust laws, not by fathers harming their children's chances in life by their courageous actions.

I want to take up the case that would be the most difficult to reconcile with my position, that of two-party, direct interactional harm, and show that rights violations do not reside in harming. This time I'll pick number (1). Surely, something is wrong with the supposed maxim "To harm someone is to violate that person's rights" if exceptions are allowed in certain cases of physical damage caused by one person to another.

A friend and I decide to have sex. We do, and have a wonderful time. Afterwards, I notice that I have acquired a bruise that is unmistakably the impression of a human hand. A bruise is physical damage. It was caused by my sex partner. So, number (1) is satisfied. Was there any violation of rights? No. Clearly not.

It might be objected, a bruise isn't much of a damage, so it really isn't a harm.[12] In case anyone thinks that this would be a worthwhile counter, the story is deliberately constructed so that it can be intensified in a number of ways.

I may have had an important professional tennis match and I may be unable to serve well with this bruise. Or, it turns out that I was married to someone other than my sex partner at the time of the livid hand impression. My spouse, on seeing the mark that I unsuc-

---

12. For an illustration of this argument, see Kleinig, "Crime and the Concept of Harm," p. 29.

cessfully tried to hide, said, "My God, you've been at it again! This time's one too many." At that point my spouse leaves—successful divorce proceedings are started, and I lose my happy home. If works of art and buildings can be damaged in a really harmful way because the physical damage makes them look unattractive, why can't I? The interesting point remains in this updated story. My sex partner harmed me by causing physical damage to me, but *between the two of us*, there was no violation of rights.

A nice feature of this sexual-escapade example is that it renders absurd what might be considered a rights-violation conception of harms. Let us assume that someone accidentally harms me. Since I did not choose to be harmed, my rights were indeed violated. However, out of generosity, I'll not claim redress for the violation of my rights—after all, it was an accident and it would be a great hardship for the person to make restitution, and so forth. But in the sex example, surely it cannot be said that my sex partner *violated* my rights by bruising me nor that only out of generosity do I *waive* my *claims* to a redress of the rights violation. Lovemaking is a shared, cooperative venture during which harms sometimes occur, but it is not logical to talk of rights violations in regard to the well-known possible consequences of acts entered into cooperatively.[13] To see the validity of this, imagine saying to a sex partner, "Oh my, you've bruised me. You know, I could take you to court for this, but relax, out of magnanimity, I won't."

The story of the bruise incurred in sex is a counterexample to the claim that all harms are rights violations. There are other, more ordinary stories than the ones so far cited that can be used to illustrate the same point. If, for some reason, I do desire to be hurt by someone else and this is done at my request and for fun or profit, that person has harmed me but has not violated my rights.

The usual stories are those of fulfillment of sado-masochistic desires. Sometimes masochists are really injured, and although the act was requested by the masochist, the functional damage counts as harm. Sometimes they are intentionally hurt by sadists or hirelings (prostitutes) who intentionally do it for fun or profit. Yet, if this is all done among adults, all of whom consented to the goings-on, rights have not been violated.

---

13. I am treating the issues of pregnancy and birth control as completely separate issues from this.

Finally, suppose an individual had persuaded some surgeon to remove a healthy spleen, and further suppose that the doctor had done it, intending no more than profit and the harm to the person. Would the doctor have violated that person's rights? No. Would the doctor have harmed the individual? Yes.

There seems no limit to such counterexamples to a theory that considers harms to be, *by that token*, violations of rights. And a large number of these counterexamples are cases of Kleinig-type harms that defeat welfare interests. So the claim that to harm me is to violate my rights ought to be rejected.

THE PROPER ROLE OF LAW

I want to illustrate an alternative view of the proper role of law. What is wrong in the case in which I am walking the streets and a roof tile falls on me? In discussing earlier examples, I suggested that what is wrong is that I've been thrust into a situation that I did not choose. I maintain that certain legitimate expectations were created when I contracted with the owner of the sidewalk to walk on it.[14] It was legitimate for me to expect, for example, that none of the sidewalk slabs were just papier-mâché imitations stretched over concealed tiger traps. I had the legitimate expectation that the sidewalk would not pitch and roll like some ill-conceived ride in an amusement park. It is legitimate for me to expect not to have to run a gauntlet of falling roof tiles, rocks, garbage, and other debris from the neighboring buildings.

I have rights. They do not come out of agreements with others, being prior to and presupposed by such agreements. But standard relations with others, which I will call "rational expectation frameworks," fix the criteria of their application to situations in everyday life. And rational expectation frameworks are a guide to those criteria.

There's nothing unusual about having the expectations which, taken together, constitute a rational expectation framework. They occur in everyday life and are part of why we call everyday life

14. I adopt the model of the laissez faire economy in which sidewalks, streets, and such are private property. This has the virtue of simplifying the story, thus eliminating the need to show a connection between the owner of the house and the person injured on a public street.

"everyday." For example, if I go into a bar and order a scotch on the rocks, then it is reasonable to expect that I'll get what I order and that neither it nor the place where I sit will be boobytrapped. There are countless examples of this.

Situations that recur frequently in human affairs have these frameworks of reasonable expectations. Generally, when I voluntarily place myself in such situations, by so doing I consent to those things predicted by the expectation framework but do not consent to things that are not, according to the framework, expected to happen. Thus, by determining what we do and do not consent to, rational-expectation frameworks determine which situations involve impositions on us of things which we have not chosen, and which situations do not. Since such impositions are always rights violating, rational-expectation frameworks thus provide criteria for determining when a right has been violated.

Let me repeat and stress that rational-expectation frameworks serve only as *criteria* for determining when someone's rights have been violated. They do *not* ground or create rights. Standard human rights theory describes the basis of human rights, and rational-expectation frameworks are not that basis.

Instead, rational-expectation frameworks are sets of states of affairs which members of a community can expect to occur together. If a person truly and knowingly enters into situation A, which has the rational-expectation framework $\{p, q, r, s, \text{not-}t\}$, then if that person objects to the consequence of an event described by 'p', that person owes an explanation why p is objectionable and further, why, knowing that p would eventuate, he/she entered into situation A. The fact that he/she entered into situation A is strong evidence that he/she *consented to p* occurring. Such consent is strong evidence that the occurrence of p does not violate his/her rights.

Similarly, if the rational-expectation framework for situation A clearly excludes t, then if t occurs when a person B enters into A and if t was a consequence of an act of a second person C toward B in situation A, then there is evidence that C has violated B's rights.

The rational-expectation framework does not *define* B's rights. Rather it serves as evidence of what B may be taken to have consented to and to have withheld consent to. Since t falls in the range of things to which B may not be supposed to have consented by entering into A, then C may be judged to have violated B's rights by introducing t into B's life in situation A. But C may be judged to have so violated B's rights *only because* C imposed the unchosen on B.

Rational-expectation frameworks are designed only to serve as indicators of what people have and have not *chosen* when they insert themselves into familiar situations. Such indicators are needed because people do not, as a rule, chatter like magpies about just what they are and are not consenting to when entering into familiar situations. So, as it is morally important to know to what thev do and do not consent, as we evaluate actions directed toward them, we need nonlinguistic criteria to fulfill the lack of information imposed by their silence. Rational-expectation frameworks fulfill this function. And a little thought will recommend the conclusion that these frameworks are, in fact, what we use in everyday life, in ordinary situations. That is how we know what our fellow participants do and do not consent to. That is how we know when we would be violating their rights (by imposing the unchosen) and when we would not.

We appeal to rational-expectation frameworks in frequently recurring situations of life. In situations that don't recur frequently in human affairs there is less of an expectation framework. Personal service contracts of athletes and entertainers may require many clauses to handle the novelties of the situations. Those contracts will be accordingly explicit and complex. My rental agreement on my simple apartment rental, on the other hand, is a standard form that can be purchased in bulk in stationery stores. In both situations, however, the participants and the courts know what to expect of the parties in countless diverse situations.

Of course, not everything falls within a rational--expectation framework. For example, I had an expectation that the bartender at the bar mentioned above might have worn a shirt today, but the *color* of the shirt was not within my expectation framework. *We all know* that I had no such reasonable expectation while we all know that we have reasonable expectations that hotel beds will not literally be beds of rocks. So there are reasonable expectations *about* what are reasonable expectations.

When we put ourselves into situations with "free variables" like shirt colors, we accept the unbound character of those variables. For example, it would be unreasonable for me to complain that my rights have been violated because a bartender's hair was parted on one side rather than the other.

Someone who for idle sport aims a gun at me and pulls the trigger, trusting to luck that there's no bullet in the chamber, imposes a risk that is no part of the background conditions of civilized life and to which no one can reasonably suppose I have consented. Such behavior is not in the rational-expectation framework of civilized life. So that person has violated my rights since my explicit statement of consent had not been obtained.

Living in an advanced industrial society involves accepting a great number of risks as part of the commonly acknowledged conditions of life. None of these risks are, in themselves, violations of rights. I have in mind situations like the following. People drive cars that can malfunction accidentally with horrible consequences for us. People's homes are stocked with potentially dangerous appliances. If I visit your house and the television set explodes, harming me, then I may expect you to pay some of my medical costs out of friendship or neighborliness, even if you had taken every reasonable precaution to maintain your television set properly.

However, you are neither civilly nor criminally liable. Nor should you have been barred from having a television set. Nor have you violated my rights. The dangers of television sets are some of the many commonly acknowledged conditions of modern life and are part of our expectation framework.

People live in unique styles that, within vague parameters of acceptable deviation, can provide us with surprising benefits or harms. You may have thought to have installed a piece of transparent hard plastic in front of your television set. The set explodes, but I, your guest, am protected. In such a case, the particular benefit is surprising, but what is not surprising is that you acted in an idiosyncratic way in a social situation to confer it. Within parameters, we accept people's capacity to be innovative in social relations. There are, however, constraints on such innovations. Those constraints are themselves part of the reasonable-expectation framework we have of everyday life. It is not reasonable, for example, to suppose that if you have a new prophylactic against cancer that involves subjecting a person to intense radiation for an hour, that you should be able to irradiate your dinner guests with it without first obtaining their explicit consent. Even if the treatment were beneficial, such a benefit is so removed from the reasonable-expectation patterns of everyday life that it would be wrong to impose it on people presupposing that they'd accept it. People can't be assumed to have consented to things outside the rational-expectation frameworks of the situations into which they put themselves. Their consent must be verified by some other means, like an explicit statement of consent, or not be pre-supposed at all.

When a situation into which I have placed myself is enriched by the inclusion of features to which I did not consent, then, if someone is not to violate my rights, I ought to be consulted and ought to have accepted those features before their inclusion.

Thus, I maintain, when a harm or a risk or anything, including the benefits of roof-tile surgery, is introduced into my life *without my consent*, my rights have been violated. This is what makes tort and negligence law proper and this is why the person who has endangered me, but not harmed me, may have violated my rights.

I contend that it is a violation of a person's rights to impose a harm or a benefit or a risk on that person to which that person has not consented. Situations into which I freely enter have rational-expectation frameworks such that in entering into the situation I voluntarily accept the predictions of that framework. These specifi-cations of expected outcomes include some incomplete specifications (people's shirt colors) and specifications that some situations won't eventuate.[15] There are even specifications of the magnitude of nov-elty that may be introduced into situations.

Government ought to protect people's rights. So, government ought to protect people from involuntary harms and benefits expe-rienced at the hands of others and from being thrust involuntarily into risky situations. In normal circumstances, unless the sidewalk owner has secured my acceptance of the risk of encountering poorly fastened roof tiles along my route, then falling roof tiles, indeed, even unsafe roof tiles (that *might* fall) along my route, constitute a violation of my rights that is actionable on discovery.[16]

My view of risks and rights allows me to say that a person who im-poses a risk on me by firing a gun near me, but not intentionally at

15. This is why my rights are not violated in the case in which I lose a tooth playing football. I accept the risk as part of the commonly acknowledged conditions of that game. And, since injuries of that scale are so probable, I accept full liability for the injury myself by choosing to play the game.

16. Of course, rather than take the case to court, I will in most cases simply stop trading with that firm. But, in some case, I will sue. And the public authorities could always press criminal charges for fraud due to failure to warn.

me, violates my rights. My rights are violated because an increased probability that I will be harmed has been imposed on me without my consent. This explanation shows, in terms of the presence or absence of consent, why I can, by law, prevent you from haphazardly firing a gun around me, but not from having potentially dangerous television sets around me. In the gun case, but not the television case, my rights are violated because of my nonconsent to being endangered by guns. The informal commonly accepted conventions of neighborhood life, based on expectation frameworks, sketch the amount and kinds of *risks*, in addition to the amount and kinds of *harms*, that we are prepared to accept as part of neighborhood life. Neighbors' tree pruning and people's cigarette smoking and television sets constitute risks of a sort and degree that we are prepared to accept.[17] (We would not accept actual damages arising out of these risky situations.) The behavior of neighborhood louts who give us some appreciable probability of being shot while sitting on our porches is not acceptable. There are borderline cases as there always are in any matter. But, again, we do know what it is reasonable to expect.

The proper role of government is not to protect us from harms but from human interactions to which we have not consented. In implementing this mandate the government will have to attend closely to the rational–expectation frameworks of everyday life. And when it detects unannounced practices or states of affairs that are outside the rational–expectation frameworks of the transactions in which they exist, then the government should step in, under its mandate, to prevent fraud and the initiation of force. But the reason that it should is not to prevent harms, benefits, or risks, but to prevent the imposition of human interactions to which we have not consented.

17. Although, as the case of cigarette smoking is designed to show, these reasonable-expectation frameworks are liable to change over time.

PART IV

RIGHTS OF FUTURE GENERATIONS

Chapter 8

GOVERNMENT REGULATION AND INTERGENERATIONAL JUSTICE

Rolf Sartorius

Whereas philosophers working within and (like John Rawls) "around" the utilitarian tradition have had much to say about our obligations to future generations, especially with respect to population and (more recently) environmental policy, those writing in the opposing tradition of natural rights and libertarianism have been conspicuously silent concerning questions of intergenerational justice. I shall attempt to partially fill this gap in a manner I believe should be welcomed by those who would defend a minimalistic conception of the state and yet take seriously the view that we not only *may* but for all practical purposes *must* turn to the state for the protection of certain fundamental human rights.[1] Any viable theory of natural rights that can account for the legitimacy of any governmental regulatory activity whatsoever must provide for activity that embraces the protection of the rights of future generations.

My strategy shall be as follows: I shall first outline what I take to be the core of the moral-political theory that sees as legitimate only governmental regulatory activity that effectively exercises "the umpirage of the law of nature," employing the coercive power of the law only to prevent coercion in the form of assault, theft, fraud, breach of contract, and so on.[2] I shall then argue that this core posi-

---

1. I shall not deal here with the question of whether or not creatures other than humans have rights or interests that the state ought to protect.
2. John Locke, *The Second Treatise of Government*, sec. 87.

tion must be extended to permit government regulation that will assure the provision of those public goods the absence of which would involve the violation of people's rights and that can neither be provided by private market mechanisms nor the application of familiar principles of criminal law, tort, contract, and so on. Next I shall argue that generally it makes perfect sense to claim that we have obligations to respect the rights of future generations. I shall then turn to the question of what rights they have, contending that the extended core position concerning legitimate governmental regulatory activity must be applied to them in a manner strictly paralleling its application to our own contemporaries. In conclusion, I shall consider what kinds of governmental regulation may be necessary to protect the rights of future generations and briefly consider the specific forms such protection might take, including that of according legal (i.e., judicial) standing to future persons.

THE CORE POSITION

What I am calling the "core" of the natural-rights and libertarian conception of the minimal state is admittedly an amalgam of elements found in the views of Locke, Hayek, Robert Nozick, and others (including Professor Thomas Haggard's brilliant contribution to this conference).[3] It consists of the following:

1. Whatever else may be said about the nature of government, its distinguishing feature, at least from the standpoint of moral and political theory, is that it exercises a virtual monopoly over the use of coercive force within the territory it controls.

2. Whatever else may be said about humanity, its distinguishing feature, from the standpoint of moral and political theory, is that merely by being human one may claim as a matter of right the freedom to act as one chooses in the pursuance of one's own goals and projects, free from the interference of others, as long as one does not coercively encroach upon the noncoercive activities of others in the process.

3. F. A. Hayek, *The Constitution of Liberty* (Chicago: University of Chicago Press, 1960); Robert Nozick, *Anarchy, State, and Utopia* (New York: Basic Books, 1974); Thomas R. Haggard, "Government Regulation of the Employment Relationship," this volume, pp. 13-41.

3. Outside of government one has the right to enforce one's rights against others by the use of coercion: acting in self-defense against, exacting reparation from, or inflicting punishment upon wrongdoers as the case may be.

4. The maximum limit upon legitimate governmental use of coercion is set by the enforceable rights that exist outside of government. In particular, the fulfillment of human needs, no matter how genuine and deeply felt, is no legitimate function of government.

5. Voluntary free-market exchange is the only just, and is indeed the most efficient, noncoercive mechanism for satisfying human needs.

6. Among humanity's natural rights is the right to acquire and transfer private property.

7. There are practically realizable conditions short of unanimous consent of the governed under which the state may claim to have legitimately acquired the right to enforce at least some of the rights of its citizens.

8. Beyond what they must do to respect the rights of others, and beyond what they may choose to do as a result of the perceived mutual advantage that presumably underlies voluntary exchange in a free market, people can and should be led by considerations of moral principle to act with charity and respect for their fellow creatures.

Before attempting to sharpen the formal conception of rights contained in the core position, and prior to arguing for an extension of it, let me comment briefly on the nature and extent to which I endorse the various elements of that position as outlined above.

The Law and Natural Rights Reassessed

First, for the purposes of the account to be offered here, the view that the law is essentially coercive is correct. But the details may prove sticky; witness, just within the recent history of the analytic tradition in jurisprudence alone, the quite different analyses of the coercive element in law offered by John Austin, Hans Kelsen, Alf Ross, and H. L. A. Hart.[4] Second, with the claim that there are *nat-*

4. John Austin, *The Province of Jurisprudence Determined* (New York: Noonday Press, 1954); Hans Kelsen, *General Theory of Law and State*, trans. A. Wedberg (New York:

tural rights, in the sense of legitimate claims that exist outside of and against government and positive law, I fully agree. But I find no reason to believe that those who have these rights are endowed with them by virtue of any characteristics that only humans possess. And with Hume, I believe that there may be a significant conventional aspect (nonarbitrary, but in *that* sense nonnatural) to some of them.[5] (See my comments on property rights below.) In line with the Kantian emphasis in much recent moral philosophy, I do not question the central fact that all normal adults under "civilized" conditions have the capacity to lead autonomous lives, free to make and responsible for those noncoerced choices that lend whatever meaning there is to their lives. Although I believe it is stretching matters a bit to construe rights against such crimes as breach of contract and fraud as instantiations of a fundamental right against coercion, I shall not attempt here to provide any more unifying an account of those basic autonomy rights I do believe we have. Placing myself within a tradition that has glorified the notion that men have the right to "life, liberty, and the pursuit of happiness," I might note that, as with Judith Thomson, it is no part of my understanding of the right to life that it entails a right to the necessities of life.[6] Neither is it part of my view that the right to the pursuit of happiness implies a right to be happy.

Leaving aside the many difficult problems with the justification of either punishment or reparation, and ignoring the significant fact that Locke (followed by our own legal system) believed that there was an important difference between the two in terms of who may exact it, let us consider the question of the enforceability of rights in the relatively unproblematic case of one using coercion to prevent coercion, the paradigm perhaps being that of one taking the life of another in self-defense.[7] It is surely the case that with respect to many of one's rights, one has (or, outside of government, would have) the right to enforce the obligations corresponding to them by the use of *appropriate* forms of coercive force (which, I hope we

---

Russell and Russell, 1961); Alf Ross, *On Law and Justice* (London: Stevens and Sons, 1958); H. L. A. Hart, *The Concept of Law* (Oxford: Oxford University Press, 1961).

5. David Hume, *A Treatise of Human Nature*, ed. L. A. Selby-Bigge (Oxford: Clarendon Press, 1896), bk. 3, pt. 2, sec. 1.

6. Judith Jarvis Thomson, "A Defense of Abortion," *Philosophy and Public Affairs* 1 (Fall 1971): 47–66.

7. Locke, *The Second Treatise*, sec. 11.

would agree, does not include the right to set bear traps for trespassers). But does this say something merely about what rights we have, or is it evidence that all significant obligations are by necessity enforceable? Hart has relied heavily on the enforceability of obligations thesis, and his view is shared by many.[8] Yet Nozick suggests a telling counterexample:

> If I cautiously insist that you first promise to me that you won't force me to do A before I will make my promise to you to do A, and I do receive this promise from you first, it would be implausible to say that in promising I give you the right to force me to do A.[9]

Just as some have claimed that having a right entails having a correlative right of enforcement, so have some claimed that having a right entails having the right to waive it.[10] Even if not a matter of entailment, this is surely typically the case. But this suggests a slight modification of Nozick's putative counterexample to the enforceability of obligations thesis. Suppose I promise you to do A and that you then promise me not to force me to do A. Have you thereby released me from my obligation to do A? I think not. Furthermore, suppose one encountered a firm defender of human rights who also claimed to be a pacifist. Could such a person be charged with being involved in a conceptual muddle? Again, I think not. Having little sympathy with the current general trend among moral philosophers to present analytic grounds for theories of right and obligation that strike me as having substantial normative content, I shall treat this element of the core position as a contingent truth about most cases of obligations.

Certain extensions of the core position for which I shall argue in the following section suggest that there are limited exceptions to the thesis, widely held by libertarians and clearly held by Locke, that government may acquire no new rights of enforcement. That aside, let me put this element of the core position in what I think is a defensible form: The upper limit upon legitimate governmental use of coercion is set by the rights of its citizens. This leaves open two possibilities that the initial formulation might be understood to exclude. First, with respect to some right X that individuals do have

8. H. L. A. Hart, "Are There Any Natural Rights?," *Philosophical Review* 64 (April 1955): 175-91.
9. Nozick, p. 91.
10. D. N. MacCormick, "Rights in Legislation," in *Law, Morality, and Society*, ed. P. M. S. Hacker and Joseph Raz (Oxford: Clarendon Press, 1977), pp. 189-209.

outside of government, there is a corresponding right of enforcement that can only be exercised by government. Second, as I believe is the case with private property rights, some natural rights have conventional aspects that depend upon the existence of, and thus could not exist outside of, government.

Another Look at the Free Market and Private Property

I maintain that a system of voluntary free-market exchange, externalities aside, is just in the sense that it provides a noncoercive mechanism for the pursuit of those individual goals that depend upon exchange relations with others and that enable the achievement of mutual benefit without violating anyone's rights in the process. Furthermore, such a system is efficient, not only in the weak sense captured by the notion of Pareto optimality, but in the stronger senses that both Locke and writers in the utilitarian tradition have associated with a system of private property rights.

Finally, I wish to consider the notion that among humanity's natural rights is the right to acquire and transfer private property. Associated historically with Locke and recently advocated by Nozick and other libertarians, the notion that one has ownership in one's body and thus one's labor, and that by "mixing" the latter with previously unowned things one thereby acquires a permanent bequeathable property right in them, I find totally mysterious. The principle that one is entitled to the fruits of one's labor, on the other hand, I find totally unobjectionable. But if one does not have natural rights of initial acquisition and transfer of the stronger sort, what grounds of complaint can one have against the compulsory transfers of property required to finance the redistributive programs of the modern welfare state? What rights could one claim were being violated in the name of the general welfare? The answer to this difficult question is a complex one, but I do believe that an answer is possible. It falls roughly into two parts; for each I can provide only the briefest sketch here.

Locke's remarks concerning the labor theory of entitlement are relatively brief and present an argument strikingly similar to that found in Hume's and Bentham's discussions of private property.[11]

---

11. Locke, *The Second Treatise*, chap. 5.

Briefly, the argument suggests that the earth's resources are a common pool to be drawn on for people's mutual advantage, providing in large measure the means for achieving the rightful individual ends of the preservation of life and the pursuit of happiness. They are to be used, of course, in the most efficient manner. This provides the ground for prohibiting not only individual waste within a particular system of property, but for requiring as a matter of moral principle— perhaps, indeed, as a matter of moral *right*—the most efficient *system* for the exploitation of natural resources. And that system is one of private rather than communal ownership, because the former provides the individual incentives required to extract the labor that for the most part accounts for the social value products have in the marketplace, typically greatly improved upon from the condition in which they are found in their natural state. Such a system, it is argued, is not only efficient in the utilitarian sense of maximizing the sum total or per capita average of human satisfactions. Despite the great inequalities in possessions the system is expected to generate, Hume contends that like other conventions associated with the artificial (i.e., nonnatural) rules of justice, it is in the long-range common interest of *each*.[12] It is only reasonable to take Hume here to be speaking, not of each particular individual, but of the situation of representative occupants of the socioeconomic strata to which a system of private property rights gives rise. Along these (Rawlsian) lines, it is significant to note that Bentham, Locke, and Adam Smith all take pains to argue that a system of private property rights, with all the inequalities it generates, works to the advantage of *the least advantaged*.[13] Having in section 40 of *The Second Treatise* argued that "the improvement of labor makes the far greater part of the value" of land, Locke goes on in section 41 to describe the system of communal property among the American Indians as one "rich in land and poor in all the comforts of life" due to the absence of the incentives to labor that arise from a system of private property rights. "And," he concludes, "a king of a large and fruitful territory there feeds, lodges, and is clad worse than a day-laborer in England." This passage is only slightly modified by Adam Smith in *The Wealth of Nations*: "The accommodation of an European prince does not always so much exceed that of an industrious and frugal peasant, as

12. Hume, *A Treatise of Human Nature*, bk. 3, pt. 2, sec. 2.
13. John Rawls, *A Theory of Justice* (Cambridge, Mass.: Harvard University Press, 1971), pp. 64f.

the accommodation of the latter exceeds that of many an African king."[14] Bentham, considering the objection that "the laws of property are good for those who have property, and oppressive to those who have none," responds that "all things considered, the protection of the laws may contribute as much to the happiness of the cottage as to the security of the palace."[15]

The view shared by these authors is not utilitarian. As already noted, strict adherence to the latter position would permit what the view under discussion prohibits—sacrifice of the least advantaged in the name of promoting the general welfare. It is not an application of Rawls's difference principle either, for it does not require that the inequalities generated by a system of private property rights be adjusted so as to *maximize* the advantage of the least advantaged.[16] What it does require is that all, especially the least advantaged, be at least as well off as they would be under any realizable system (honoring the principle that one is entitled to the fruits of one's labor) other than a system of private property rights. The principle in question, aptly described as a principle of justice, both lies at the foundation of, and provides a basis for interpreting, the so-called Lockean proviso that the initial acquisition of previously unowned resources leaves "enough and as good for others."[17] Clearly, what the proviso must address is not the distribution of land (by Locke's time virtually all land in England was owned by a very few), but rather the fruits of productive resources (including land) that provide the necessities of life and the means for the pursuit of happiness. Given Locke's belief in the great efficiency of a system of private ownership and in its justice, the proviso is *more than* satisfied, for not only are the least advantaged classes as well off as they would have been prior to the appropriation of most if not all of the land by the (industrious) few; they are *better* off.[18]

According to Hume, basing title on first possession is not just conventional; it comes very close to being *arbitrary*, resting upon the "slightest" of "analogies"—presumably the analogy suggested by

14. Adam Smith, *The Wealth of Nations* (New York: P. F. Collier & Sons, 1909), p. 78.

15. J. Bentham, *Theory of Legislation*, ed. R. Hildreth (Boston: Weeks, Jordan & Co., 1840), p. 114.

16. Rawls, *A Theory of Justice*, pp. 82f.

17. Locke, *The Second Treatise*, sec. 33.

18. My interpretation of Locke builds upon, although it goes beyond, that of C. B. Macpherson, *The Political Theory of Possessive Individualism* (London: Oxford University Press, 1962); pp. 211–14.

that principle of association of ideas having to do with contiguity.[19] Although the labor theory of original acquisition may *appear* less arbitrary, I believe Hume is correct in suggesting that the right systematic method of initially dividing previously unowned natural resources is whichever one works best by providing incentives. First possession, first mixing of labor, equal division, division by lot — all are real moral possibilities, none of which can be claimed as a matter of natural right. This also applies to inheritance. While Hume seems to consider the right of bequest a necessary part of the desired incentive structure,[20] Bentham claims that while redistribution within generations would destroy the security of expectations upon which the incentive structure depends, intergenerational redistribution based upon confiscatory inheritance taxes would not.[21] The important point is that they agree, I believe rightly, that this, like the question of initial title to unowned resources, is an empirical question.

Having sketched my view of the core position, I now turn to the question of what rights are being violated when government engages in compulsory redistribution — typically, although of course not exclusively — through the device of compulsory taxation. My response has two parts, and although they may be merely restatements of the same basic points, nonetheless I find it preferable to state them separately.

Although there may be no natural rights to initial acquisition and transfer of property of the sort proposed by Locke, Nozick, and others, one can at least claim a right to the fruits of one's labor. With respect to the ownership of natural resources and their products, one can claim the right to a just and efficient system of property rights that entitles one to the equivalent value of one's labor in addition to what (under such a system) one rightly possesses. Accepting the arguments in terms of the just incentive structure reviewed previously, I believe that a system of private-property rights embedded within the framework of a largely unregulated free-market economy is that system. And thus I believe that one can claim a right to it. But what of *redistribution* within such a system, either intra- or intergenerational? Here, in the intragenerational case especially, I would appeal

19. David Hume, *An Enquiry Concerning the Principles of Morals* (LaSalle, Ill.: Open Court, 1966), sec. 3, pt. 2.

20. Ibid.

21. Bentham, *Theory of Legislation*, p. 122.

to the arguments of Hume, Bentham, Nozick, and others claiming that redistributive programs may undermine the incentive structure upon which the entire system rests, even if they do not violate the principle that one is entitled to the fruits of one's labor. Although no one program alone is likely to have this effect, the combination of a number of such programs, coupled with the general insecurity that results when government is conceded the right to engage in compulsory redistribution, may undermine the system of private property to such an extent that people are denied *the kind of system* to which they are rightfully entitled.

Locke and other contract theorists have thought it important to argue that government could have been created through a process of explicit agreement (although, of course, they knew that it never was). Nozick, rejecting contractarianism, has argued that government could arise through largely invisible-hand processes in which no one's rights would be violated. Concern, indeed, preoccupation, with the question of how a legitimate government might emerge from a nonstate situation has led most recent commentators virtually to ignore what political theorists like Locke and Hume had to say about what would already exist in a nonstate situation through a system of private property. Recall, then, that for Locke, money would have been introduced by tacit consent into the state of nature, resulting in the emergence of a market economy based upon a system of differential private-property rights. For Hume, the rules of justice in general, including the rules concerning the acquisition and transference of private property, represent conventions that would arise without explicit agreement in a nonstate situation. For both Hume and Locke, government has as one of its primary functions the protection of private property, in other words, the protection of the system of private property as it would and could exist prior to the existence of government. Now, if one could argue that the kinds of conventions and implicit agreements leading to a system of private property in a nonstate situation would preclude compulsory transfers for the purposes of redistribution, one would have a powerful argument indeed for denying government the right to engage in compulsory redistribution. Unfortunately, it is not limitations of space alone that prevent me from offering such arguments here, but I seriously recommend this line of argument be developed by those attracted to contractarian and other developmental-type explanations of the origins of social institutions. At the nontheoretical level, at least this much seems clear: the massive forms of compulsory redistribution associated with the programs of the modern welfare state could not exist outside the framework provided by the equally massive coercive apparatus of the modern state with its particular bureaucratic forms and legislative structures. Clearly, such a framework could not exist in a nonstate situation. Thus, whatever forms of redistribution for which such a framework is necessary could not have existed in a system of private property in a nonstate situation either.

Government's Right to Rule

The view that there are realistic conditions under which government may claim a right to rule (corresponding to which would be a prima facie moral obligation of obedience to law on the part of its citizens) appears to be just as widely held among libertarians as it is among other political philosophers. Without restating here arguments that I and others have given elsewhere, let me simply indicate that I flatly reject this view of the legitimacy of government.[22] Rather, I take government to be an inescapable historical given, and, rejecting the notion that some may have a right to rule, recognize two questions as having central importance to political philosophy: (1) What individual rights must government seek to protect? (2) What intitutional forms are most likely to secure the effective protection of those rights?

On the more positive side, I take seriously the notion of government as enjoying a "trust"; as exercising a "guardianship." An individual may be appointed the guardian of the interests of an orphaned child merely by claiming to be able and willing to look after those interests; no special relationship need exist between that individual and the child conferring a special title to direct the child's life in important respects, and the child is not viewed as having any special obligation to do what the guardian commands. The important question for the guardian is which interests of the ward ought to be recognized and what order of priorities ought to be imposed upon them in case of conflict. The main difference in the case of the state, is that its role is confined to protecting *rights* rather than promoting

22. Rolf Sartorius, *Individual Conduct and Social Norms* (Encino, Calif.: Dickenson Publishing Co., 1975), chap. 6.

interests. I do not ask government, then, "By what right do you rule over me?" There is no such right. Rather, I ask government, "Do you rule rightly?" And by this I mean, "Do you rule so as to secure the rights of those over whom you rule?"

I fully agree that the minimal state may provide the framework within which individuals and voluntary associations of individuals can and should act with consideration toward their fellow creatures in a manner that goes beyond respecting their moral rights. As R. M. Titmuss's discussion of blood donorship suggests, though, the existence of free markets in commodities like blood may drive out the charitable giving of those things that would otherwise be viewed by potential donors as literally priceless.[23] If this analysis is correct, it is interesting and not unimportant, but surely no more than that. No one has ever seriously contended that a free society is totally cost-free.

Rights and Obligations

Before considering the various ways in which I believe the core position must be extended, let me elaborate upon my view of the concepts of "right" and "obligation" in terms of which the core position is stated. In line with recent defenders of extremely diverse rights-based theories about what particular rights people have, I am adopting the following formal conception of what is a justified claim of right, whether it be a claim of moral right against other individuals or a claim of political right against government: A claim of right is one whose satisfaction takes priority over the satisfaction of competing claims based upon considerations of promoting overall welfare, be it that of the individual or of society at large.

Since few would be willing to claim that there are any moral or political rights that are absolute, most (including myself) would wish to add the following "escape clause" as a qualifier to this conception: Failure to satisfy a claim of right may be justified if the consequences of satisfying it would be extremely severe. Severity of consequences in such a qualifier may be understood in one of either two ways: (1) in a straightforward utilitarian sense of welfare—the very

23. R. M. Titmuss, *The Gift Relationship* (London: Allen and Unwin, 1970). This theme is developed by Peter Singer, "Altruism and Commerce: A Defense of Titmuss Against Arrow," *Philosophy and Public Affairs* 2 (1973): 312–20.

kind of consideration that a claim of right is designed to defeat in the *normal* case; or (2) in a limited sense associated with the prevention of a much (not just marginally) more extensive violation of rights than that involved in the violation of the right in question.

Whatever the nature of the escape clause, given this formal conception, claims of right "trump" utilitarian arguments in matters of morality and politics. At least according to Ronald Dworkin, in law, cast as arguments of principle that generate claims of legal right, they cannot be defeated by arguments of social policy. Indeed, Dworkin claims that "this sense of a right (which might be called the anti-utilitarian concept of a right) . . . marks the distinctive concept of an individual right against the State which is the heart . . . of constitutional theory in the United States."[24]

Although not part of the purely formal conception of rights described above, there is a closely related claim of substantive moral principle that at least Rawls is prepared to defend and to which I wish to return in my discussion of intergenerational justice. In claiming that the principles of distributive justice are "absolute" regarding considerations of utility, Rawls has meant to do more than emphasize the priority that claims of right take over counterclaims based upon the promotion of welfare. In addition, he contends that the benefits accruing to the beneficiaries of an unjust institution or social practice must be "tossed out" in the course of any appraisal of the overall moral merits of that institution or practice.[25] Even where utilitarian calculations may be appropriate in the context of institutional choice, satisfactions that rely on violations of the principles of justice deserve no weight whatsoever.[26] Generalizing on Rawls's position, one might claim that where the violation of any kind of right is involved, the benefits that accrue to the violators (or, more broadly, to the beneficiaries of their violation) should be given no weight in the overall appraisal of the acts, practices, or institutions responsible for their violation.

Related to the above substantive claims about the relationship between rights and utility is an issue concerning the kinds of trade-offs permissible among rights themselves. Just what sort of action-guiding principle is appropriate for dealing with claims of right? The pri-

---

24. Ronald Dworkin, *Taking Rights Seriously* (Cambridge, Mass.: Harvard University Press, 1977), p. 269.
25. John Rawls, "Justice As Fairness," *Philosophical Review* 67 (1958): sec. 7.
26. Ibid.

mary choice seems to be between a principle treating rights as "side constraints" on action and one that treats them as "goals" (in the sense of claims that are to be maximally satisfied). Nozick has argued convincingly that adopting a maximization principle with respect to rights—for example, to act in a way that maximizes satisfaction (minimizes violation) of claims of right—will be open to essentially the same sort of objection as is utilitarianism because some persons' rights will be sacrificed for others. Familiar cases involving the punishing of innocents in order to prevent great *harm* to others, for instance, can easily be redescribed in terms of the maximally efficient means for minimizing the violation of people's *rights.*[27] Thomas Nagel, in his review of Nozick's *Anarchy, State, and Utopia*, elaborates upon the reasons for rejecting a "utilitarianism of rights" despite the fact that, like myself, he clearly does understand claims of rights to be qualified by a suitable escape clause.

> The fact that a right can be overridden to avoid sufficiently serious consequences does not mean that its violation can be assigned a disvalue comparable to the disvalue of those consequences. For that would give the occurrence of such a violation greater weight in a calculation of outcomes (e.g., when the question is what may be done to prevent such violations by others) than it in fact has. Therefore, although rights may on occasion be overridden, the violation of some people's rights cannot automatically be justified because it leads to a reduction in the more serious violation of other people's rights. This issue arises in connection with preventive detention, wiretapping, and search and seizure, all of which might be useful in the prevention of robbery, murder, assault, and rape.[28]

It is quite compatible with the purely formal conception of rights to claim that people have *welfare rights*; those who believe that they do might for obvious reasons reject the view that rights function as side constraints and opt rather for some form of maximization principle with respect to rights. But at least with regard to the quasi-Kantian autonomy rights with which we are here primarily concerned, the position taken by Nozick and Nagel seems to be correct. Side constraints, as Nozick claims:

> express the inviolability of other persons. But why may not one violate persons for the greater social good? Individually, we each sometimes choose to

27. Nozick, *Anarchy, State, and Utopia*, pp. 28–29.
28. Thomas Nagel, "Libertarianism Without Foundations," *Yale Law Journal* 85, (November 1975): 145n.

undergo some pain or sacrifice for a greater benefit or to avoid a greater harm: we go to the dentist to avoid worse suffering later; we do some unpleasant work for its results; some persons diet to improve their health or looks; some save money to support themselves when they are older. In each case, some cost is borne for the sake of the greater overall good. Why not, *similarly*, hold that some persons have to bear some costs that benefit other persons more, for the sake of the overall social good? But there is no *social entity* with a good that undergoes some sacrifice for its own good. There are only individual people, different individual people, with their own individual lives. Using one of these people for the benefit of others, uses him and benefits the others. Nothing more . . . . Talk of an overall social good covers this up. . . . To use a person in this way does not sufficiently respect and take account of the fact that he is a separate person, that his is the only life he has. He does not get some overbalancing good from his sacrifice, and no one is entitled to force this upon him. . . .[29]

Utilitarianism, with its characteristic neglect of the distinctiveness of persons, is perhaps in the best position to provide the philosophical underpinnings for the redistributive programs of the modern welfare state. The opposing conception of rights as side constraints, respecting the individuality of autonomous persons, is perhaps best understood as the core of the moral-political theory that would limit governmental regulatory activity to the prevention of coercion (broadly construed). This includes the enforcement of those voluntary agreements central to the operation of a free market based on the existence of a system of extensive private-property rights. It is to the extension of that core position that I shall now finally turn.

THE CORE POSITION EXTENDED

It has now become commonplace to consider necessary some form of compulsory taxation, statutory prescription, or the direction given by regulatory agencies to assure the provision of public goods that are provided neither through the operations of the free market nor by resorting to the prohibitory or compensatory measures of traditional civil and criminal law. In general, the paradigmatic case is one in which it is impossible to charge potential beneficiaries for the enjoyment of benefits from which they cannot be excluded. Realizing this, rationally self-interested individuals, attempting a free ride

29. Nozick, *Anarchy, State, and Utopia*, pp. 32–33.

on the benefits they hope to realize through the voluntary contributions of others, will find there is no ride to be taken at all. Assuming that each would receive benefits outweighing the individual's fair share of the costs of contributing toward the provision of some public good, the situation may be formally represented as a "many-person" prisoner's dilemma in which the optimal strategy choice for each leads to a non-Pareto-optimal outcome. Rational individual choice leads to a social state in which all are worse off than they might otherwise have been. Government regulation in such cases is seen as a means of forcing people to help themselves. Indeed, some have construed it as a form of justified paternalism.[30]

I will not review here the details of an analysis of the public-goods problem that I have developed at considerable length elsewhere.[31] Rather, I shall review some of the conclusions of that analysis that can be sustained by argument and explore their implications for the core position.

The Public Goods Problem

It is often assumed that the free-rider problem arises due to individuals acting selfishly and that recognizing principles of an enlightened social morality would lead people to cooperate voluntarily in the provision of public goods.[32] If this were correct, in those cases where the absence of a public good could be viewed as a violation of individual rights, government regulation would be no different than in those standard cases envisioned by the core position. The use of coercion would be justified as a means of ensuring that individuals fulfilled their obligations to respect the rights of others. But I believe this view of the matter is profoundly mistaken.

Consider the case of the overharvesting of a potentially renewable resource such as a fishery or an animal herd. Assume that ownership

30. Cf. Gerald Dworkin, "Paternalism," in *Morality and the Law*, ed. Richard Wasserstrom (Belmont, Calif.: Wadsworth Publishing Co., 1971), pp. 107–26.

31. Rolf Sartorius, "The Limits of Libertarianism," in *Liberty and the Rule of Law*, ed. R. L. Cunningham (College Station: Texas A&M Press, 1979), pp. 87–131; Frank Miller and Rolf Sartorius, "Population Policy and Public Goods," *Philosophy and Public Affairs* 8 (Winter 1979): 148–74.

32. As in Garrett Hardin, "The Tragedy of the Commons," *Science* 162 (December 1968): 1243–48.

is fully privatized among a large number of individuals, each owning part of a large territory throughout which members of the species roam according to their individual migratory patterns. This is surely the most favorable case for the core position, since many public-goods problems would not exist but for *public* ownership. Now the so-called Lockean proviso requires each to harvest an amount that leaves enough, in terms of quantity *and* quality, for others; in cases like the one in question I shall assume that at a minimum this requires that overexploitation not occur to the extent that the reproductive capacity of the species is destroyed. Perhaps maximum sustainable yield represents the policy that ought to be adopted by those who have the fishing or hunting rights in question.[33] Economic analysis shows that rational self-interest may lead each to adopt a policy that will destroy whatever capital that individual has in the fishery or animal herd.[34] Even if ownership in parts of the herd is so fully privatized so as to prevent migration, individuals, given the right investment opportunities, may find it in their economic interests to systematically deplete their capital in the species, reinvesting the return elsewhere. Following such a policy leads to the total destruction of the resource, and presumably, according to the Lockean proviso, violating the rights of others. But consider: the overharvesting of a fishery or animal herd to the point where it can no longer reproduce represents a significant threshold effect for which no individual can be held responsible, at least where sufficiently large numbers of individuals are concerned. Each individual could reason as follows: (1) if there are enough people trying to conserve the resource, I can take as much as I wish, or (2) if other people are *not* trying to conserve the resource, I might as well take while the taking is good. Whatever any individual does will not determine whether or not the threshold is crossed; thus, whatever any individual does, the Lockean proviso has not been violated. But if each one reasons this way, the proviso has, nonetheless, been violated. The rights of other would-be fishers and hunters have been violated.

33. Mary B. Williams, "Discounting Versus Maximum Sustainable Yield," in *Obligations To Future Generations*, ed. Brian Barry and R. I. Sikora (Philadelphia: Temple University Press, 1978), pp. 169–85.

34. See Daniel Fife, "Killing the Goose," *Environment* 13 (1971); Colin W. Clark, "The Economics of Overexploitation," *Science* 181 (1974). Both papers are reprinted in *Managing the Commons*, ed. Garrett Hardin and John Baden (San Francisco: W. H. Freeman and Company, 1977), pp. 76–81, 82–95.

But are there not independent moral principles requiring individuals to act in a manner that would assure compliance with the proviso? I think not. The act-utilitarian principle surely will not do for the reasons already noted—no one individual can be deemed responsible for the bad consequences associated with the relevant thresholds being crossed and the proviso being violated. A principle of moral generalization, Kantian or utilitarian, would handle such cases, as would perhaps a rule-utilitarian morality. But I know of no generally defensible versions of such theories. And even if there were an acceptable version of a fair-play principle of the sort defended by Hart and Rawls, it would be sufficient only to generate cooperation within an ongoing general practice of cooperation and would not be capable of generating such a practice in the first place.[35] A natural duty to support and help establish just cooperative practices might be invoked here, but even the chief proponent of such a principle admits that it engenders cooperation toward the provision of public goods only where there is some reasonable assurance that others will cooperate as well.[36] And what is proposed as a solution to the assurance problem is government regulation!

Principles of Cooperation

Finding themselves in a situation where they will either act to their own mutual detriment or in a manner that will violate the rights of others, would not rational and moral individuals *agree* to regulate their activities to assure the provision of the kinds of public goods in question? Could not Garrett Hardin's solution to "the tragedy of the commons," that of "mutual coercion, mutually agreed upon," be taken to represent a nonobjectionable interpretation of Rousseau's notion that it might be right for people to be "forced to be free"? I think not, for agreement to act cooperatively toward the provision of a public good is itself a public good, and the dilemma of collective action can equally well arise for it.

I have elsewhere suggested that elaboration of a proposal originally made by Colin Stang might lead to the formulation of a moral prin-

---

35. See Hart, "Are There Any Natural Rights"; Rawls, "Justice and Fairness"; Nozick, *Anarchy, State, and Utopia*, pp. 90–95.
36. Rawls, *A Theory of Justice*, sec. 23.

ciple that would generate cooperation toward the provision of public goods.[37] It is designed to avoid the difficulties associated with rule-utilitarian and generalization arguments that stem from their failure to take into account others' behavior and to solve the assurance problem associated with the ostensible duty of supporting and establishing just institutions and social practices. Assuming that there is a moral obligation to keep promises and not to lie, the required assurances would be provided by individuals making conditional promises based upon unconditional declarations of their desires and intentions. Individuals who perceived themselves to be in a type of prisoner's dilemma with respect to some public good, G, would have to make some form of declaration, explicit or implicit, of the following: "I prefer that G be obtained and intend to do my fair share of cooperating in its provision if, but only if, I have reasonable grounds for believing that enough others will also cooperate so that it will actually be provided. I thus promise to take initial steps toward cooperation and promise to carry them through if I receive similar assurances from enough others."

Although it is hard to avoid the charge that any such principle is an ad hoc construction designed to solve a problem apparently otherwise insoluble in terms of what people are *obligated* to do, I believe such a principle does have some merit. Especially if confined to the provision of those forms of public goods necessary to ensure the protection of people's rights, it does seem to capture the notion, especially prevalent now among students of serious environmental problems,[38] that "we" have an obligation to adopt policies that will protect people's rights to a not overpopulated planet having sufficient resources to allow decent living standards, and so on. The problem raised by the public-goods aspects of many of these problems, of course, is the cashing out of the "we" in terms of individual responsibility, and that is just what the proposed principle does.

But only in part. For the kinds of regulation required to enable the provision of many public goods, due to the thresholds involved, typically do not involve outright prohibitions of certain kinds of conduct but rather rationing schemes designed to maintain certain kinds

37. Colin Strang, "What If Everyone Did That?" *Durham University Journal* 53 (Fall 1960): 5–10, reprinted in *Ethics*, ed. Judith Thomson and Gerald Dworkin (New York: Harper & Row, 1968); Sartorius, "The Limits of Libertarianism," pp. 127–28.

38. Mary Williams, "Discounting Versus Maximum Sustainable Yield," is a good case in point.

of activities at certain (below threshold) levels. Harvesting a renewable resource at maximum sustainable yield and maintaining a certain level (zero or otherwise) of population growth are prime examples. Many such schemes have of course been proposed, including the somewhat attractive idea of issuing marketable rights to engage in the activities in question. Unfortunately, although it may be plausible to claim that government regulatory activity in such areas is just a special case (given the proposed principle) of government employing coercion to ensure that individuals carry out their obligations by respecting the rights of others, it is not plausible to claim that the particular mode of allocating the burdens of cooperation (as well as some of the possible windfall benefits) represents what is naturally right and obligatory in a nonstate situation. As even Nozick has seemingly admitted, there is "in a state of nature . . . no central or unified apparatus capable of making, *or entitled to make*, these decisions."[39] If government may properly exercise its regulatory powers to ensure the provision of public goods through the operation of some centralized rationing mechanism, then it would appear to be exercising a power no individual could rightfully exercise in a nonstate situation. Although given the proposed principle that it will be enforcing preexisting rights and obligations, it will also be exercising new rights in the process.

If neither the proposed principle nor any other is available to ground an obligation to cooperate voluntarily toward the provision of public goods whose absence would constitute a violation of people's rights, then government regulation designed to ensure the provision of such goods must of course be understood to represent an even more radical extension of the core position. For although it could again be viewed as protecting preexisting *rights*, it could not also be said to be enforcing preexisting correlative *obligations.*

RIGHTS OF FUTURE GENERATIONS

But for the fact that numerous philosophical analyses of the concepts of right and obligation (as well as more general theoretical constructions) have implied the contrary, there would seem to be no need to argue that members of future generations have moral rights.

39. Nozick, *Anarchy, State, and Utopia*, p. 74 (emphasis added).

Should I construct a diabolical device that will cause terminal cancer in all those living in Santa Barbara fifty years from now, surely I have violated the rights of all those who will be living then, not merely the rights of those who will be living then who are also living now. If the contrary is implied by the sort of general moral theories that would base morality upon relations of reciprocity, a feeling of extended sympathy, or a hypothetical contract among members of a single generation, so much the worse for those theories.[40] Likewise for analyses of the concept of right which would deny rights to members of future generations because future people do not exist now or because it is impossible for us to know exactly what their interests will be or because they are in no position to waive whatever rights might be ascribed to them.[41] Like us, members of future generations will have a vital interest in preserving their lives and in enhancing their ability to revise and alter their own individual living patterns, whatever particular tastes and values those patterns may represent.[42] They are entitled to be such autonomous agents, and such entitlement provides reasons for action that cannot be defeated by counterclaims based simply upon considerations of promoting the general welfare, whether that welfare be our own *or theirs.* If it would be wrong for us to harm the vital interests of some or all members of future generations as a means of maximizing our own welfare, it would be equally wrong for us to adopt policies that would ensure, say, the enslavement of *some* of our descendants as a means of maximizing the welfare of other ones. *Future* generations of course do not exist *now*; they have no interests now, vital or otherwise, and they can make no claims upon us. But the nature of the vital interests they *will* have is a valid basis for claims upon us as to how we ought to behave. These claims have the same role and weight in the sphere of morality and in the justification of action as do the moral right claims of our contemporaries. In brief, given the account of rights as side constraints that I have associated with the core position, members of future generations have rights in just as definite a

40. Cf. Brian Barry, "Circumstances of Justice and Future Generations," in *Obligations to Future Generations*, ed. Barry and Sikora, pp. 204-48.

41. Cf. Gregory Kavka, "The Futurity Problem," in *Obligations to Future Generations*, ed. Barry and Sikora, pp. 186-203.

42. Cf. John Rawls, "The Kantian Conception of Equality," *Cambridge Review* 12 (February 1975): 94; "Reply to Alexander and Musgrave," *Quarterly Journal of Economics* 18 (November 1974): 641.

sense as we do. And since we are assuming the existence of future *persons*, it can be said that they have *the same rights.*

We are in a position to violate the rights of members of future generations in essentially the same ways that we may violate the rights of those who are living now. As the core position must recognize, an individual living now might commit an act that would be *virtually certain* to violate the rights of those not yet living. Or, what I take to be unproblematic, the action of an individual living now might present such a high *risk* of harm to the vital interests of those not yet living that the act would constitute a violation of their rights. (I violate your rights if I subject you to Russian roulette with my six-shooter even if the gun does not go off.)

As the *extended core position* must recognize, each member of *a group of individuals* might act in a manner that *is virtually certain* to result in the violation of the rights of those not yet living. But because of the thresholds involved, no individual can be held responsible or said to have a moral obligation to act any differently. Or, what I again take to be unproblematic, each member of a group of individuals might act in a manner that would present such a high *risk* of harm to the vital interests of those not yet living as to constitute a violation of their rights (although, because of the thresholds involved, no individual can be held responsible). Just as Rawls has noted that "collective saving for the future has many aspects of a public good,"[43] so it may be said that, more generally, the protection of the rights of members of future generations has many aspects of the dilemma of collective action with respect to the voluntary provision of public goods. If, as I argued earlier, government regulation is both necessary and morally permissible to ensure the provision of those public goods whose absence would represent the violation of people's rights among contemporaries, it surely must be equally so where future generations are concerned.

GOVERNMENT REGULATION AND INTERGENERATIONAL JUSTICE

I would be the first to acknowledge that the public-goods argument for government regulation has been overworked and that regulation

43. Rawls, *A Theory of Justice*, p. 295.

in response to perceived externalities occurring outside of the pricing mechanism provided by private markets may itself involve the imposition of significant externalities upon those regulated.[44] My argument is limited to those cases in which the failure to provide public goods can plausibly be claimed to involve the violation of individual rights; given my understanding of what rights people have, this is a significant constraint. I believe that future generations have a *right* not to be born with the birth defects that may be caused by the leakage of our radioactive wastes or the accumulation of PCBs and other mutagens we are dumping into the environment.[45] Furthermore, many of the rights of those yet unborn are being violated by the actions of presently existing individuals and corporate and governmental agencies, either acting in isolation or (albeit unwittingly) as collectives. If government both can and should act as guardian of their interests, how may it do so?

What comes immediately to mind is the legislative prohibition of activities that endanger the rights of future generations or the regulation of these activities through agencies like the Environmental Protection Agency. Although such measures have their place, they have their obvious shortcomings as well. Outright statutory prohibition may bar activities whose harms could be offset by covering the costs of the damages they cause. Regulatory agencies are notorious for their bureaucratic inefficiency and apparent arbitrariness in decision making. Both are liable to all the difficulties surrounding democratic decision-making procedures. I would like to conclude my discussion by briefly exploring two alternatives that might go a long way toward protecting the rights of future generations in ways that might minimize the extensive interferences with individual liberty associated with familiar types of more or less direct regulation.

Many activities known to be harmful or to involve a high risk of harm are perceived as having sufficient social value to be permitted to continue, but only on the condition that those choosing to engage in them insure against the eventuation of those harms, thus assuming the responsibility for compensating those who become injured. The cost of the insurance, where business activities are in-

44. Bruce Johnson, "Planning Without Prices: A Discussion of Land Use Regulation Without Compensation," in *Planning Without Prices*, ed. Bernard H. Siegan (Lexington, Mass.: Lexington Books, 1978), pp. 63–111.

45. Cf. R. and V. Routley, "Nuclear Energy and Obligations to Future Generations," *Inquiry* 21 (Spring 1978): 133–79.

volved, is passed on to the consumers of the goods and services produced by the harmful or risky activities. In the case of noneconomic activities like driving motor vehicles, compulsory insurance forces individuals to internalize some of the costs of their activities that would otherwise remain as externalities, and provides at least some assurance that those who are harmed by motor vehicles will be compensated for the losses they sustain.

However messy may be the details of any complete analysis of principles of risk and compensation, our understanding of how such general principles operate among contemporaries would at least seem to be clear enough to warrant the suggestion that they are capable of intergenerational application as well. Only some of the risks that our present activities impose upon future generations may involve harms that are compensable, and among those that are, the cost of insuring against them might not be worth the benefits. But I suspect there are many activities involving risks of harm to future generations whose riskiness could be offset by insuring against the eventuation of the risks involved. Modern governments have found no difficulty in devising methods for leaving future generations with the huge financial liabilities that result from deficit spending; I am confident that with sufficient ingenuity they could find ways to leave future generations with sufficient financial assets to repair at least some of the costly but repairable damage that our activities will cause. Especially if financed through a transfer tax upon the exchange of marketable rights to engage in activities that involve a serious risk of repairable environmental damage, such an insurance scheme might effectively protect some of the rights of future generations in a manner requiring minimal governmental regulation.

Where government itself is the culprit, either directly engaging in or encouraging activities that involve a violation of the rights of future generations (activities that enjoy considerable popularity because of their perceived benefits to us), there is little chance that the executive or legislative branch will see to it that government regulates itself. The development of nuclear policy, both military and civilian, with the risks attendant upon the storage of radioactive wastes that will remain lethal for thousands of years, is all too real a case in point. But what of the judiciary? Christopher Stone has argued that natural objects ought to be accorded the status of legal personhood as are other nonhuman legal persons such as ships, corporations, and governmental entities, and Justice William O. Douglas, for one, seems to have found the argument legally compelling.[46] As with natural objects, according legal standing upon *future persons* would enable potential guardians of their interests to sue on their behalf. As with other persons who have legal rights they are unable to claim for themselves (e.g., infants), the fact that the right holders have no power to claim or enforce their rights for themselves is more rather than less reason to take those rights seriously and to do everything possible to devise institutions that will secure them. Members of future generations have rights, but the asymmetry of power between them and us is complete. They can neither bargain with us in the market nor press their claims of right against us in courts of law. If *we* have a right that government protect *our* rights through an effective exercise of the guardianship with which it is entrusted, *they* have a similar right. My suggestion is that judicial recognition of that right may be required to fully secure it.

46. Christopher D. Stone, *Should Trees Have Standing?* (Los Altos, Calif.: William Kaufmann, Inc., 1974), includes the opinions of the U.S. Supreme Court in *Sierra Club* v. *Morton.*

Chapter 9

REFLECTIONS ON THE RIGHTS OF FUTURE GENERATIONS

Randall R. Dipert

It has become increasingly common, in both popular and academic circles, to invoke obligations we have to future generations. The environmentalists have been at the vanguard of this movement, pointing out such serious problems for future generations as our storage of nuclear waste and our exhaustion of key natural resources. The environmentalist argues: Haven't we an obligation not to bequeath to our descendants rusty barrels of dangerously radioactive material scattered all about? Haven't we an obligation to leave our descendants a reasonable supply of natural resources, including pristine wilderness? With these questions answered in the affirmative, the usual next step—one that often comes too easily—has been to argue for some form of government regulation to enforce these obligations.

SOME CLAIMS ABOUT FUTURE RIGHTS

Philosophers have been somewhat slow in examining these often appealing arguments.[1] The utilitarians faced the problem first, being sensitive (as one might expect) to questions of *whose* happiness we should maximize: Should our hedonistic calculus include the plea-

---

1. See J. B. Stearns, "Ecology and the Indefinite Unborn," *The Monist* 56 (1972): 612–25.

sures of future individuals? Others followed.[2] However, as Professor Rolf Sartorius notes, there has been little or no attention paid to obligations owed future generations by those who advance a "classically liberal" conception of the state.[3] For example, one would search in vain in Robert Nozick's recent book for a discussion of the rights of, obligations to, and government institutions designed to protect, future generations.[4] This lacuna has led to a general lack of attention paid to the *rights* of future generations, as opposed to looser obligations owed them; the protection of those rights, a defender of the minimal state would maintain, forms the only legitimate activity of government.

Sartorius's motive for appealing to the rights of future generations is to provide some protection for future generations within such a classically liberal conception of the state. In particular, there are many for whom this commonly expressed argument has little force:

> If we act in a certain way (build nuclear reactors, mine coal, etc.), then we shall do harm to future individuals.

> Therefore, we should not act in this way, and furthermore, there should be government institutions to prevent us from acting in this way.

Even for a utilitarian, one must additionally show that more harm than good is done. However, for one who maintains a conception of the meaningfulness and centrality of rights and embraces a political theory holding that the only proper function of government is to protect these rights, the problem with vague appeals to harm is still greater. For such a classical liberal, one must show that, (1) in acting in a certain way, one is violating the rights of individuals; and (2) in establishing government institutions to protect these rights, one does not create a system that systematically violates more rights than it protects. It would then follow that it is legitimate to establish government institutions that protect these rights.

The bulk of Sartorius's paper, then, is an attempt to satisfy the constraints of a classically liberal view of permissible government activity by demonstrating that future individuals have such rights. I do not see that he addresses the second proposition at all; namely,

---

2. For example, R. M. Hare, "Abortion and the Golden Rule," *Philosophy and Public Affairs* 4 (1975): 201–22, esp. p. 219; and the discussion of the "just savings principle" in John Rawls, *A Theory of Justice* (Cambridge: Belknap, 1971).

3. Rolf Sartorius, this volume, p. 177.

4. Robert Nozick, *Anarchy, State, and Utopia* (New York: Basic Books, 1974).

that the system with such institutions must protect rights more extensively than it violates them. We shall return to this question.

TROUBLESOME CLAIMS

I wish now to make a number of observations on some general difficulties in claiming, as Sartorius does, that future generations have rights. We shall move from these observations to an attempt to vindicate the deep and widespread intuitions that we have some duties and responsibilities to future generations, without positing that future individuals have rights here and now. Finally, we shall examine the prospects for Sartorius's conclusion that government regulatory activity is necessary to enforce the obligations, duties, or responsibilities to future generations.

A number of striking facts come to mind when we consider the future individuals to whom we are obligated and whose rights we allegedly must respect. For one thing, there are probably a lot of them. Arguably, there are an infinite number of them. This raises the distinct possibility that any rights we assign them—particularly if these include so-called positive rights (a possibility Sartorius refuses to discount)—will overwhelm any rights we have.[5] For example, if there is some positive right to health care, food, or any scarce resource, then *all* of our resources should be directed toward medical research and the storage of medical supplies and food. Only by this means can we hope to ensure that we are not violating the rights of future generations in the hard times that are sure to come eventually. And if one thinks for a moment that *our* rights or desires have any significance in this plan, remember that the infinite number of future individuals will surely outweigh our finite rights and desires. One could "discount" future generations according to how distant they are from us. But one finds no hint of such a proposal in Sartorius's paper, and if these rights are assigned on the basis of human rights, such a procedure would appear to be illegitimate. Future individuals a thousand years hence are no less human, and will have no fewer rights than future individuals a hundred years hence; certainly we cannot discount the rights of distantly future generations merely be-

5. Sartorius, this volume, p. 177.

cause it would be inconvenient for us to respect them as much as possible.

Second, the notion on which Sartorius must found his argument is extremely troublesome; namely, "Future individuals have rights now that must be respected." It is true that we fall easily into saying things like, Individuals in future generations have moral rights, too. But on the other hand, this sounds a great deal like saying my unborn daughter has blonde hair. The truth of the matter is that she *will have* blonde hair, and the truth of the previous assertion is that future generations *will* have moral rights.

The temptation to speak of our duty to respect the rights of future generations probably arises because many feel that we have obligations or duties concerning these future generations. But because we have an obligation *concerning* them, it brings us nothing but trouble automatically to say it is an obligation to them, these nonexistent entities.[6] There are many cases in which one has obligations concerning persons or things (even quite strong ones) but not necessarily *to* them. Furthermore, if we mean only that we *should* be concerned with the well-being of future individuals, or that we have a *responsibility* to them, it is not at all obvious that this is enforceable — in other words, that it would legitimize government institutions to enforce our concern — or that this feeling arises because of their rights.

In short, there are many halfway houses to explain the widespread and natural concern we have for future individuals before we arrive at saying these nonexistent individuals "have rights." We might have obligations concerning them but not to them, and these "obligations" might not be enforceable.[7] In addition, whatever obligations we have to future generations might not arise because of *their* rights (which are as yet nonexistent) but because of the rights of existing individuals. All of these points will be developed later in the essay.

Some important issues concerning the rights claimed for future individuals can be isolated by asking two questions: (1) Has every possible future individual a right to life? (2) Are there other rights of future individuals that we must respect? With regard to the first question, Sartorius jauntily places himself in the tradition that claims all

---

6. See Stearns, "Ecology and the Indefinite Unborn."

7. Either because they are not the sort of obligations that are enforceable — that is, not based on existent rights — or because to enforce them effectively would create institutions that violate more rights than they protect.

people have a right to "life, liberty, and the pursuit of happiness," and then spends much of the paper ensuring that future individuals have all the same rights we do.[8] It might thus seem that we are violating the rights of these unborn individuals by not engaging constantly in procreative activity. This is absurd and incompatible with Sartorius's views on population control expressed elsewhere.[9] It thus appears necessary, but difficult, to separate the rights future individuals have from those rights we have but they don't — such as the right to life. One could perhaps argue that as part of the right to life there is a right to the protection of existing life, but not to the creation of life. This, however, seems ad hoc and less satisfactory than granting an unrestricted right to life only to those who now exist.

Having concluded that future individuals do not now have a right to life, contrary to Sartorius's suggestions, we ask, are there other rights of future individuals that we must respect? Sartorius is more explicit here, suggesting that future individuals have a right to be free from birth defects (when caused by us and capable of being eliminated).[10] If future individuals lack a "right" to be created in the first place — which is quite plausible — the easiest and surest way of guaranteeing that no violations of these rights will occur is to guarantee that there are no future generations! While there are times in human history when this might have been shrewd advice, as a universal principle it cannot be sound. Our duty to sterilize would follow not just from certain knowledge that rights will be violated, or even from our estimation that it is probable that rights will be violated, but from the mere possibility that rights will be violated.

If future individuals now have rights, then we are obligated not to have children, and government institutions should ensure this. This is such a strange and clear conclusion that it provides good reason to believe future individuals do not now have rights. Or alternatively, it provides better support for government sterilization agencies than for the environmental protection agencies Sartorius envisions.

8. Sartorius, this volume, p. 177.
9. Fred Miller and Rolf Sartorius, "Population Policy and Public Goods," *Philosophy and Public Affairs* 8 (1979): 148–74. For the difficulty with a "right to life" see R. De George, "The Environment, Rights, and Future Generations," in *Ethics and Problems of the 21st Century*, ed. K. E. Goodpaster and K. M. Sayre (Notre Dame: University of Notre Dame Press, 1979); and Joel Feinberg, "The Rights of Animals and Unborn Generations," in *Philosophy and Environmental Crisis*, ed. W. T. Blackstone (Athens: University of Georgia, 1974).
10. Sartorius, this volume, p. 199.

The natural response to this argument might be that it is impossible as a practical matter to sterilize the world, or that as a matter beyond our control, future generations will exist. I suspect this is not so, and that if we were to set it as our goal, it would not be difficult to effect this drastic solution to the protection of the rights of future generations. If the question is the practical concern of how *best* to protect the rights of future generations, I doubt whether it is *easier* to gain complete compliance with restrictions that protect the alleged rights of future generations than it is to make sure there are no future generations.

A discussion of what is practical or probable, however, misses the point. Such a discussion evolves into the consideration of whether future generations should have *legal* rights now. It becomes a question of whether we should behave *as if* future generations now had some rights. Sartorius seems to be engaged in just such an enterprise, and at the end of this essay, we shall examine the conditions under which legal rights should be granted to future individuals (and whether Sartorius has met these conditions).

My claim at this point is that *one* way to protect the rights of future generations is to ensure that they will not exist. By comparison with the estimation of how our present activities will damage distant generations, or even an estimation of what future generations will value (oil might again be considered the dirty, useless substance it was before the late nineteenth century), it is also the *surest* way. We can be sure that no matter how hard we try to free the environment of substances and conditions that, for example, produce birth defects, some future babies will have birth defects. If all babies have the right to be born free of defects, then some babies' rights will be violated—by us, who allow them to exist. This is such a strange conclusion that Sartorius's theory cannot be sound.

There is another, metaethical reason why we cannot admit obligations based on respecting the rights of future individuals as if they existed; perhaps for these same reasons we cannot admit that we have the same obligations to all future individuals. If we really think big, there are probably an infinite number of moral, that is, rights-bearing, creatures in the universe. However, the possibility of ethical theory, and certainly of a legal system, requires us to limit our horizons just enough to make moral theory possible. Assuming there are an infinite number of presently existing rational creatures, for the utilitarian there is an infinite amount of pleasure and an infinite amount of pain no matter what actions we take. At most, we might rearrange the amount of pleasure here or there. Similarly, for the rights theorist, there are an infinite number of infractions of individuals' rights throughout the universe. Any actions we take, laws we make or punishment we exact, will change only slightly the distribution of these infractions. Almost all political and moral philosophers have sought to keep speculation focused on our corner of the universe, to limit our horizons just enough to make moral theory possible. The contemplation of future individuals and their rights destroys this possibility, and so threatens to make moral and political theory impossible or to involve us in distasteful problems of discounting the lives and rights of future individuals.

OBLIGATIONS TO THE FUTURE

These considerations have not been intended to imply that we do not, or cannot, have obligations *concerning* future individuals. They do entail, I have argued, that we do not have obligations to future individuals in exactly the same way that we have obligations to respect the rights of our contemporaries.

The sources of our enforceable obligations to future generations, as well as our interest in and responsibility for them, are diverse. A great many of us have a deep interest in the well-being of future generations. Perhaps this interest in future generations is, as Jonathan Bennett has suggested, quite inexplicable in terms of other general or theoretical principles such as "maximizing pleasure" or "respecting human rights."[11] Certainly, simply applying these principles to future generations is extremely problematic.

We might even have a more abstract interest in the future development of civilization in all its aspects and in the continuation of the human race. Perhaps a concern for future individuals is not universal; yet it is quite common. When any interests are important and common, we typically find mechanisms for their protection in the law. These mechanisms can include tort law or, more explicitly, contracts. So we would expect such guarantees for the respecting of these interests: "I promise to protect the future welfare of your descendants

---

11. Jonathan Bennett, "On Maximizing Happiness," in *Obligations to Future Generations*, ed. R. I. Sikora and Brian Barry (Philadelphia: Temple University Press, 1978), p. 66.

if you will do the same for mine." Or, we can join together and form an organization dedicated to the improvement of morals, music, or to the improvement of the condition of all humanity. There is altogether too little of this, we might say, too little groping for common interests, and the required legal apparatus is not well developed. Perhaps we need more trust funds and more mutual pacts to refrain from doing harm to others' interests in future generations.

Many of the enforceable duties we have concerning future individuals probably derive from explicit—and perhaps even implicit—contracts among those of us now living who have a deep interest in the future. I agree with many who argue that we should not act in a way that contributes to the exhaustion of the earth's energy resources, and we should not act in a way that will bring about predictable birth defects and other forms of suffering for future individuals. These are not obligations *to* future individuals, although we might confusedly describe them as such. Rather, they arise from (1) my interest in the future, and (2) my usually all-too-tacit agreement with, as Thomas Schwartz terms them, my "like-minded contemporaries."[12]

What I am sketching here is not without its difficulties. First and foremost is the public-goods problem of the sort Sartorius has explored in his "Limits of Libertarianism": Why would any individuals, let alone all individuals, initiate or consent to an agreement to limit their consumption of energy, their procreative activities or their pollution, when the benefits to them are so tiny and the chances of others' nonconsent high?[13] This, however, is a much more general problem than the one with which we are concerned here. It is a game-theoretic difficulty concerning how *our* interests about the future can be realized and does not concern the interests and rights of future individuals—except indirectly. Talk of obligations to future generations in this connection is a red herring. Note also that it is extremely unlikely for any individual to have an interest per se in the misery of future generations. Thus discussion and negotiation are possible.

12. Thomas Schwartz, "Obligations to Posterity," in *Obligations to Future Generations*, pp. 3–13.

13. R. Sartorius, "The Limits of Libertariansim," in *Law and Liberty: Essays in Honor of F. A. Hayek*, ed. R. Cunningham (Indianapolis: Liberty Press, 1978).

LEGAL RIGHTS OR NATURAL RIGHTS?

I do not see that any special regulatory agencies of the sort Sartorius attempts to justify would be legitimate. At most, owing to special expertise required to adjudicate complex issues about the future, special legal institutions might be needed to enforce future-oriented contracts.

It might further be arguable that because of a widespread interest in the *eventuality* of future generations and thus because of the probability that there *will be* future generations, we should give future generations some legal rights. A legal right in some cases does not simply reflect a natural right, but is a complicated entity deriving its legitimacy from its contribution to the effective protection of natural rights in an applied system of justice. Thus a corporation and other "legal fictions" have some legal rights and standing. A corporation does not have these legal rights because it has natural rights, but (arguably) because "pretending" that it does have these rights produces a system in which natural property rights of individuals are better and more efficiently protected. Similarly, the legal right that evidence seized by improper means is inadmissible in a court of law is not a natural right. But pretending that there is such a right (arguably) more efficiently protects the natural rights of property and privacy.

I think there is little question that future individuals do not now have natural rights. Hence, within the framework we have been using, there is no justification for government institutions to protect these rights. In particular, environmental agencies cannot be justified because they protect "future people's natural rights."

We must then take Sartorius's paper as a long argument for why future individuals should be given some legal rights: an argument for why we should pretend that they *had* some rights.[14] Some cases are

---

14. Compare Feinberg, "The Rights of Animals and Unborn Generations," whose case very much resembles Sartorius's. Feinberg argues that in spite of the metaphysical difficulties (they do not now exist) and the practical difficulties (along with animals, fetuses, those in a coma, etc., they cannot now defend their own cases) we should give future generations rights. I take this also as a proposal to treat future generations as if they now had rights — that is, grant them legal rights. The questions remain of which rights they are to have, how they are to be administered, and their interaction with the broader system of justice; thus there is no concrete proposal or argument for any particular legal rights. Incidentally, I suppose one reason many authors are so cavalier about the distinction between natural and

clear. If a perverse terrorist places in an airport a bomb that will go off in 200 years, what do we do? (Let us assume that the option of evacuating the airport in 200 years—a proposal akin to universal sterilization—is not open to us.) The terrorist has not obviously violated or threatened the lives of anyone now living. We should probably treat the terrorist "as if" the intention were to violate the rights of someone now living. This would be equivalent to giving indefinite future individuals some legal rights now.

It is clear that such a system would do what we expect of a system of justice: discourage and punish rights violations in an ongoing, efficient, and not unjust way. But until the legal rights we are proposing are crystal clear, until the way they interact with other proposed legal rights is understood, and until the nature of the agencies administering them is concretely outlined, we must be extremely hesitant in accepting proposed legal rights. Whereas the straightforward transformation of natural rights into legal rights is usually unproblematic, the standards are necessarily higher for accepting claims that a legal right will in the long run maximize natural rights. Vague claims that such legal rights will probably "promote" natural rights (i.e., limit their future violation) are simply too weak. Such claims would in other contexts lead one to accept a variety of draconian legal rights that would, in unforeseen ways, destroy natural rights. (Various "registration" proposals come to mind: work cards, ID cards, computer files, etc.) The consideration of a legal right when there is no clear natural right is necessarily a difficult practical matter. Even if we grant legal rights to future individuals, we are faced with two previously noted puzzles: (1) Why not ensure that there are no future generations? (Short answer—perhaps our natural right to procreative activity outweighs the more tenuous legal rights of future generations to a comfortable existence.) (2) Which legal rights can we afford to grant to the possibly innumerable members of future generations? (Short answer—very few, certainly no positive rights.)

The exact nature of the legal rights proposed by Sartorius is not clear. Their utility in enforcing a respect for natural rights is unexamined. And the nature of the regulatory agencies supposedly necessary to administer these legal rights is nebulous. Consequently, even

---

legal rights is that they are utilitarians of some stripe, for whom any "rights" are just ways of referring to a bundle of obligations most efficiently treated as a package; that is, they believe natural rights do not exist.

as a proposed legal right we must reject Sartorius's proposal. He has, therefore, failed to establish a need for government regulatory agencies to protect the rights—natural or legal—of future generations.[15]

15. I thank Tibor R. Machan for the suggestion that we must separate "legal rights" from "natural rights" (although the development is my own) and for many other useful suggestions. I also thank Dale Jamieson and Florian von Imhof for helpful discussions.

PART V

LEGITIMACY OF REGULATION

Chapter 10

REGULATION AND PATERNALISM

Steven Kelman

In a renowned passage in *On Liberty*, with immense intuitive appeal, John Stuart Mill argued:

> The sole end for which mankind are warranted . . . in interfering with the liberty of action of any of their number, is self-protection . . . the only purpose for which power can be rightfully exercised over any member of a civilized community, against his will, is to prevent harm to others. His own good, either physical or moral, is not a sufficient warrant. He cannot rightfully be compelled to do or forbear because it will be better for him to do so, because it will make him happier, because in the opinions of others, to do so would be wise, or even right. . . . The only part of the conduct of any one, for which he is amenable to society, is that which concerns others. In the part which merely concerns himself, his independence is, of right, absolute. Over himself, over his own body and mind, the individual is sovereign.[1]

Paternalism is a doctrine stating that it is justified to restrict people's liberty of choice, without their consent, even insofar as their actions affect only themselves, when such individuals are not considered to be in a position to know their own best interests and the behavior imposed is believed to be in their best interests. Opposition to paternalism plays an important role in the current national debate over the appropriate scope for government consumer protection regulation, especially of safety and health. It is frequently applied in

1. John Stuart Mill, *On Liberty* (London: Oxford University Press, 1912), p. 15.

condemning proposals to ban saccharin or laetrile. It is pronounced likewise against proposals to require people to wear seatbelts or motorcycle helmets. And it appears in criticisms of safety standards for lawn mowers or autos, since such standards, although they neither ban nor mandate use of the product in question, do require that consumers pay for certain safety features if they wish to buy the product. The antipaternalistic contention is simple. If people know the risks of, say, saccharin and choose to run these risks in order to obtain some perceived benefits, who are we to interfere with that choice?

This paper will consider conceptual justifications for government consumer-protection regulation, taking into account objections to paternalism. First I will present reasons for being critical of paternalism. I will then argue why, even if objections to paternalism are accepted, there are frequent occasions when regulatory officials are justified in requiring that consumer products meet certain safety standards or even in banning them. Finally, I will discuss whether the judgment against paternalism ought to be absolute.

The force of the argument to be made and most of the examples selected involve regulation of consumer products for purposes of safety or health. However, some of the arguments will also be applicable to other public-policy domains that raise issues of paternalism, such as the use of in-kind as opposed to cash-transfer payments.

ARGUMENTS AGAINST PATERNALISM

The case against paternalism rests on two broad categories of reasons.[2] According to utilitarian ethics, an act is right if it produces greater net satisfaction in the world than possible alternative acts under the same circumstances. The utilitarian argument would claim that paternalistic acts are wrong because decisions made paternalistically for people will produce less satisfaction than those decisions people make themselves. According to rule-based (deontological)

2. Economists should note that the following is a normative discussion of how people *ought* to act, not a positive discussion of how they *do* act. Positive discussions by economists generally assume self-interest, while normative discussions by moral philosophers generally assume "a moral point of view" that is disinterested. An economist would find it pointless to condemn those who did not make certain moral judgments; a philosopher finds such condemnation appropriate.

ethics, right and wrong are not definable simply in terms of the satisfaction they produce. An act might be wrong simply because it violates a moral principle, independent of its consequences for satisfaction. A deontological argument would contend that paternalistic acts are wrong simply because they violate a moral duty to treat people with respect and to not violate their human dignity. This is over and above any dissatisfaction such lack of respect or violation of human dignity may produce.[3]

The Utilitarian Case

There are a number of grounds for the utilitarian argument that paternalism will not maximize people's satisfaction. First, choices made paternalistically for us are less likely to promote our own satisfaction than ones we make ourselves. In addition, the pain the paternalistic intervenor may inflict to get us to behave in a certain manner is a source of dissatisfaction. Furthermore, the very act of choosing for oneself may itself produce satisfaction and interference with such choice may produce dissatisfaction. Finally, even if an individual paternalistic intervention might increase a person's satisfaction, the long-run consequences of a social decision to commence such intervention would still produce less satisfaction.

The first argument suggests that paternalistic choices are less likely to be good choices. It is often difficult to determine what choice under a given set of circumstances is best suited to make an individual happy. Yet *somebody* must decide what choices are most conducive to that end. The individual involved seems the most logical candidate. After all, we devote regular attention to the subject of our own best interests. We can therefore be expected to know them better than do paternalistic intervenors, for whom our interests are generally a subject of only fitful attention. Furthermore, we are the ones who stand to bear directly the costs of bad choices we make, thus providing an incentive to concentrate when making choices.[4]

---

3. The deontological argument probably seems strange at first, to economists especially. On the distinction between utilitarian and deontological approaches generally see any standard text in moral philosophy, such as Richard Brandt, *Ethical Theory* (Englewood Cliffs: Prentice Hall, 1959), chaps. 15-17. A further discussion appears below in this paper.

4. By postulating that an individual's act affects only that person, we make the utilitarian calculation identical to the calculation of what is in the person's own best interests, because by hypothesis the net change in the sum total of satisfaction in the world is equivalent to the effect of the act on that person's own happiness.

The second argument notes the pain that the paternalistic intervenor may inflict (fines, imprisonment, ridicule, or whatever) to get us to behave a certain way.[5] Much of the horror that accompanies reactions to paternalism reflects the experience of the twentieth century, when brutal dictators have resorted to mass murder in pursuit of schemes they felt were in the best interests of the people, but which the people were "too shortsighted" to appreciate.

The third utilitarian argument suggests that the act of choosing for oneself may itself produce satisfaction, while interference with such choice produces dissatisfaction. Choice, like puzzle solving, may produce satisfaction because it provides an occasion to demonstrate one's faculties. More important, interference with that process of choice produces dissatisfaction because adjudging individuals incapable of making their own decisions implies a lack of respect for their worth as human beings. Our own choices, by contrast, give expression to our worth because they demonstrate the uniquely human capacity to make reflective and self-conscious choices. Furthermore, the paternalistic intervenor claims superiority over us, and this too engenders resentment.

Even if paternalism increased satisfaction in a particular case, the long-run consequences of commencing intervention might still produce less satisfaction. This fourth argument notes that one paternalistic intervention may have a strong effect on the general tendency to intervene in people's choices. This general tendency to intervene occurs most frequently not for benevolent reasons, as in cases of paternalism, but because of the selfish advantages that may be obtained through intervention.

Utilitarian arguments against paternalistic acts, like all utilitarian arguments about whether an act is right or wrong, are crucially dependent on predictions about the consequences of such an act in terms of people's satisfaction. Thus, if it turned out, empirically, that paternalistic intervenors *did* generally have a better sense of what was good for us than we did, or that people *did not* become unhappy when others intervened in the making of individual choices, then these utilitarian arguments against paternalism would fall.

5. The reminder that any punishment causes suffering and that this suffering must be included in calculations about the rightness of an act that includes the infliction of punishment comes originally from Jeremy Bentham. H. L. A. Hart uses the argument at several points in his discussion of the enforcement of morality, a discussion similar but not coterminous with discussions of paternalism, in *Law, Liberty, and Morality* (Stanford, Calif.: Stanford University Press, 1964).

The Deontological Argument

Deontological arguments, however, would not fall. For, in deontological ethics, a statement such as, "It is wrong to violate the dignity of human beings," stands as an ultimate ethical proposition, not as a judgment contingent on maximizing satisfaction.[6] Paternalism might be wrong to a deontolotist simply because it violates human dignity.[7] To be sure, one still must define what acts violate human dignity. Such debates can be lively ones, and they will be as controversial as well. But establishing the statement, "It is wrong to violate human dignity," sets a framework for the implications of the debate. It also clearly opens the way for arguments about what constitutes human dignity that are independent of effects a given act has on satisfaction. Thus, it makes sense to say, for example, that the Soviet government violates human dignity by not permitting free speech, even if nobody in the Soviet Union were made dissatisfied by such a denial.

The distinction between a moral principle and a utilitarian argument that violating human dignity causes dissatisfaction becomes clearer if situations are imagined, as proponents of deontological ethics propose, in which the hypothesized link between violations of human dignity and dissatisfaction is severed. For example, a negative utopia such as that presented in *Brave New World*, where some drug alters the human mind in a way that people no longer experience any pleasure simply from having the occasion to give expression to their human dignity, nor any pain when others fail to show respect for them, might illustrate this point. The question is whether, under such conditions, a simple violation of a person's human dignity, assuming the act had no other consequences, would still be wrong. One might also imagine two men stranded on a desert island, one of whom is unconscious. The conscious man discovers that if he keeps the unconscious man in a container partly filled with excre-

6. W. D. Ross, *The Right and the Good* (London: Oxford University Press, 1930).
7. It should be noted that the wrong of violating human dignity is separate from the unhappiness produced *in others* by the knowledge that somebody's human dignity has been violated. It might be noted parenthetically that utilitarian arguments in which the unhappiness caused by wrong acts is included in the utilitarian calculation presuppose that the act would be considered wrong in the first place. A utilitarian would not believe the act to be wrong unless it did not maximize satisfaction. In a utilitarian world, unhappiness over wrong acts, then, could never determine the outcome of a utilitarian calculation.

ment, the combined smell of the man and the excrement keeps annoying mosquitos away. Assuming that the unconscious man suffers no permanent ill effects from being stored in excrement, that there are no other humans on the island to observe the spectacle, and that this act has no effect on the tendency of the conscious man to act in similar ways in the future when he might be faced with others not in a similarly helpless state, is it right for the conscious man to store the unconscious man in excrement? Or is it wrong, because doing so violates the human dignity of the unconscious man, even if it does not make the unconscious man unhappier and does increase the satisfaction of the conscious man, who is spared annoyance by mosquitos? As a final example, one might imagine two states of the world with an equal sum total of satisfaction. In one world, this sum of satisfaction has come about from a series of acts that all affirm human dignity. In the other world, the *equivalent* sum of happiness has resulted from a different series of acts, many of which violate human dignity. Should we choose the first world over the second or be indifferent between them?

Those who believe it is wrong to violate the human dignity of the drugged person in the *Brave New World* situation or of the unconscious man on the desert island, or who choose the dignity-preserving world over the dignity-violating world with the same sum total of satisfaction, have grounds for arguing against paternalism not dependent on empirical predictions about what makes people happy. The most plausible (in my view) version of deontological ethics, that of the philosopher W. D. Ross, suggests that there are certain "prima facie duties," such as the duty to keep promises and the duty to do justice, that create grounds for making an act right, independent of its consequences for the sum total of satisfaction. By "prima facie" is meant that an act reflecting a prima facie duty should be performed unless a stronger duty overrides it. Thus, to cite a classic example, if it is wrong to lie and wrong to allow murder to take place, how do I act if I know Jones is in the next room and a knife-brandishing maniac rushes in asking if I know where Jones is? Or, to return to one of the examples above, if it is wrong to store the unconscious man in excrement in order to keep away annoying flies, would it also be wrong to do so to keep away killer bees?

In the deontological ethics of Ross, the necessity of making trade-offs among duties in deciding what is finally right is not eliminated, because duties frequently conflict. In fact, one of the prima facie duties Ross enumerates is the duty of beneficence, or the duty of maximizing net satisfaction, which thus incorporates by reference (so to speak) all of utilitarianism. That it is prima facie wrong to violate a person's human dignity by paternalistic acts then does not necessarily demonstrate that paternalism is wrong in every instance. But it does cast further doubt on the rightness of paternalistic acts. Note the implications of this argument: if showing respect for people has value not because of its effect on anybody's satisfaction, but simply because showing such respect is right and violating human dignity is wrong, then paternalistic interventions might be wrong even if they made the person subject to them happier. They might be wrong because the net satisfaction the intervention produces does not outweigh the wrong of violating human dignity.[8]

DECISIONMAKING COSTS AND VOLUNTARY RENUNCIATION OF CHOICE AUTHORITY

When there are costs associated with deciding what choice to make, situations exist in which it is rational for individuals to renounce their own authority to make certain choices for themselves and to hand over such authority to third parties willing to make the choices in the individuals' interest. Such third party choices are not paternalistic, because they are not made against the individuals' wishes. They introduce a new category, separate both from choices one makes oneself and from choices made paternalistically in one's be-

---

8. Since the violation of the person's human dignity serves by hypothesis to increase the person's happiness, it seems intuitively difficult to accept the view that we ought to condemn the act for violating that person's human dignity. Such a claim is, however, necessary if we are to make an argument for favoring person A over B in cases where A's act causes B greater unhappiness than it brings A happiness. (See footnote 25). It is also necessitated by the intuitions, which are probably more strongly held, cited in the text. That an act can be wrong even if it brings about more good than an alternate act is what the statement that "right" is not reducible to "good" is all about.

To complicate matters further, there might be cases in which people's choices may violate their *own* human dignity, for example, by selling themselves into slavery. In such cases, there might be deontological grounds for interfering with an individual's act, again for the reason that it is wrong to violate human dignity. Such intervention would not be paternalistic, because it would not be for the person's own good, but to prevent a wrong from being committed. The complications such arguments may involve argue for the importance of developing a logical structure (such as that presented in moral philosophy) for making sense out of very complicated moral issues.

half. Much government safety regulation of consumer products, I believe, falls into this category.

The probability that one would want to renounce the authority to choose increases the more decision-making costs for the person exceed those for the third party, and the closer the third party's choice parallels the one the person would have chosen.

The situation in which voluntary renunciation of the authority to choose is rational may be illustrated by a simple example. Imagine that a person could, without bearing any decision-making costs, simply go out and choose, impulsively, to buy a product with certain features. Let's say that such a choice would produce a net benefit of ten units of satisfaction. Imagine further that perfect information could be gained about the different features of the various product types that are available. After obtaining and processing this information, the individual would be able to make a better choice — say, one that provided fifteen units of satisfaction. But if gathering and processing the information cost eight units of satisfaction, the net benefit from the choice, after decision-making costs were taken into account, would be only seven units. In such a case, the "impulsive" choice, yielding ten units of satisfaction, would be preferable to the "better" but decision-costly choice, which yields only seven units of net satisfaction.

But these may not be the only two alternatives. Suppose someone else can gather and process the same information much *more cheaply than that individual can* — for two units of satisfaction (units that presumably would be billed to the person in some way). Armed with this information, the third party would make for the person a decision yielding only thirteen units of satisfaction. (The third party has gathered and processed the same information that the individual did, but the resulting decision may not yield as much satisfaction, even though the third party is supposed to act in the person's best interest, because of a faulty judgment about exactly what those interests are. Or perhaps the third party seizes the opportunity to judge what is best for the person, or acts self-interestedly and imposes a decision that better satisfies his/her own interests.) The net benefits of authorizing the third party to make the decision in this case would be eleven units (thirteen units for the decision minus two units of decision-making costs). Of the three alternatives — uninformed choice by consumer, informed choice by consumer, and informed choice by third party — the last yields the highest net benefits. This is so despite the fact that, if one looks simply at the benefits of the choice itself and not at decision-making costs, the informed choice by the consumer would have appeared to be the most advantageous one.

Information-gathering Costs

The costs of decision making include information-gathering costs, information-processing costs, and possible psychological costs of choice. Information-gathering costs include the costs of determining the relevant features that vary among the different product types and the different values these variables take among the different product types. Information-processing costs include the costs of calculating the implications of the different values for a judgment of the product's benefits, given one's preferences. Psychological costs include, for example, the frustration that may be felt from information overload or the trauma that may be experienced from having to make difficult choices.[9]

An immense disservice to intelligent discussion of the safety regulation of consumer products occurs because of the tendency to base such discussions on a small number of controversial examples—saccharin, seatbelts, laetrile. A statement such as, "People know that it's riskier to drive without seatbelts than with them, and if they choose to take that risk to avoid the discomfort of wearing the belts, that should be up to them," may be seriously made. People know the product feature about which they are making a choice (that is, they know what seatbelts are). They know what values the variable can take (the seatbelts may be worn or not worn). They know the implications of these different values for their judgments about the choice (wearing seatbelts decreases risk but may increase discomfort).

The problem is that such individual dramatic examples are unrepresentative of the universe of choices that consumers would have to make for themselves in a world where they had to make all decisions about the safety features of products they themselves buy. Statements about consumers knowing the risks of seatbelts or saccharin and choosing to bear them are plausible. Statements such as the following are far less so. "People know that if the distance between the

---

9. Throughout this part of the discussion, I will consider the case of an individual consumer. Both decision-making costs and the gap between the fully informed decision an individual would have made and the choice a third party makes may vary among individuals, of course. I take up the aggregation question in a situation with such variation among individuals at the end of this section.

slats on the infant crib is 2 3/8 inches there is little risk that an infant will be strangled by falling through the slats, while if the distance is 3 1/4 inches the risk is much greater, and if they choose to take this risk in order to get a crib that is less expensive, that should be up to them." We might ask ourselves if we would feel confident identifying which substance is by far the riskiest of the following four that may be present in food: calcium hexametaphosphate, methyl paraben, sodium benzoate, and trichloroethylene. Or we may feel less confident in making decisions about what safety features to buy to guard against power lawn-mower accidents or to protect against a radio exploding or electrocuting us. If we do know, how confident do we feel that we understand the risks associated with various levels of the substance? Is five parts per million of benzene hexachloride a lot or a little? If the bacteria count in a frozen egg is one million per gram, should we be alarmed?

What these examples suggest — and they could be multiplied many times — is that consumers do not ordinarily have anything approaching perfect information for judging the safety of most consumer products themselves, in spite of the misleading impressions created by widely publicized regulatory controversies over such issues as saccharin and seatbelts. Compared with their knowledge of product features such as appearance, convenience, or taste, knowledge of safety features is typically very small.

One conclusion sometimes drawn is that lack of knowledge demonstrates lack of concern. If people don't know about safety features, it is sometimes argued, that means they don't care about them. This conclusion doesn't follow from the premise. When information gathering costs something, the amount of information gathered depends not only on the perceived benefits of the information but also on how costly it would be to gather. I may "care" about two product features equally, but if information on one is cheap to obtain and information on the other is expensive, I will gather more information on the first feature than on the second. Information on product features such as appearance or convenience is often relatively easy to get. Information on a product's appearance is garnered by simple observation. For a product that doesn't cost very much and that is frequently repurchased, experience is a cheap way to gain information about the product's convenience or taste.[10] I may buy a certain

10. This point is made in Philip Nelson, "Information and Consumer Behavior," *Journal of Political Economy* 78 (March 1970).

brand of orange soda or paper tissue and try it. I will then know whether I like it.

By contrast, gathering information on safety features is often very costly. Frequently, arcane or technical facts must be understood, and the recourse to experience is not available in the same way as with many other product features, since using a risky product does not always lead to an accident, while drinking a brand of orange soda will always provide information on its taste. Furthermore, to experience the pain of an injury or illness is a very high cost to pay for gathering information about a product's safety. As Victor Goldberg has noted sardonically, "Learning from one's own experience is even more impractical if the injury is a very serious one. In the extreme case of a fatal accident, of course, the learning experience might be profound, but the learning curve is abruptly truncated.[11]

It would be rational for an individual to hand over decision-making authority to a third party when the latter can gather the information more cheaply than can the individual. This would appear to apply often in the case of safety features. The cost to each consumer of gathering safety information is likely to be much less with an expert third party gathering it for a large group of consumers than with each consumer doing it individually. It may be easier for an expert to discover and evaluate different technical safety features. Since only one gathering process need occur, its cost can be divided among the large group for whom it is undertaken, rather than separately borne by each consumer assembling similar information individually.

Information-processing Costs

Information-processing costs represent the second set of costs associated with the act of choosing. These costs involve taking information about a product feature and evaluating its significance in light of one's preferences. Memory and other cognitive limitations make it costly or simply impossible to process large amounts of information about something, even if the information is available. Information-processing costs clearly vary for different people and situations, but the more information that must be processed, the higher the processing costs. Furthermore, there is evidence that at some point "infor-

11. Victor P. Goldberg, "The Economics of Product Safety and Imperfect Information," *The Bell Journal of Economics and Management Science* 5 (Spring 1974): 686.

mation overload" may occur, when the brain has too much information to process. Under the circumstances, one's skill at evaluating information can decrease so much that one's choice is less indicative of one's preferences than a choice made with less information, but better processing.[12] Overload may occur not only when we must process lots of information for one choice, but when we must process a little information for many choices.

Psychological Costs

There may be psychological costs associated with choice as well. To be sure, there are many instances, as noted earlier, in which people relish the opportunity to choose. In other instances, people might not relish the process, but fear that choices made by a third party are likely to be so inferior to their own choices that they are willing to bear possible psychological costs. But this is not always the case. Life would be unbearable if we had constantly to make all decisions for ourselves. Information overload may produce not only poorer quality evaluations but also a feeling of frustration deriving from the realization that we are not processing information as well as we usually do. Furthermore, there are some kinds of decisions people find very unpleasant to make. These might include choices that are complicated, ones that involve thinking about distasteful things, or ones in which all the alternatives are disagreeable. Everyday experience is filled with instances in which people try to avoid making unpleasant decisions. Linus, in the Peanuts comic strip, expressed the trauma that can accompany a difficult choice when he said, "No problem is so big or so complicated that it can't be run away from." Yet, as Irving Janis and Leon Mann have noted, "In the extensive writings by social scientists on decision making we find hardly any mention of this obvious aspect of human choice behavior."[13] (Some of the same people who argue against proposals for, say, greater employee participation in choices currently made by management, on the grounds that most workers would prefer not to be psychologi-

12. See, for instance, Jacob Jacoby et al., "Brand Choice Behavior as a Function of Information Load," *Journal of Marketing Research* 11 (February 1974): 65.
13. Irving L. Janis and Leon Mann, *Decision Making: A Psychological Analysis of Conflict, Choice, and Commitment* (New York: The Free Press, 1977), p. 3.

cally burdened with such choices, forget about this burden when proposals for government regulation of consumer products are made.)

With safety issues, the costs of information processing and the psychological costs of choice (like those of information gathering) frequently are likely to be lower for an expert third party than for the individual. Decisions about safety, because they involve so much technical information, are likely to involve information overload that makes processing costly. In addition, many people may find such decisions unpleasant to make. They require that one contemplate the prospect of illness, disfigurement, or even death. They also necessitate thought about tradeoffs between saving money and taking risks — thoughts that most people also find unpleasant, as can be seen by looking at how politicians, agency officials, and even business spokespersons themselves squirm when such topics are raised. In fact, this unease may be one of the main reasons that safety decisions are delegated to government. (The argument that people prefer not to think about injury is sometimes used as a justification for paternalistic interventions in the safety area, on the grounds that "people don't like to think about these things, so they won't take safety enough into account." The argument here is different. It depends on a determination by individuals themselves that since thinking about illness or injury is unpleasant, they wish to renounce to a third party their authority to choose.) An expert third party can generally process information much more cheaply per consumer, both because of that expertise and because the cost of processing can be divided among a large group. A third party's charge per consumer for bearing any psychological costs of choice (presumably in the form of a wage premium required to attract people to such work) is also likely to be far less than the cost an individual would have to bear alone. These costs are lowered further because the third party's expertise and experience reduce possible frustration from information overload. Furthermore, the trauma of dealing with difficult choices is counterbalanced by the satisfaction arising from the power to make decisions affecting many people. Finally, people who find it less traumatic to make difficult choices might gravitate toward such work.

One point ought to be made about decision-making costs before proceeding. It is unrealistic to believe that many consumers consciously tote up the difference between their own and third party decision-making costs in determining whether to renounce voluntarily the authority to choose. If consumers do not even know about the existence of a feature by which a product might be judged, it is hard to conceive of them "deciding" how much it would cost them to gather information. Instead, the consumers' judgments are of a much grosser sort. They know enough to realize that they are quite ignorant about the whole area of product safety and that obtaining information will be costly. They might also conclude that they find thoughts about illness or injury unpleasant. On this basis, they may decide that they want product safety choices *as a whole* to be turned over to a third party. Thus, Milton Friedman's objection that government safety regulation "amounts to saying that we in our capacity as voters must protect ourselves in our capacity as consumers against our own ignorance" is unconvincing.[14] In our capacity as voters we need know only that we are ignorant or reluctant in our capacity as consumers about certain issues.

How similar would the choice made by a third party be to the person's own fully informed choice? Cited earlier, this is another consideration that can influence the decision to relinquish voluntarily the authority to choose. There are reasons to believe that government officials, when deciding what protective features to mandate, often assign safety a higher weight than does the average consumer. This is because the organizational mission of these agencies is to promote safety and because many agency officials are recruited from safety and health professions whose ideologies stress such protection.[15] On the other hand, there is also reason to believe that the disparity will normally not be extreme. "Safety" is a value attributed high weight whenever people discuss it consciously; indeed, environmentalists have shifted the focus of their political efforts from woods and streams to safety and health out of a conviction that the latter two strike the most responsive chord among large numbers of Americans. At the end of this section I shall return to the subject of the weight people attach to safety. But there is still the possibility that the value assigned to safety by many consumers will differ sharply from that of government officials, and this is the main reason why consumers might be reluctant to allow government the authority to choose product safety features.

14. Milton Friedman, *Capitalism and Freedom* (Chicago: University of Chicago Press, 1962), p. 148.
15. For a discussion of these points, see Steven Kelman, *Regulating America, Regulating Sweden* (Cambridge: MIT Press, 1981), chap. 3.

OBJECTIONS TO THE ARGUMENT THUS FAR

Different objections might be raised to the argument developed so far. One argument, frequently heard, maintains that if the consumer's problem in making choices about safety features is a lack of information, then government should see that information is provided, rather than mandate safety features or ban products. To do more, the argument goes, would be to throw out the baby of individual choice with the bathwater of imperfect information. (A more radical argument could be made as well: that market forces will see to it that consumers are provided with appropriate information and so there is no need even for government intervention to mandate information.)

Others might argue that voluntary renunciation of consumer choice to some third party need not justify *government* standards or product bans. Consumers might hire a personal agent to make the choice for them. Or the government might be limited to certifying those products that meet what the agency considers appropriate safety standards. All these methods, it is argued, allow voluntary renunciation of the authority to choose without mandatory government regulation.

Is Provision of Information Sufficient?

Consider the argument that government's role should be limited to information provision—or even that such limited role as that is unjustified. For the government to mandate provision of information or to provide such information itself does indeed lower information-gathering costs. To require its dissemination in nontechnical form lowers these costs further. And to make the information conveniently available (as part of labeling) lowers it still further. These steps do sometimes lower decision-making costs enough to make it worthwhile for consumers to retain their authority to choose (for example, in the area of product quality, where the psychological costs of choice are low and preferences differ widely among consumers). In such cases, government should restrict its endeavors to such tasks. But in other situations, these practices would still not lower decision-making costs enough to make it rational for a consumer to retain the authority to choose. Consumers might still be frequently confronted with columns of fine print presenting large numbers of product features and risk information about each. The information-processing costs of evaluating this information in the light of one's preferences remain unaffected by the cheaper information-gathering. Any psychological decision-making costs are, similarly, unaffected.

A more radical argument against any government role even in information provision suggests that anytime products vary in some feature considered important by a number of consumers, the producers of the product with the more attractive features have an incentive, if markets are competitive, to provide consumers with information about those features. Since competitors whose products lack such features cannot make similar claims, consumers will become informed, through producer efforts, about whatever features are valued by a significant number of people.[16]

Such a mechanism clearly does operate at times. Manufacturers of low-tar cigarettes or margarines with a high polyunsaturated-fat content advertise widely these features of their products. Manufacturers who have removed antioxidants from their potato chips promote them as being additive-free. But to show that this mechanism works sometimes is not to show that it is sufficient to obviate any need for a government role. It has a chance of working mainly when consumers *already know* something about the feature in question. Most consumers know that cigarettes and saturated fats are hazardous. This kind of knowledge makes it much easier for producers to advertise the superiority of their products. In cases where producers would need to create awareness of these features from scratch, such advertising is far less likely to be done. In part, this is because if one producer spends money on such awareness advertising, the benefits of creating awareness could be reaped by competitors whose products also perform well in the relevant area, without the competitors having to bear the significant costs of educating consumers. Furthermore, the distrust consumers have of self-serving claims by producers might discourage them from accepting the information.

Alternatively, it may be argued that if ways exist to make information-gathering cheaper, by using experts to gather the information, and by sharing the costs among large numbers of people, market

16. This argument appears in Richard A. Posner, "The Federal Trade Commission's Mandated Disclosure Program," in *Business Disclosure: Government's Need to Know*, ed. Harvey J. Goldschmid (New York: McGraw-Hill, 1979).

incentives would exist for private firms to arise that specialize in performing such information-gathering functions, thus rendering unnecessary a government role. Again, this mechanism does operate to an extent. *Consumer Reports* does product testing, but this information is not as accessible as, say, information on a product label, and the cost to the consumer of locating it must thus be added to the information-gathering costs the private organization bears. Also, the decreasing marginal cost of disseminating information once it is gathered means that marginal-cost pricing will not meet a private firm's cost, while pricing at higher than marginal cost will mean that an inefficiently small amount will be produced. This market failure suggests the preferability of public provision.[17] There are still, then, likely to be instances in which individuals would wish to renounce voluntarily their authority to choose to a third party.

Why Government?

I shall now consider objections that the third party need not be the government. Consumers might let friends they trust or expert agents they hire make decisions in their interests.[18] Mandatory government regulation, the argument continues, is a poor vehicle for making decisions that a consumer chooses to renounce, because it binds not only those who prefer not to make the choice themselves, but also those who *would* have wanted to do so.

Certainly there are instances in which choices by consumer-appointed agents might be preferable to decisions by government. Consumers use doctors as agents, for instance, and to some limited extent retail stores act as agents as well. That these agents can be apprised of the client's individual preferences certainly offers an advantage. By contrast, a government agency must make a single choice, despite existence of diverse preferences among citizens. But in other instances looking for, paying, and monitoring a privately hired agent might be more expensive than having the government undertake the same tasks. This greater expense might outweigh the

17. On this point, see Nina W. Cornell et al., "Safety Regulation" in *Setting National Priorities: The Next Ten Years*, ed. Henry Owen and Charles L. Schultze (Washington: The Brookings Institution, 1976), pp. 465–66.

18. See George Stigler, *The Citizen and the State* (Chicago: University of Chicago Press, 1975), p. 12.

advantages of a choice personally tailored to the client's preferences. Furthermore, the private provision of information-gathering by an agent creates the same public goods problems as any private provision of information. And to seek an agent in any individual instance, a person must have enough knowledge of the existing characteristics by which to judge the product in question to realize the need for an agent in the first place.

Government Certification – An Alternative to Regulation?

Perhaps authority to choose could be renounced without requiring mandatory government regulation by asking the government to certify the safety of products. Consumers who wished to renounce their authority to choose could simply buy the certified product. In certifying a product, the government would decide on appropriate safety features, but it would not be mandatory that all products include these features. Only those that did, however, would be certified. Consumers who decided to buy a certified product, would, in effect, be allowing the government make the decision for them. But those who wished to decide for themselves would have the choice of buying a product without the certified safety-feature package.

Choosing to buy certified products might be an appropriate form of voluntary renunciation of the authority to choose. But it might not be a consumer's preferred alternative. The most important reason for preferring mandatory regulation to certification is the fear that, despite one's general resolution to buy only certified products, one might be tempted in individual cases to depart from that resolution and buy noncertified ones. The concept of "temptation" – of doing something one doesn't "really" want to do – is a difficult one for the standard economic paradigm in which, a person, voluntarily choosing x over y, is considered better off because the choice shows a preference for x over y. Therefore, the individual should be glad of the opportunity to make the choice. In fact, though, some people fear that at some future moment they might act "in a moment of weakness" in a different way than they would have under normal circumstances. Even if we end up not "giving in to" temptation, we might wish to be spared temptation to avoid the anxiety costs of realizing that one might, at any time, give in. Thus, some people might well prefer mandatory regulation to certification out of a fear that in many specific instances, when faced with a choice between one product (say a can of soup or a lawn mower) that is certified and another that isn't, they might "take a chance" and get the cheaper, noncertified one, although as a general matter of considered reflection, they would wish to buy only certified products. People frequently choose at times to have an alternative withheld from them just to avoid future temptation.

If there are psychological costs accruing from the very *thought* of choosing something that one would ordinarily shun, the most tragic aspect of temptation is that once one has been tempted, one may be better off giving in. This may well be the case in situations that tempt one to risk life and limb to save a few dollars. Imagine a situation in which one unit is the perceived net benefit (at the moment of temptation) of choosing a cheaper, more dangerous product over a more expensive, safer one. But the pangs from just considering the choice cost two units. Since these feelings are experienced whether or not the choice is made, once a situation clearly presents itself, consumers might as well choose the cheaper, more dangerous product to "cut their losses." But there is still a loss of one unit that would not have occurred if the possibility of choice had never been presented.

There are other reasons for consumers to prefer regulation to certification as well. If consumers must decide in each case whether to buy a certified brand, there are still significant decision-making costs. Even after deciding to buy only certified brands, they must still remember to check for the certification every time an unfamiliar product is purchased. Given the number of times people buy unfamiliar products, this may add up to a significant annoyance. Imagine also the situation of the consumer buying an unfamiliar product with no apparent certification. This may be because the product has no significant safety or health aspects that need to be regulated, and thus it has not been subject to certification. Consumers who wish simply to trust the judgment of the government agency and buy only certified (or regulated) products need do no checking if the product is subject to mandatory regulation. Either the product will possess the safety features the regulation requires or it will not have been regulated because it was deemed to have had no hazardous aspects that needed regulation. In either case, consumers can proceed without further ado to buy the product. If the signal to consumers is *only* a certification, however, absence of certification requires further investigation by those who wish to buy only certified products. They must find out whether that particular product has actually failed certification, or whether the product type just has not been subject to certification. Again, more effort is required than consumers may wish to expend. They may thus favor regulation to certification. (This might be resolved, in part, by placing the certification on products that had no certification standards to meet, but this would probably reduce the general perceived value of the certification in the eyes of many consumers.) Finally, consumers who wanted to see a higher level of concern for their welfare demonstrated by the government might prefer regulation to certification because the former demonstrates a higher level of concern.

Certainly, there are people who would rather have government set mandatory safety standards than hire private agents to certify product safety. Yet it still might be protested that others who would prefer to make the decisions themselves (or to hire their own agents or choose with the help of government certification) should not be forced to pay for safety features they don't want.

Balancing of Harm

Under the circumstances, one group or the other will end up being harmed. Either those opposed to mandatory safety standards are harmed by being forced to buy products with mandated features, or those favoring mandatory standards are hurt by having to do without the mandatory standards they seek. Whether the ultimate social decision responds to the wishes of the first group or the second has, then, external effects on the group whose wishes are denied. Those seeking mandatory regulation are demanding something that will help themselves and hurt those who would prefer to choose for themselves. The latter group, then, may be seen as passive victims of the acts of those demanding regulation. The prima facie duty to do justice suggests sympathy with passive victims against active encroachers. Nevertheless, considerations of the size of the groups seeking and wishing to avoid regulation, as well as the nature of the interference contemplated, are relevant to such judgments. Regarding the size of the groups in the case of government safety regulation, rather clear survey data exist. In a 1974 poll, respondents were asked whether the government should "make sure that each packaged, canned, or frozen food is safe to eat." An overwhelming 97 percent agreed, a degree of unanimity hard to replicate for any government policy. In a 1976 poll, respondents were asked a similar question about government product-safety standards and 85 percent agreed.[19] As for the extent of interference, it is not generally great. Those opposed to regulation face the annoyance of having to pay extra money for safety features they would have preferred to avoid. Their homes are not burglarized. They are not restrained by physical force from moving around wherever they wish. Their fortunes are not decimated. My own conclusion is that it would be wrong to prevent the vast majority of Americans who prefer to do so from turning over to the government product-safety decision making.[20]

The figures on the percentages who wish to turn over safety decision making to the government also shed light on a question briefly examined earlier. Would decisions made by government safety regulators and decisions that fully informed consumers would themselves make be sufficiently similar to make it rational for consumers voluntarily to hand over such choices to regulators? If government agencies did frequently make decisions that wildly departed from those consumers would make themselves, one would expect the survey results to have been dramatically different. Instead, they show a clear vote of confidence for the efforts of government agencies regulating product safety.

There remain instances of public outcry over issues like saccharin. A wise agency official might well conclude that such outcries signify withdrawal in the specific instances of consumers' general delegation

---

19. These figures are from U.S. Department of Health and Human Services, Food and Drug Administration, *Consumer Nutrition Knowledge Survey, Report I* (Washington, D.C.: FDA, 1976), p. 39; and Seymour Martin Lipset and William Schneider, "The Public View of Regulation," *Public Opinion* 2 (January 1979): 11.

20. A case could probably be made for allowing the establishment of certain stores (with warnings prominently posted) that sell only products that do not meet regulatory standards. This would allow those who wish to buy such products the opportunity to do so without subjecting others to serious temptation problems. There would be important implementation problems with such proposals, however, especially with fraud at the manufacturing level (labeling noncompliant products as compliant ones) or at the distribution level. Also, if the external effects of a person's choices are an important part of the justification for regulation in a specific instance (to be discussed below), then the individual's own choice might be overridden. These problems make the establishment of such outlets for noncompliant products hardly a top-priority item on the consumer-protection regulation agenda.

to government the authority to choose. It is not irrational for consumers to decide generally to relinquish that authority, but to wish
to reclaim it when they feel sufficiently informed or when the
agency might make a decision sufficiently different from their own.

To deny people the option of delegating to government agencies
decisions they would prefer not to make does liberty a disservice.
Those who oppose such an option appear to place choice on a pedes-
tal as a supreme value. But in doing so they set it up for a fall.
Almost 40 years ago Erich Fromm remarked upon some people's
desire, reflected in their support for Nazi and Communist totalitarian
movements, to "escape from freedom." [21] People might want to
escape from freedom, Fromm wrote, if they felt overwhelmed by
constant demands to make choices they felt unable to handle. If
people think they have only two options, either having to make
choices they would rather delegate or giving up their freedom entirely, many might choose the course, abhorrent to all who value liberty, of relinquishing freedom. Ironically, those who would refuse to
allow people the option of delegating choices to the government
often defend this view with paternalistic arguments. They might contend that liberty of choice is such an important value that people
must be required to give it priority under all circumstances, whether
they wish to or not, or that people must be protected against the
gradual loss of ability to choose that might result from relinquishing
too many choices. Those who truly value liberty of choice will be
eager to allow people to delegate to the government choices they
don't wish to make, so that they can better husband their choice-
making resources for decisions they genuinely wish to make themselves.

EXTERNAL EFFECTS AND THE OVERRULING
OF A PERSON'S OWN CHOICE

John Stuart Mill affirmed in *On Liberty* that the restriction against
hindering a person's authority to choose applied to acts affecting the
individual alone and not to those affecting others. This distinction
has, however, come under withering attack. Government intervention in people's decision making may occur not out of a paternalistic

21. Erich Fromm, *Escape From Freedom* (New York: Rinehart, 1941).

desire to overrule individuals' choices for their own good, but out of a desire to protect others against the negative consequences of those choices. Thus, banning saccharin or requiring people to wear seatbelts might be justified on nonpaternalistic grounds even if people didn't want these decisions made by the government, because of the effects bladder cancer or auto accidents have, not on those individuals themselves, but on others. The distinction between intervention on paternalistic grounds and intervention to protect others against the negative consequences of a person's behavior is often lost in the general public debate on regulation, in which opposition to both kinds of intervention tend to get lumped together as complaints against "government interference." Thus, the resentment of businessmen toward the Occupational Safety and Health Administration's or the Environmental Protection Agency's regulations should not be confused with resentment toward bureaucrats who believe they are better able to decide what is right for people than are the people themselves.

The Scope of External Effects

The discussions of external effects such as pollution in introductory economics textbooks tend to obscure the issue, because they imply that most actions lack external effects. That "no man is an island" dashes any attempt to make such neat categorizations. Clearly, the argument for freedom of political speech, an argument often made in terms similar to the one against paternalism, can hardly be made on the grounds that free speech affects no one else. The famous argument by Lord Devlin against allowing pornography was based on the external affects of these actions on social cohesion.[22]

The inevitability of external effects extends to actions in the private sphere as well. Words we speak everyday, small gestures we make, even the tone of our voices—all may profoundly affect the feelings of those around us who value our friendship or our love. The clothes we wear, the opinions we express, the plays we attend, the colors we paint our houses—all may give joy, or offense, to those around us. If I choose to patronize one business, my action has an

22. Lord Patrick Devlin, "Morals and the Criminal Law," reprinted in *Morality and the Law*, ed. Richard A. Wasserstrom (Belmont, Calif.: Wadsworth, 1971).

effect on other businesses that lose my patronage. Even if we are passive, our passivity has effects on others. Words we fail to say or gestures we fail to make can affect another person as much as words we do say or gestures we do make. Whenever we are passive we affect others who could have benefited from our aid. The person who sees a fire starting in a building and continues on without calling the fire department is hardly in a position to say that this failure to act had no external effects.

If a person gets sick or injured, or dies, as a result of purchasing an unsafe product, clearly the action of buying the product had external effects on friends and loved ones. If a person is insured, other policyholders foot the bill.[23] If a person is not insured and suffers great financial hardship, other members of society still end up paying. When the victim of unfortunate circumstances appears before us, the rest of us either pay cash to help the uninsured victim — or else pay in the form of guilty feelings occasioned by turning our backs, even if we attempt the justification that the victim was solely responsible for the unhappy situation. The fact that we end up either saving people from the really bad consequences of their choices or feeling guilty if we don't is an argument, based on external effects and not on paternalism, for intervening in the original choices. Consequently, we require people to insure for their old age, give the poor in-kind rather than cash transfers, or mandate safety regulations.

None of this means that our every move should be subject to government restrictions. Just about everyone who has thought seriously about the implications of the ubiquity of external effects has come to the conclusion that society must determine which acts individuals have a right to commit or refrain from doing, despite the harm such acts may inflict on others, and which acts are too harmful to permit unhindered or undone, despite the fact that an individual might prefer to commit or refrain from committing them.[24]

23. That situation is only partly remedied if the policyholder falls into an experience category with a higher premium. It is sometimes argued that only the existence of government-provided health insurance creates the external effect from accidents that may be used to justify government intervention. This contention is then used to illustrate the general view that government regulation pyramids on itself, one regulation soon requiring another, with the implication that the process should never be started. The use of government-provided health insurance to argue for this contention is unwarranted. First, there exist important external effects from an accident other than bills paid by other insurance policyholders. Second, this problem exists whether insurance is governmental and mandatory or private and voluntary.

24. See, for instance, Hart, *Law, Liberty, and Morality*, Jethro Lieberman, "The Relativity of Injury," *Philosophy and Public Affairs* 6 (Summer 1977); Guido Galabresi and

Maximizing Net Benefits

To decide in a given case whether an individual should have the right to make decisions about what risks to take, despite the harmful consequences such decisions can cause others, raises difficult questions that cannot be answered deductively. It will not do to argue, as is sometimes done, that external-effects arguments must never be used to justify restricting risks because it would be possible to use such arguments to eradicate all exercises of liberty. For the fact is that *everyone* recognizes that at some point the external effects of an individual's acts become great enough to justify taking away the individual's right to act. Thus, all agree that murder or assault are not rightful displays of liberty. We cannot escape a messy balancing process in which the extent of the external effects produced by a person's action, the importance of the act for the individual, and possible deontological considerations regarding prima facie duties, are weighed against one another.

One way of balancing these elements is to apply the utilitarian criterion of maximizing net benefits: A person would be assigned the right to act if that individual valued the action more than those bearing the costs of the act valued being spared those costs. Such an approach might appear to offer scant shelter for small groups whose acts or failure to act produce even the slightest cost to a large group. But this view underestimates the scope for liberty of choice that would likely result from such a calculation. First, it fails to consider the effects of many different, potentially discomforting or offensive acts performed by many different people, with the strong probability that within this universe of acts a person will be both perpetrator and victim. Most people usually feel more dissatisfaction in being prohibited from doing something they wish to do than they feel happiness in stopping another's act they find offensive. I may not like your pink polka-dot shirt, but I probably don't dislike it enough to outweigh the distaste I would feel if you could stop me from wearing my favorite motorcycle jacket. I may be unhappy seeing part of my insurance dollar go to pay for injured lawn mower users who bought mowers without any safety features, but I would be more unhappy if

---

A. Douglas Malamed, "Property Rights, Liability Rules, and Inalienability," *Harvard Law Review* 85 (April 1972); and any of the "property rights" writings by Chicago school economists, such as Harold Demsetz, "Toward a Theory of Property Rights," *American Economic Review* 57 (May 1967).

I were told I had to sleep between seven and eight hours a night because people who do so tend to live longer. Therefore a basis exists for agreements to tolerate each other in cases where the harm produced by one person's acts involves small cost, discomfort, or offense. This is the basis of the hoary doctrine, "Live and let live." Second, as Mill argued in *On Liberty*, the existence of many varied "experiments in living" confers external benefits on others. They can learn about a wide portfolio of possible choices they themselves might make (and something about the consequences of choices) at a much lower cost than if they were required to try out everything for themselves. Third, if some are offended by polka-dot shirts or distasteful political views, others derive satisfaction from living in a diverse society. I may not skydive or attend ballet, but I am happy to know that such alternatives exist around me. Or people may derive satisfaction from living in a society where the liberty to choose is valued highly and derive offense from the knowledge that the exercise of liberty is being constantly curtailed. Finally, interference with liberty of action has enforcement costs, and these costs increase with the extent of interference.

A Nonutilitarian Case for Choice

A nonutilitarian case may also be made that people have the liberty to choose even in some instances where the benefits to them do not outweigh the costs to others. Grounds for such a right might be that it is prima facie wrong to violate human dignity by restricting a person's liberty. Thus we might conclude that A has a right to act a certain way, even though A's act causes B greater unhappiness than it causes A happiness, because interfering with A's liberty would violate A's human dignity.[25] Nonutilitarian judgments on rights become extremely complicated and end up raising the most profoundly difficult

25. The statement that it is prima facie wrong to violate human dignity is being used here to justify a social decision about rights that will favor A's good over that of B. Note that it is intuitively easier to accept the use of the moral principle that it is wrong to violate human dignity to decide that a policy should favor A's good over B's good even though B's good is greater because doing otherwise would violate A's human dignity, than it is to accept the view, presented earlier, that a policy that produces x-1 units of goods for A may be ethically superior to one producing x units of good for A because the first policy preserves and the second violates A's human dignity. In the former case, we are, at least, maximizing A's good (although sacrificing B's), while in the latter case we aren't maximizing anybody's good.

issues in moral philosophy. Thus we might conclude, contrary to the above example, that A does *not* have a right to act a certain way, even though the prohibition causes A greater unhappiness than it causes B happiness, because the harm that B would have been caused had the act been permitted would have violated B's human dignity far more than the interference with liberty violates A's dignity. Those bearing costs through the acts of others might also be regarded as victims of injustice, because they have suffered harm without deserving to do so. In such cases, the prima facie duty to do justice may argue for not granting people the right to act as they wish even though such acts might provide net benefits.

One approach to the problem of external effects is to grant people the right to act as they wish, while charging them for the monetizable costs of their behavior. Thus, smokers might be charged higher insurance rates, or accident victims not wearing seatbelts might be denied a portion of insurance recovery. The applicability of such an approach is limited by administrative costs that may outweigh its savings, by the nonmonetary nature of many harms, and by discomfort in placing an implicit price tag on certain behaviors.[26] However such approaches ought to be considered when not excessively costly.

Complex considerations must be applied in deciding in situations involving external effects whether the right shall be assigned to the person wishing to act or to others bearing the costs of the act. Such considerations have occupied lawmakers and judges for centuries, and they cannot be wished away with formulas or slogans. I have argued that there are, indeed, instances where the external effects of people's actions may justify overriding their own decisions. I have also tried to present both utilitarian and nonutilitarian grounds for being relatively cautious about such restrictions. Beyond that, one can only conclude that situation-by-situation determinations must be made, with attention to the concerns presented here.

PATERNALISM PROPER

Up to this point, various nonpaternalistic justifications for government regulation of consumer product safety have been considered.

26. On reasons for the latter, see Steven Kelman, *What Price Incentives?: Economists and the Environment* (Boston: Auburn House, 1981), pp. 54–84.

It remains to be discussed whether intervention may ever be justified strictly on paternalistic grounds.

The argument presented earlier against paternalism had both utilitarian elements, based on predictions that paternalistic interventions were unlikely to satisfy the person on whose behalf the intervention took place, and nonutilitarian ones, based on the wrongness of violating human dignity regardless of its impact on happiness. If the empirical predictions of the utilitarian argument turn out to be correct, both arguments against paternalism tend in the same direction. There is then no trouble concluding that paternalistic acts are wrong.

But what if the empirical predictions turn out to be incorrect? It is certainly not hard to imagine that in some cases individuals might ultimately be happier with certain choices made for them than with different choices made themselves, even if they don't realize it initially. People themselves often come to regret the choices they have made. There remains the effect of one particular intervention on the general tendency to intervene, a tendency that one would not wish to encourage. This argument has some force, but society already has considerable experience intervening in people's liberty of choice—generally because of the costs such acts may impose on others—and it has proven possible to commence such intervention without liberty disappearing. The argument about the effect of one intervention on the tendency to intervene has greater weight when applied to potential restrictions of freedom of political speech, where such intervention is far less common. Individual paternalistic acts might, then, be possible without leading society down the proverbial slippery slope.

Suppose that, in fact, some paternalistic interventions might increase long-run happiness. If one wishes to go beyond utilitarianism (as I believe one should), the question then becomes one of balancing such net satisfaction against the prima facie wrongness of violating human dignity. One should be very hesitant about letting the good that might come of paternalism outweigh the wrongness of violating human dignity. That it is wrong to violate human dignity is something about which we feel rather strongly. Given the difficulty of deciding what choices will make people happiest, our certainty that we are indeed making a better choice for individuals than they would make themselves must generally be much less.

The Choice Process

Relevant considerations in making such balancing judgments are provided by a closer look at the nature of the choice process. Standard choice theory suggests that the process of choice involves listing valued goals, weighing them in comparison with each other, and calculating what choice will best maximize their attainment. Preferences have both *direction* and *intensity*. How unhappy people are with a choice imposed on them, and how much the choice may be regarded as interfering with their human dignity, depend crucially on how deep are their convictions about the preferences underlying the choice made. Generally, an important difference in the conviction and permanence of preferences would seem to exist between preference direction and preference intensity. The direction of preference—what things we like and what we don't—seems to be something with genuine existence and permanence. I do not believe that any number of years of indoctrination in the point of view that asceticism is good would succeed in convincing any significant number of people to like it. That I like steak and dislike spinach, that I like tennis and dislike jogging, that I like reading the comics and dislike reading the editorial page—each of these preferences is real and substantial.

The same cannot be said for the precise weight ascribed to preferences in any individual choice calculation. I like both apples and oranges, but *how much* more do I like the one than the other? I like both convenience and safety, but how much of one am I willing to give up for the other when the two conflict? To give the precise weighting ascribed to preferences the same status as the direction of those preferences may be to cast a puff of smoke in stone. Sometimes the difference in weightings is large enough to be relatively stable. But often weightings are likely to be unstable and weakly held. Considerable evidence suggests that the discomfort associated with trading off among positively valued but conflicting objectives often produces sequential attention to goals, in which attention is paid to only one of the positively valued goals at a time. Which goal is chosen depends on the vagaries of chance—on what stimuli are received at the time of choice and what one's mood happens to be.[27]

27. See Richard Cyert and James March, *A Behavioral Theory of the Firm* (Englewood Cliffs, N.J.: Prentice Hall, 1963), p. 118.

Such a process favors attention to goals that are most immediately apparent (and thus easier to perceive). If an absolute rule is adopted that prohibits paternalistic intervention in individual decision making for the purpose of overriding preference direction, such a rule would forbid intervention when the decision is likely to have genuine significance for the individual and when violation of human dignity would be greatest. Paternalism might be more justified when its purpose is to revise choices among objectives that have similar directional valuations but different weightings. Attaching too much importance to the exact weight individuals give preferences in any particular choice may sanctify something that people themselves hardly appear to sanctify.

This is even more true in regard to the outcome of an individual's calculatory process. A choice depends not only on preferences and their weights, but also on beliefs about the world and on the acuity of an individual's calculative apparatus. Two people who have exactly the same preferences weighted exactly the same way, but who have different opinions about the likelihood of rain tomorrow, might make different decisions about whether to buy tickets to a baseball game for the next day. If no substantial information exists to determine whether it *will* rain tomorrow, we would not be able to say that one has made a better decision than another. However, suppose that one person but not another believes in the gambler's fallacy or feels exempt from the law of gravity. In such cases, we are in a position to say that the first person will make poorer decisions than the second in instances where such knowledge of the world is less accurate. Similarly, two people with the same preferences, one of whom has digested Howard Raiffa's *Decision Analysis* while the other hasn't, might well make different decisions about what to do in a given situation. One would be in a position unambiguously to state that the person using decision theory made a better choice than the person not using decision theory, given the preferences that both share, because the former was better at calculating than the latter.[28]

Intervention on the grounds of incorrect factual knowledge or defective calculative abilities is of course the basis for intervention

28. For discussions of choices that do not maximize attainment of a person's own preferences due to incorrect facts or defective calculation, see Amos Tversky and Daniel Kahneman, "Judgment under Uncertainty: Heuristics and Biases," in *Benefit-Cost and Policy Analysis*, ed. Richard Zeckhauser et al. (Chicago: Aldine, 1974) and Amos Tversky, "Intransitivity of Preferences," *Psychological Review* 76 (January 1969).

in the decisions of children and of the mentally deranged. Refusing ever to intervene in such instances entails consequences that virtually everybody would regard as intolerable. We would have to refuse to stop individuals (to use Robert Nozick's example) who claim they wish to live, but who believe they can float in air after walking out a fifteen-story window. We would have to refuse to stop individuals who say they want to find the quickest way to get from Boston to New York but have concluded from looking at the map that the shortest route goes via Hong Kong, from getting on a plane to the Far East.

The initial reaction might be that paternalistic intervention is always justified in cases of incorrect facts or defective calculation. But such intervention does still raise the problem of violating human dignity. There is also a danger that intervenors will have trouble distinguishing between cases of incorrect facts or defective calculations and other kinds of cases. They may also consciously overestimate the incidence of such cases so as to justify otherwise unjustifiable interventions. Finally, caution is indicated because intervention on grounds of superior calculative ability can open the way for intervention by the superiorly gifted in the decisions of the normally gifted.[29] These considerations necessitate a cautious attitude toward paternalistic intervention even in cases involving incorrect facts or defective calculations. But they do not dictate an absolute prohibition.

The Context and Consequences of Choice

The question of paternalism involves other issues as well. One is the broader context of individual choice. If the alternatives among which a person is able to choose, given constraints imposed by circumstances, are either limited or generally unpalatable, the value ascribed to liberty of choice is likely to be diminished. A poor person may be excused for not rejoicing at the liberty to choose between jobs as a dishwasher and a ditchdigger. In such instances the best way to increase the value of the liberty to choose may be to take steps to widen the range of choice. A second, broader question raised by paternalism involves the quality of relationships among people. There

29. This point is made forcefully in "Paternalism and the Mildly Retarded," *Philosophy and Public Affairs* 8 (Summer 1979).

is a danger that our remonstrances against intervening paternalistically may discourage concern for the fate of others. Mill, while opposing paternalism, recommended that people be given advice by others about how best to live. Yet, while remonstrances against paternalism may not be *logically* inconsistent with concern for others, they may nonetheless act *psychologically* to extinguish such concern.

The purpose of this paper has not been to defend or criticize any specific example of government safety regulation but to defend the justifiability in principle of such regulation against accusations that it inevitably involves paternalism and hence should be condemned. I have agreed with the general condemnation of paternalism while suggesting nonpaternalistic justifications for such intervention and arguing that there are certain cases where cautious paternalistic intervention might be justified.

That government safety regulation can be justified in principle does not necessarily mean that the regulatory activities of the Food and Drug Administration or the Consumer Product Safety Commission have, on balance, been justified in practice. My own belief, though, is that they clearly have been. Establishing the case for such a proposition would require going through a representative sample of the regulatory interventions these agencies have undertaken and analyzing them in light of the conceptual criteria for intervention presented here. This does not imply that some individual regulations have not been excessively or insufficiently protective, or that some things that have been regulated should never have been regulated while others not regulated should have been. The view that such regulation is to be condemned in principle as paternalistic has constituted a significant part of the attack on consumer product-safety regulation. That bulwark of the case against such regulation thus falls.

Chapter 11

ON THE RATIONALE OF GOVERNMENTAL REGULATION

Nicholas Rescher

THREE BASIC PARAMETERS

The theoretical justification of state intervention in the sphere of individual action and initiative depends on three basic issues: Is it *right*? Is it *desirable*? Is it *expedient*? A negative response to any of these questions would suggest that the state's abridgement of individuals' liberty to conduct their affairs in their own preferred ways is inappropriate. Rightness, desirability, and expediency are severally necessary and jointly sufficient to legitimate state regulation of individual affairs. Let us examine these three parameters of the problem more closely.

The Issue of Right?

The state has always impinged heavily on the lives of its individual subjects. It has taxed them, impressed them into its service, dictated where they can and cannot live, and, not infrequently, appointed the time and means of their death. Obscure existence outside the range of the state's sight has usually been the best way to remain outside its reach. "Fortunate," said one of the caliphs, "is the man whom I do not know and who does not know me." But what is, is not necessarily right, and so the big question remains: To what extent is it right and proper for the state to interfere by way of regulation and control in the actions and dealings of its members.

Is it right for the state to take onto itself this or that mode of regulation or control of the activities of its citizens—to fix the rules of the road, say, or to stipulate retirement ages, or to limit the opening hours of bars? Such questions pose the difficult normative issue of the basis on which one is to proceed in determining whether a state acts rightly or legitimately in adopting a certain regulative measure.

Two alternatives arise at this point. On the one hand, one can take the view that it is somehow written large in the scheme of things that the state should exercise certain regulative functions and these only; that this is somehow determined by the general principles of the matter. Such a position in effect has it that it is somehow engraved on bronze tablets delivered from on high—to put it in caricature—what the proper regulative business of the state actually is. The virtually insuperable difficulty here is that of getting hold of the bronze tablets, or, rather, of establishing the general principles that are to effect the determination at issue.

On the other hand, a more relaxed view of the matter is also possible. That is, one can take the view that the proper business of the state is to discharge whatever regulative functions it is assigned by its citizens through the due processes of the political decision-making apparatus at their disposal. If the public wants to charge public authorities with the licensing of TV sets, the monopoly of postal services, or the monitoring of banking transactions, then so be it; the activities and regulations at issue have thereby automatically become part of the "proper business" of the state. The question "Is it right and proper that the state should restrict or regulate the activities at issue?" is on this view effectively settled when the public uses the valid political processes at its disposal to mandate those responsibilities to the state.

But this rather laissez faire approach to the question of the right of the state to take on certain restrictive and regulating functions does not resolve the issue of justification. What it does is simply to displace the entire weight of concern to the issues of desirability and expediency. Beyond question, much can be said for the view that, if and when a viable consensus of the public (acting through the channels of the duly established political process) charges the state with a certain regulative mission, then the question of inherent rightness is closed—for this position bypasses any problematic aspects beyond "the general will" in regard to the normative appraisal of the legitimation of state action.[1] But of course, even with such a view the issues of "Is it desirable?" and "Is it expedient?" still remain wide open. These considerations now come to the center of the stage.

The Issue of Desirability

The question "Is it *desirable* for the state to exercise a certain controlling or regulative function?" comes down to this: Is it manifestly in the best (real) interests of the substantial preponderance of its members that the state should assume this function—in short, is it in "the public interest"? In concrete cases the answer to this question may sometimes be *yes* (e.g., fluoridating water supplies, licensing the construction of nuclear power stations, controlling the distribution of drugs). But sometimes it may be *no* (mandating a certain retirement age) and sometimes *maybe* (prohibiting the use of studded tires on private vehicles, prohibiting the acquisition of gold or of foreign exchange by private individuals). The status of these particular examples is unimportant: they are meant to be no more than suggestive. What matters is the general principle at issue, namely that the question of desirability turns on the devising of a cogent case to show that a *successful* carrying-through of the measure at issue will indeed serve the best interests of a preponderant majority.

It is important, however, to recognize that even after this question of desirability has been settled in the affirmative, the issue of feasibility yet remains wholly untouched, for the question of desirability takes the hypothetical form. Even if the measures at issue were implemented in an efficient, effective, and (relatively) inexpensive manner, would worthwhile results thereby be anticipated? And the important question yet remains very much open, whether this hypothesis—or anything like it—is realized or indeed realizable. It is to this concern that the issue of feasibility is addressed.

---

1. In actuality this position is overly simplistic since its conception of rightness is too legalistic and overlooks the underlying issue of justness. Certainly the measures of control or regulation at issue could be unjust—in being discriminatory, for example. For the methodological purposes of this essay we may, however, adopt a suspension of disbelief in this regard.

The Issue of Feasibility

Even if it is "desirable—in the sense of contributing to "the public interest"—it is still reasonable to raise the question of whether it is actually possible for the state to realize this desideratum. Can the mice bell the cat? Is the state actually in a position to discharge this mission efficiently and effectively? Prohibition was an arrangement that arguably satisfied the criteria of desirability. But it soon came to grief, shattered on the rock of feasibility.

This matter of efficiency and effectiveness poses large and ramified problems. For one thing, it is important to realize that the question of efficiency and effectiveness is generally not so much absolute as relative, a matter of a comparison between alternatives; that is, the question is not just whether the state can achieve the desired results with some degree of adequacy, but whether other, less awesome mechanisms for their realization might actually be superior in this regard. In particular, we must recognize that potent forces are generally at work to militate against the state's assumption of a function when other, less dramatic alternatives may be substituted; this is true regardless of how desirable it is to accomplish the function. These constraints are indicated by the following sorts of considerations:

1. The state—an inherently sluggish and cumbersome agency—is hard to coax into an area of concern, and, once settled there, is even harder to oust when circumstances so develop that this becomes desirable.

2. The state is, in general, a comparatively problematic mechanism of purpose realization, because its pursuit of any given goal is inevitably fraught with political complications.

3. The actual agents through which the state effects its actions— officialdom and its bureaucracy—are generally too insulated against consumer feedback to emerge in fact (rather than theory) as effective servants of the public.

4. The state operates at a disadvantage in that by proceeding within an all-embracing monolithic framework, it loses the benefits of efficiency gained through rivalry and competition among smaller units of operation.

A large variety of considerations of this sort militate toward the conclusion that whenever an agreed-upon goal can be pursued without the state assuming the responsibility of implemention, then this should be done on grounds of feasibility.

In general and *in abstracto* the issue of feasibility turns on matters of cost-effectiveness. Its governing concern is with the question, "Are the specific measures of regulation and control so operable that the benefits at issue with *desirability* are achieved at a practicable cost?" And the costs at issue must be estimated not just in economic terms but in social terms as well, including such matters as a diminution of the liberty of the individual.

THE RATIONALE OF STATE INTERVENTION

Let us pause to consolidate the implications of the preceding deliberations. They indicate that it only makes sense to assign a regulative function to the state — even an inherently meritorious one — when certain conditions are met:

1. Exercise of the regulative function at issue would actually be desirable in terms of the public interest.
2. There is reason to think that the state will prove (in absolute terms) reasonably efficient and effective in achieving the regulative functions at issue, and moreover that it will prove (in relative terms) more efficient and effective than alternative mechanisms would.
3. The overall costs and negative effects incurred through the state's assumption of control are significantly outweighed by the benefits resulting from such control.

From this analysis, then, it emerges that a complex series of conditions must be met if state control or regulation of the personal or economic dealings of its citizenry is to be properly legitimated. Specifically, a convincing case must be established for believing that (1) in the absence of the particular control or regulations there is a real risk of significant harm to individuals or of serious impairment of the public interest; (2) there is reasonable assurance that this danger will be avoided or significantly diminished by the controls at issue; (3) no alternative device less awesome and less cumbersome than actual state intervention is available for attaining the desiderata; and (4) the overall costs and disabilities of implementing the particular controls and regulations in an acceptably efficient and effective way do not exceed the benefits being realized.

Such a process of assessment involves a number of distinct but important factors: (1) the gravity of the potential risk; (2) the probability of the potential risk's realization; (3) the cost of the proposed measures (including the realization that we may be paying an assured price for averting a merely possible danger); and (4) the likelihood that the proposed measures will actually *avert* the potential risk (and not simply deflect it into other channels).

These considerations illuminate the difficulties inherent in establishing a legitimating rationale for measures of state control and regulation. Indeed, they establish a powerful presumption against all such measures. But this presumption is certainly not indefeasible. Although the difficulties in question are real, they are not insuperable. Consider an example of the current standard security measures of weapons control imposed on airline passengers. They do exact from all concerned a price in terms of increased expense, added delays, and some degree of invasion of privacy. But they do provide a substantial benefit in terms of diminishing the inconvenience and safety risks involved in aircraft hijackings. Accordingly, one can reasonably argue in this case that the benefits outweigh the costs and that such controls and regulations are legitimate.

On the other hand, there can be little doubt that this is not true of much current governmental regulation in the economic and social areas. Instances of major expenditures in time, energy, and resources for the realization of minor or nonexistent benefits are legion. To take just one example, the annual cost to society of the paperwork generated by the federal government's insatiable demand for information was estimated at some $100 billion in 1977. Certainly the vast bulk of this cannot be justified on cost-benefit considerations of the sort operative in validating measures of governmental regulation and control.

With respect to feasibility, it must surely be conceded that in some instances we cannot be assured of knowing beforehand if the state can actually administer particular regulations or controls efficiently and effectively—whether, for example, governmental funding of scientific research facilities in colleges and universities will help or hinder the research process it is designed to facilitate. The dangers are certainly there. A program of statutory regulation often makes a leap in the dark — creating a monster that dwarfs the evils it is designed to remedy. (Prohibition affords a good example of this.) Whenever possible it is wisest to proceed by a slow and tentatively experimental process, lest relatively minor evils be traded for even greater ones. (And one of the real problems is that in this sphere of governmental action a "slow and experimental process" is well-nigh impossible to realize.)

QUESTIONS OF PRESUMPTION

It is important to recognize that regulation and control are matters of degree that admit of infinitely varied shadings and gradations. At the top of the scale we have the state's determination as to whether a certain type of good or service should be banned altogether (the sale of fireworks, the screening of pornographic films, the purchase of armaments by private individuals). At the next level come controls over who can provide or receive certain goods or services (child-labor laws, licensing of professionals or airlines or radio stations, licensing of purchases of certain "dangerous" products, etc.). Then come regulations about conditions of operation (closing times for bars). Near the bottom come the mere requirements to provide information (regarding certain banking transactions, for example).

Now in a democratic society there must always be a strong presumption against the control and regulation of individual action by the state. The need for a maximum range of individual liberty is axiomatic within the democratic ethos.

Recognition of the fact that regulation and control *can* be justified is simply the first step toward recognizing that they *must* be justified — that they are not proper and legitimate unless we make sure cost-benefit conditions are satisfied, conditions such as those illustrated in our preceding discussion. The presumption is always against government intervention and in favor of things being allowed to run their own course.

Accordingly, even in cases where state regulation and control is desirable and feasible, it is also desirable that it be accomplished at the minimum level of intervention. Every move toward control or regulation, and every step up the ladder of increased intervention levels must prove itself in terms of benefits to be actually realized.

But while there is a presumption in favor of unfettered liberty, this is certainly a defeasible presumption. We do not operate an unfettered free market in the provision of medical services, or of land utilization because the school of bitter experience has taught us that the consequences are unacceptable. And this is the important factor, for it takes a clear and present danger—a very real risk of some substantial sort—to reverse this standing presumption in favor of "the liberty of the subject."

THE RECENT AGGRANDIZEMENT OF STATE FUNCTIONS

Historically the state has sought to intervene in the affairs of its citizens when necessary for: (1) the survival or aggrandizement of the state itself; (2) the physical safety and well-being of its citizens; (3) the peaceable and orderly settlement of interpersonal dealings; and (4) the creation of major public works and facilities. Considerations of the first kind would yield such measures as the impressment of seamen, conscription in time of war, and the launching of colonies. Those of the second kind would underwrite the quarantine of the victim of a dangerous communicable disease or the maintenance of police forces or the construction of aqueducts. Considerations of the third kind lead the state into the regulation of inheritance, the mechanisms of commercial transaction (including, for example, the management of the coinage, the regulation of property transfers, and other aspects of the economic interaction of one person with another). Finally, those of the fourth kind bring the state into the business of building roads, constructing harbors, or exploring distant shores.

However, the past hundred years have seen a major change, with the state assuming substantial functions beyond the four traditional areas of national security, public safety, the settlement of interpersonal disputes, and public works. Specifically, the state has come to assume responsibility for the *economic well-being* of its citizenry and for the "quality of life" in a broader, noneconomic sense that embraces various *social desiderata*, particularly those of promoting equality of opportunity and access.

In respect to these latter items, the question of expediency that has preoccupied us throughout these pages now becomes especially significant; for this question looms extra large with respect to these "new" state functions, seeing that, historically speaking, the state has not evolved with a view to handling these new functions, and that it has had to develop new and sometimes problematic devices to meet them—especially by developing a vastly enlarged and diffused regulative bureaucracy. To clarify this issue, it is useful to look somewhat closely at a particularly important special case: the pursuit of egalitarianism.

EGALITARIANISM AS A SPECIAL CASE

The realization of egalitarian arrangements is something that by its very nature invites state intervention. For only action and coordination at the grandest and most inclusive level can assume uniformity of procedure and process. Thus, a great part of the modern state's best efforts at control and regulation is motivated by the pursuit of justice, fairness, equality of access and distribution, and other such egalitarian goals.

It is at this point that the potential discord between desirability and expediency comes into prominence, for the pursuit of egalitarianism, doubtless laudable as an end, can run into trouble when the correlative measures of regulation and control come to exert—as they inevitably must—a powerful feedback impetus upon the process being controlled. Thus rent-control measures can lose their effectiveness if they engender economic distortions that eliminate the availability of rental property. Or again, there is no point in promoting equality of access to medical services by means that seriously diminish the quality or quantity of the services being delivered.

There is, in sum, no sense in striving for equality of access and distribution by means that degrade significantly the resources available for distribution. A society can only distribute the goods and services it manages to produce. But the egalitarian ethos of our time all too easily fails to deal realistically with this factor of productivity. Consider the following two distributions of shares to individuals:

Patently Scheme I effects the fairer (indeed a perfectly fair) distribution. From the standpoint of "justice in the narrower sense" it has the clear-cut advantage. But that Scheme II is superior from the standpoint of the interests of all concerned is equally clear: everyone would be the gainer by its adoption. Despite its less *fair* distribution, the advantage from the standpoint of "justice in the wider sense" lies with this scheme. An adequate theory for the evaluation of distributions cannot confine its attention to fairness alone, but must also take into account the crucial factor of production.

Examples of the sort previously indicated underline the critical importance of a principle of production for determining the expediency of regulatory and control measures. Due heed of these factors soon forces the recognition that we must be prepared to acknowledge the superiority of "unfair" distributions whose unfairness "pays for itself" by conducing to the general advantage. We may well be prepared to tolerate discrepancies in the fairness of a distribution in contexts where these *could only be removed by exacting an unreasonable price* from all or most or the least well-off of the individuals involved.

In this connection it is necessary to reemphasize the deliberation already mentioned that the pursuit of inherently desirable ends can run into problems of expediency when it exacts too great a price in the attainment of other desiderata. It can—and often does—happen that measures that, inherently and in themselves, are incontestably desirable create a systematic feedback so that their operation exacts a price not commensurate with the expected benefits. And this sort of phenomenon can totally undermine, on grounds of *expediency*, the legitimacy of measures of control and regulation that aim at inherently proper and desirable objectives.

Chapter 12

THE PETTY TYRANNY OF GOVERNMENT REGULATION*

Tibor R. Machan

"I wonder how they let people like them grow so powerful?"
—*Anne Frank*

Supporters of government regulation of business have seldom argued their case without defending the general idea of government intervention in the marketplace. There are a few, however, who have clearly explained why they believe government regulation is required. Joan Claybrook, who was head of the National Highway Transportation Safety Administration in the Carter Administration, stated that government regulation aims "to protect legitimate health and safety rights against incursions such as pollution and latent defects." By her account, government regulation is a matter of moral requirement.

> Safety regulation is normally imposed following gross abuses that the marketplace does not correct. Its purpose is to prevent the recurrence of certain harm, not to punish. . . . What about the rights of individuals to breathe clean air, to drink clean water, to secure drugs and food that do not have unnecessary side effects or cause illness, to have a job that does not foster concern, to drive an automobile without unnecessary exposure to death or crippling

*I have benefited from the critical comments of Milton Friedman, Robert Hessen, Eric Mack, Randall Dipert, Eugene Bardach, and Mieczyslaw Maneli, though I may not have made the best use of their suggestions. Marty Zupan has helped me with the editing of this essay.

injury? These are the rights of the citizenry which regulation is designed to defend.[1]

Even many fervent critics of government regulation believe that the practice is sometimes justified. They share Irving Kristol's view that "no reasonable person is *in principle* opposed to all government regulation."[2] But I beg to differ and wish to affirm that government regulation is wrong in principle because any bona fide instance of it— as distinct from instances that really amount to judicial processes or managerial functions of government—infringes upon human liberty, something to which everyone has a natural right, including members of the business and professional community, who are most thoroughly regulated.

I won't be able to make a full case against government regulation in this essay. Moral conceptions, arguments, principles, and so forth, are embedded in broad theories touching on numerous aspects of philosophy, psychology, economics, and other disciplines.[3] It is not possible to cover all this ground here. But enough can be considered to appreciate that there are very strong reasons for regarding the institution and practices of government regulation as morally impermissible.

---

1. "Joan Claybrook Response," *Regulation*, (March–April 1981): 3–4.

2. Irving Kristol, "A Regulated Society?" *Regulation* (July–August 1977): 12. Murray L. Weidenbaum, chairman of the Council of Economic Advisors to President Ronald Reagan, answered the question, "Would you do away with regulation altogether?" by saying, "Of course not. Unless you're an anarchist, you believe that there is a role for government in setting rules. The question is: What are the legitimate limits? Should the Federal Government be concerned about the cleanliness of our environment, about the safety in workplaces, about eliminating discrimination, about the safety of products? Those are the principal areas affected by what I call the new wave of regulation. In a complicated modern society, there is an important role for government in these areas. But in each of them, Congress has enacted an excess of regulation, and the agencies in charge have promulgated an excess of rules, with the result that the basic objectives of the laws are not achieved in many instances." *U.S. News & World Report*, 14 June 1976, p. 31. F. A. Hayek, a prominent advocate of the free market and liberalism in the classical sense, also allows for considerable government regulation. He makes room for it in the "certification by government or others of the quality of some goods and services which may include a kind of licensing of particular activities by government." *Law, Legislation, and Liberty*, vol. 3 (Chicago: University of Chicago Press, 1979), p. 62.

3. But see John Rawls, "The Independence of Moral Theory," *Proceedings and Addresses of the American Philosophical Association*, vol. 47 (Newark, Del.: American Philosophical Association, 1975), p. 21.

MORAL GROUNDINGS

Ultimately the soundness of a moral position can only be established by developing a positive theory and showing that it compares favorably with alternatives. Here only a reasonably complete outline will be presented of the positive case that I consider sound. But it should be noted that the case for government intervention in the economy, and for government regulation in particular, is never made in great detail. Thus, perhaps even a sketchy presentation of the case against this institution will suffice. It will at least suggest that there are serious moral problems with government regulation worth some careful reflection and perhaps even radical changes in the organization of our government.

The substantive ethics underlying my thesis can be classified most fruitfully as eudaemonistic individualism or, alternatively, classical egoism.[4] This position rests on a recognition of ethics as a natural field of concern, arising from basic questions human beings ask about reality and their relationship to it. To wit, it is natural to ask how individuals should act, alone or in one another's company. It is natural because human beings lack the instincts that enable other living things to carry on with no concern for truth and falsehood, right and wrong. Once a person makes the choice to live—explicitly or implicitly, overtly or tacitly—then, as a rational being, it is imperative to

---

4. For a statement of this ethical position, see my "Recent Work in Ethical Egoism," *American Philosophical Quarterly* 16 (January 1979): 1–15. See also David L. Norton, *Personal Destinies: A Philosophy of Ethical Individualism* (Princeton, N.J.: Princeton University Press, 1976).

It must be noted that there is a crucial issue that is quite controversial and bears directly on the present discussion, namely, whether human beings are capable of self-determination, self-initiated free action? Or, on the contrary, are human beings, as the noted contemporary philosopher Willard Van Orman Quine—as well as the "scientific socialist" Karl Marx—contends, just the last interesting event in a causal chain? Is Quine right that "the will is a link in the causal chain," and that "the will is determined"? Is he right that "we can admire good voluntary actions and condemn others in the same way in which we admire a fine painting or disapprove of a bad one without ever thinking that they ever came about spontaneously to existence, without causal connections behind them"? (Quoted in Jiri Weiss, "Philosopher Quine Merges Abstract and Material Beliefs," *The Stanford Daily*, 1 April 1980, p. 2.) No, for then even this belief would be caused in others, with no independent way to resolve any such disputes. And while we admire paintings, we do not hold them responsible for being accomplished, as we hold a philosopher responsible for writing a well-argued, superior treatise in ontology or ethics. See my *The Pseudo-Science of B. F. Skinner* (New Rochelle, N.Y.: Arlington House, 1974), for more on this issue.

find out how to do this living, how to conduct oneself. Life requires guidelines, or principles of action, and ethics is concerned with the most basic principles of volitional human action.

The ethical individualist holds, furthermore, that the purpose served by ethics helps determine *which* principles of action are right for human beings. Ethics addresses the question, "How should I, a human being, live my life?" Put most directly, the most adequate answer is, "One should live so as to succeed at the project of living." And because of *what* one is — a human being who lacks instincts but has a mind — living successfully requires that one live rationally, being aware of and responding to things as they are. The generality of this answer is unavoidable, of course, since it must ultimately apply to every human being in order to best serve the purpose of guiding *human* conduct. It must also be fully accessible to anyone who is not crucially incapacitated, thereby making possible its universal implementation.

Political questions in turn arise with reference to living in the company of other human beings simply as human beings, not as parents, cousins, friends, colleagues, and so on. "How should we act toward others simply in virtue of their being human beings with whom we associate as fellow members of a human community?" or "What are the basic principles of conduct that our ethical stance requires us to adopt in such a situation?" Political theories aim to answer such questions. They seek to identify the basic principles of community life as such, not principles of personal conduct or family relations or even professional associations. In other words, the basic principles of *justice* by which citizens ought to abide are at issue here.

The most promising answer to the central political questions comes in the form of the Lockean natural-rights tradition, albeit supported by the ethics outlined above, an ethics with which Locke was not in agreement. On the basis of eudaemonistic individualism, the Lockean natural-rights theory can be shown to be a sound set of normative principles of human community life.[5]

The ethical individualist-Lockean case may be put roughly as follows: Each person is a *morally* independent and responsible being. They each have the task of making their lives the best they can be. The principles of a just community — which are to guide the interac-

---

5. See my review of Norton's *Personal Destinies*, which establishes this point, in *American Journal of Jurisprudence* 24 (1979): 213–26.

tions of such persons when they live among others—must accord with these facts. Natural rights are precisely the principles that most faithfully heed, in a social context, every individual's moral nature.

Now a community's government is the means by which rational people would attempt to secure the protection and preservation of their natural rights. The division of labor justifies government on prudential or practical grounds: a group of specialists in crime prevention, law enforcement, military defense, adjudication of disputes about various rights, and the whole system of derivative laws—all are probably more successful in reducing rights violations in a community than is unorganized action, aiming at self-defense and rectification of wrongs, undertaken by people sporadically. But an organized instrument of protection is also morally required by the fundamental purpose of politics: a rigorously defined legal system can best serve to secure the *administration of justice* in accordance with the *principles of justice*—that is, the maximum observance of due process of law in the service of justice among persons.

There are numerous other values a person should pursue in society besides the security of natural rights. That value, however, is the only bona fide public, or general-community, good—the only objective pursued legitimately by political, in other words, enforceable, legal organization. Safety, prosperity, science, art, education, recreation, security in old age, international cultural exchange, and so forth, are without doubt important and valuable to numerous members of the community at some time (and now and then to all at the same time). Still, only the protection and preservation of the natural rights of each person is of universal moral and political importance at all times and a pursuit that qualifies as bona fide public action.[6]

What natural rights individuals have is, in the end, the crucial question for purposes of determining whether government regulation is morally justified. To ascertain what our natural rights are, we must consult our concept of human nature. What makes people the distinctive beings they are is that *they are able to think and indeed require thinking for their survival as human beings.* Of course, thinking requires more than merely responding to stimuli, exhibiting reflex action, or even engaging in daydreaming. Rather it is conceptualizing, using more and more complex ideas, theories, explanations, predic-

6. I argue this point in full in my "Rational Choice and Public Affairs," *Theory and Decision* 12 (September 1980): 228–59.

tions, and other mental constructs in coming to terms with human life and reality. So, roughly, human nature consists of a biological entity having a mind whose goal is guiding its conduct. This does not mean that people must be intellectuals or mathematicians to qualify as human beings, only that they must have the capacity to engage in creative thought, even if they exercise this capacity only minimally.

It is by the competent, sustained use of their minds *in their particular lives* that people can achieve human excellence—this is how they can live a morally commendable life. So the conditions for living such a life in the company of other human beings are conditions morally required, morally right for people to respect and uphold. Natural rights identify these conditions. What is, so to speak, naturally right for human community life involves what by nature is the proper way of life, generally, for human beings. And this would be to engage, as a matter of free choice or individual decision—not forced by others—in the rational conduct of one's life. Those conditions, in turn, that make the exercise of this choice possible—that is, make it humanly possible for people to pursue a morally excellent life—are the basic rights all persons have and should, indeed, seek to protect and preserve.

As John Locke suggested, it is because of their basic freedom and independence—or their nature as self-made, autonomous beings at the crucial level of moral excellence—that individuals have the basic right to life, liberty, and property. In plain terms, this means that no one has the right to murder, assault, or rob another. It is morally impermissible to terminate willfully another's life, to thwart another's actions, and to seize another's belongings, for these are the materials with which a person can either achieve or fail to achieve moral excellence. If a society's legal system does not guard against those who would thwart people's pursuit of morally excellent lives, then such a society is, to that extent, defective.

Given these unavoidably brief considerations of the moral basis of a good human community, how are we to evaluate the institution of government regulation? Does it or does it not qualify as a proper function of government, as justified political practice?

REGULATING MARKETS
IS REGULATING PEOPLE

To regulate something is to adjust and steady its motion intentionally. Regulation of economic affairs would involve, in part, adjusting an ongoing process—manufacturing, marketing, selling, testing, and so on. But this by itself does not tell us what *government regulation* is, since regulation per se might ensue without government intervention. There are dress-code regulations in schools and banks, there are rules that govern the way cars must be driven at the Indianapolis 500, yet these are not imposed by government. Private organizations such as the Better Business Bureau of Consumers' Research might manage to achieve the regulation of business by persuasion or even boycotts.

Government regulation is distinctive because it brings about adjustments in the various economic processes without requiring the consent of those whose activities are being regulated. When cigarette advertisers were required to place a warning on cigarette packages, they were not asked to do so, or urged, or even cajoled into this practice. It was required of them under penalty of law.

Of course, some who defend government regulation would declare this a misstatement of the situation because, in fact, government regulation of the safety conditions of the workplace or of cigarette smoking is simply a kind of protection of people's basic rights, and thus does not require the consent of the regulated. And indeed, if, in a trade, the customers have the right to ensure that the sellers look after their safety and health fully, this interpretation would be correct. But there are reasons to doubt that government regulation is but an extension of the protection of people's rights, and I will say more about this later. For now it seems clear enough that government regulation involves forcing people to behave in certain ways.

When a private organization tries to induce greater care on the part of some manufacturer, the manufacturer may choose to heed or to ignore the advice.[7] Even a boycott would only involve refusing to

---

7. It has been argued by some that the choice to select from alternatives in the marketplace is quite illusionary. See, for example, Andrew McLaughlin, "Freedom Versus Capitalism," in *Outside Looking In*, ed. Dorothy James (New York: Harper & Row, 1972), pp. 120–40. But this contention rests on the false thesis that human beings are unable to resist advertising pitches and that their will or "consciousness is . . . from the very beginning a social product," quoting Karl Marx, *Writings of the Young Marx on Philosophy and Society*, ed. Loyd Easton and Kurt H. Guddat (Garden City, N.Y.: Anchor Books, 1967), p. 422, whose views McLaughlin, as many others taking his stance, is repeating here. See, for example, Lawrence Crocker, "Coercion and the Wage Agreement," *The Personalist* 59 (January 1978): 78–81, who thinks that refusing to sell equipment at a normal price to people suddenly threatened by fire or refusing to employ out-of-work laborers at a wage rate above what would merely enable them to subsist, are forms of coercion. Crocker, however, confuses the circumstances that force people into helpless situations with the people who offer them help for returns that may be difficult to meet, so that the "coercion" of

trade with a manufacturer who would not be legally prohibited—if he could afford it—from continuing the production of his goods or services. Government regulation, on the other hand, legally requires that, for example, a productive process abide by certain (enforceable) rules, regardless of whether the producer is willing. If, for example, government requires adherence to a dress code in schools, one cannot simply ignore the regulation by finding a school where no dress code is observed. All schools must abide by the regulation—as is the case with government regulation of education that requires teachers to possess government-issued certificates or credentials.

In summary, to regulate people's economic activities, the government must designate agents schooled in legal coercion to enforce economic directives—to carry out inspection, supervision, and so forth. The method involved is the method distinctive of government, namely, force; the ultimate consequence of resisting government regulation is that punishment will be imposed. Such regulation is distinctive in that it *forcibly* directs people's activities toward the specified goal(s).

MUDDLES OF GOVERNMENT REGULATION

We often include under the rubric "government regulation" activities that are, strictly speaking, quite distinct. Some are judicial, some managerial. For example, the Securities and Exchange Commission not only regulates the sale of stocks and bonds—for example, by prohibiting insider trading—but it also adjudicates disputes involving allegations of fraud. The Federal Communications Commission not only regulates the content of Saturday morning children's programming and advertising on television but is also responsible for adjudicating conflicts of property-rights claims in the electromagnetic spectrum. On the other hand, the Department of the Interior engages in the management of government-owned parks, forests, and lakes, apart from regulating the use of pesticides or the mining of coal.

---

events is attributed to the coercion of *people*. See Jan J. Wilbanks, "Free Enterprise and Coercion," *Reason Papers* 7 (Spring 1981): 1–19. For a better treatment of the issue see Robert Nozick, "Coercion," in *Philosophy, Science and Method*, ed. Sidney Morgenbesser, et al. (New York: St Martin's Press, 1969), pp. 440–72, in which Nozick considers whether any degree of coercion can result when something greatly valued by one person isn't granted by another. My view is that coercion involves rights violation, which, in turn, requires the use of physical force or its threat, since this form of intrusion—unlike advertising or refusal of assistance or kind treatment—is caused by the perpetrator and is *unavoidable*.

As to the judicial issue, the distinction is important because in determining whether government has the proper authority to carry out regulatory activities, one need by no means dispute its proper authority to engage in various judicial functions. Moreover, when attempting to identify the consequences of government regulation per se, it is important to know the precise nature of such regulation. Legal definitions alone will not suffice here, since the law is not an internally consistent system.

The managerial functions, too, need to be distinguished. Let us assume that government owns or manages for the owners (the public at large) some sphere, such as the postal service or the highway system. When it sets rules and regulations for the activities in that sphere, it does so as a function of its proprietary or managerial responsibility and control, not as a regulatory function as described above. The Food and Drug Administration does not have or claim proprietary rights and responsibilities in the manufacture of medicine, yet is legally charged with regulating that process. The Department of Transportation does, however, own—or the public it officially represents owns—the interstate highway system, even if the law states the matter less directly. As such, the Department of Transportation is performing its managerial functions by setting rules and regulations for the use of the national highway system.

All this must be kept in mind as we try to understand what constitutes government regulation, which we can summarize by stressing its two crucial interdependent features: the adjustment and direction of some human activity that is deemed quite legitimate (such as selling cars or manufacturing drugs), by threatening or actually using physical force (via the machinery of law enforcement).

THE IMPETUS FOR GOVERNMENT REGULATION

Modern government regulation—as distinct from feudal mercantilist management of the realm—evolved slowly and is rarely defended explicitly, especially in terms of moral considerations.[8]

The central legal concept that has fostered government regulation in the United States is that of police power of the various states.[9]

---

8. See Louis M. Kohlmeier, Jr., *The Regulators* (New York: W.W. Norton, 1965). For a detailed descriptive and analytic discussion, see Barry M. Mitnick, *The Political Economy of Regulation* (New York: Columbia University Press, 1980).

9. See Ernst Freund, *The Police Power* (New York: Arno Press, 1977).

Ironically, this concept, introduced into the U.S. legal system from England via the common law, relates directly and naturally to feudalist societies, including monarchies, and not to constitutional republics or democracies.

However, in its transposition from England to the United States, the idea of police power has been bolstered by implicit philosophical and normative support for government regulation. Those supporting elements initially arose in a context of political and economic ideas that encouraged laissez faire capitalism. This system had at one time been promulgated as a virtual utopia, a cure-all for society's ills—if not by its major defenders, then at least by its more zealous publicists. The earliest theoretical justification for capitalism promised that the system would foster both prosperity and virtue.[10] When this line—advanced, for example, by Frederic Bastiat, Montesquieu, Sir James Stewart, James Millar, and Adam Smith, plus numerous less well known thinkers—began to be cast within a "scientific" framework, the part stressing virtue and morality tended to diminish. Increasingly, the scientistic intellectual community began to stress material progress as the central promise of implementing the system. Laissez faire would unchain the productive drives of capital and labor, enhance the "free flow of commerce," and lead to ever-rising prosperity.

But laissez faire, both as practiced and as conceived, could not secure the widespread, indeed uniform material progress its optimistic utopian advocates promised. It did not satisfy some of the popular notions regarding the outcome of a truly just or progressive economic system—for example, equalization of wealth distribution; eradication of social distinctions; elimination of such influences as natural talent, circumstances, background, and so on. The system did, of course, give rise to great, though not uniform, prosperity. But its critics, relying on well-entrenched moral notions, could always point to problems. They lamented the lack of care the system was said, in fact, to promote concerning the unfortunate, the many who could not compete well or those with handicaps. Many believed that unfettered competition often led to market failures—for example, to pernicious monopolies, to booms and busts that caused instability and unemployment, and to generally chaotic economic conditions.

---

10. Albert O. Hirschman, *The Passions and the Interests: Political Arguments for Capitalism Before Its Triumph* (Princeton, N.J.: Princeton University Press, 1977).

By the early 1880s the courts began to invoke the police-power concept to support government intervention (e.g., in labor disputes). As early as 1867 one could read about complaints of twenty years of excessive government intervention—for example, protectionism, blue laws, and so on—by advocates of free trade.[11] Legislatures, in turn, began to pass interventionist laws that the courts eventually upheld. At first the arguments advanced seemed mainly legalistic, making reference to such quasi-economic, quasi-constitutional notions as the "free flow of commerce."[12] Gradually, however, an intellectual climate emerged that reflected the moral sentiments of paternalism. By the turn of the century, the ideas conveyed by John Maynard Keynes in the following passage had considerably taken hold. For him the laissez faire idea

> implies that there must be no mercy or protection for those who embark their labour in the wrong direction. It is a method of bringing the most successful profit-makers to the top by a ruthless struggle for survival, which selects the most efficient by the bankruptcy of the less efficient. It does not count the cost of the struggle, but looks only to the benefits of the final results which are assumed to be lasting and permanent, once it has been attained. The object of life being to crop the leaves off the branches up to the greatest possible height, the likeliest way of achieving this end is to leave the giraffes with the longest necks to starve out those whose necks are shorter.[13]

Apart from some of the economic reasoning advanced in support of the practice—reasoning that shied away from explicit normative considerations—government intervention, as distinct from centralized planning, was thus defended largely on grounds that protection was morally required for those left without adequate means of their own in the prevailing relatively free market. In the end, interventionism and its offspring, government regulation, were supposed to be the partial remedies for the alleged shortcomings, many of them moral, of the free market. Government intervention and regulation was to help those thought to be harmed by the operations of a competitive, unregulated market.

11. Charles Astor Bristed, *The Interference Theory of Government* (New York: Leypoldt & Holt, 1867). Bristed chides the government for twenty years of illicit growth!

12. Ibid.

13. John Maynard Keynes, *The End of Laissez-Faire* (New York: Hogarth Press, 1927), p. 40.

When government regulation is defended today explicitly on moral grounds, there are clear suggestions of the prevalence of such considerations. Regulatory programs are said to "deal with the injustices that prompted their creation in the first place."[14] Consumer-advocacy agencies are justified on grounds that such bodies "will promote justice and fairness."[15] Ralph Nader believes that "it is important to look at regulation issues in terms of the needs of society . . . we should ask ourselves what human purposes regulation fulfills, whether it is just or unjust."[16] And it is argued that "simple cost-benefit calculations may be less important than more abstract conceptions of justice, fairness, and human dignity."[17]

THE CONSEQUENCES OF GOVERNMENT REGULATION

Government regulation of the economic activities of members of a community means, as I have noted already, the forcible institution of legal guidelines for production, trade, and consumption (for purposes specified by Congress, state legislatures, city councils, and so on). What are the results of such regulation within a community? More specifically, what consequences of moral significance can be seen to result from this kind of government activity?

Specifying the *moral* significance of government regulation helps to focus on those of its aspects that relate to the principles of a sound moral point of view, whether or not they are widely accepted or given support by prominent figures in the community. Thus, to answer our central question, we need to scrutinize some samples of government regulation. At times it will also be necessary to speculate on what could have occurred had the regulation in question not been imposed, on what actions people might have been free to take without the legal barriers government regulation created for them, or

14. Steven Kelman, "Regulation That Works," *The New Republic*, 24 November 1978, p. 16.

15. Roger Noll, "Agency for Consumer Advocacy," in *Regulatory Reform*, ed. W.S. Moore (Washington, D.C.: American Enterprise Institute, 1976), p. 44.

16. Eileen Shanahan, moderator, *Government Regulation: What Kind of Reform?* AEI Roundtable, September 11, 1976 (Washington, D.C.: American Enterprise Institute, 1976), p. 2.

17. Kelman, "Regulation That Works," p. 19.

without government's preemption of their efforts. It will not be denied here that some of the desired goals of government regulation could be valuable to many people. It is one thing, however, to consider whether some measure leads to good results and another to determine if it is the morally appropriate means of attaining those results.

In 1975, Michael Jacobson wrote to the Food and Drug Administration complaining that, because possibly dangerous dyes and preservatives have been used in alcoholic beverages without notice to drinkers, some action should be taken by the agency.[18] He argued that "consumers have a right to know what is in their foods and beverages."

In this case, the FDA responded by turning to another agency, the Treasury Department's Bureau of Alcohol, Tobacco, and Firearms. It asked the bureau to require the labeling to which Jacobson claimed the public has a right. Members of several industries objected to the proposed requirement because it would increase their production costs and cause related problems.

In this simple case we can already detect the distinctive nature and consequences of government regulation by contrasting Jacobson's proposal with other alternatives. Making a *recommendation* to the producers of the beverages concerning how they might label their products is not what distinguishes a government regulatory act. Nor would government regulation be involved if Jacobson had gone to court and demonstrated that the commonsense meaning of the beverage excludes any dyes or preservatives. The first method could contribute to the safety of the consumer by *persuading* manufacturers to make sure they do not mislabel their products. The second method would achieve the same goal by taking the issue before a court and applying rules of evidence to show that present labeling techniques are fraudulent.

Neither an appeal to voluntary cooperation nor a demonstration of the violation of some basic right of prospective buyers — for example, to be free of fraudulent exchange — was involved in this case. Instead, on grounds of *possible danger* — not even very probable or likely danger — to consumers, it was proposed that all the members of an industry be compelled by law to change their conduct. The emphasis here is on the compulsion and its circumstances. *If* fraud on

18. Reported in *The Wall Street Journal*, 15 July 1975.

the part of the industry members were shown and they were compelled to cease committing fraud, this would be a case of defensive, retaliatory, and perhaps punitive, hence justifiable, force. But no fraud has been demonstrated. Still, members of the industry were to be coerced, something the criminal courts disallow even when a mere technicality separates a known murderer from being condemned and punished.

Had some other right been violated? Jacobson alleged that "consumers have a right to know what is in their foods and beverages." If consumers do have such an enforceable right, there would be grounds for compulsion.

In considering whether they do, the first thing to note is that, until purchased, the foods and beverages do not rightfully belong to the consumer but to the manufacturer or seller. Consumers do have the right to know *what* it is they are purchasing when they exchange their money for some commodity or service. This right derives from basic rights against fraud and from the nature of trade. When Joe offers Bill some item for another, the prospect of knowing the items involved—that is, their nature as determined by what they accomplish in use (as best understood in customary discourse by reference to the prevailing "reasonable man" standard)—is required for the trade. If, for example, additives change the nature of some beverage, say wine, so that it is no longer that beverage but some other, say vinegar, it is possible to show fraud, unless the change is made evident prior to the exchange. With demonstrable fraud, regulation would be redundant. Most traders, however, are not defrauded into accepting each other's wares. True, when Bill agrees to some trade, he has a right to receive the item for which he bargained, as distinct from something else. Suppose Joe informs Bill that something is a certain (type of) item, knowing (or being responsible for knowing) that it actually is not that item. If Bill then purchases it, under normal circumstances this can be considered fraud. (The details of handling this within the law may require further distinctions, such as whether the trade is contractual or merely promissory.)[19] If Bill is

19. That fraud constitutes a species of property rights violation may be appreciated by considering that it involves, not merely breaking a promise (which is a moral wrong but not a violation of rights), but the wrongful acquisition of values based on legally sanctioned misrepresentation of values given in exchange. For more on this see Murray N. Rothbard, *Man, Economy, and State* (Los Angeles, Calif.: Nash Publishing Company, 1970), pp. 157–58, 702. See, also, my "Ethics and the Regulation of Professional Ethics," *Philosophia* (forthcoming).

assured by Joe that an item is of a certain type and it actually is, but Bill wishes to know its entire composition, Bill is not prevented from requesting the information and can refuse purchase if it is withheld. But this is not to say that Bill has an enforceable right to know the entire composition of the item—as distinct from having the right to obtain an item that has *not* been misrepresented (by a reasonable man standard).

In the case under consideration, Jacobson is just wrong—consumers have no right to know what is in their food. Such a right would require that others, at their expense, furnish the information, but no one has shown that people owe it to each other, as an enforceable obligation, to carry out such acts of benevolence. The mere *possibility* of something being dangerous—as distinct from the presence of a demonstrably strong probability of harm—is inadequate grounds for bringing the force of law to impose burdens on members of an industry in the absence of the proven commission of injurious crimes. True, it is sometimes not objectionable to use force in the face of danger (or even apparent danger); for example, when one responds with adequate force to deter someone who points a gun that is, in fact, unloaded. Yet even in such a case the clear probability of injury or rights violation, from the point of view of the respondent, needs to be demonstrated, antecedently, to ensure that the act was indeed defensive or deterring and did not employ excessive force. In cases of clear and present danger, as in all others, the onus of proof is rightfully on those claiming the warrant for the use of force, not on those against whom it is used. This is standard policy in most criminal law and has good moral support in the principle that only those should suffer the willful imposition of burdens by others—coercion, penalties, punishment—who have first violated someone's rights.

There is no rational reason why the same approach should not apply to the treatment, by government and individuals, of people in the business world—manufacturers, producers, advertisers, and the rest.[20] A refusal to do so is contrary to the dictates of "justice, fairness, and human dignity." And among the more clear-cut harmful consequences of the sort of injustice and unfairness advocated by Jacobson is the likelihood that those who are operating only marginally—breaking even in the free market—will be forced out of busi-

20. See Michael S. Baram, *Alternatives to Regulation* (Lexington, Mass.: Lexington Books, 1981). See also, R. W. Poole, Jr., ed., *Instead of Regulation* (Lexington, Mass.: Lexington Books, 1981).

ness. Such people are unable to assume productive functions beyond the current range of industry activity and are left with only two alternatives: to continue producing the items in question without adding the labeling information and thus accept the serious risk of being fined or imprisoned (both considerably burdensome); or to withdraw from the industry, thereby risking a loss or diminution of their investments. (I use "risking" here simply to allow for the unlikely possibility of escaping without any serious adverse effect, however remote this may be.)

Producers who do add labeling information will incur additional costs (very likely) requiring some cut in production or increase in revenue. In either case, these producers will (very likely) distribute the losses in a way that will enable business to continue. Some customers will be priced out of the market, or some employees will be laid off, or the owner(s) will reap lower returns on their investments than they would have without the imposition of new labeling requirements.

These so-called economic consequences of government regulation are by now familiar to its proponents as well as to its opponents. What is often forgotten in economic analyses, however, is that actual individuals are involved and that in bringing about economic dislocations, regulatory provisions create actual life changes for those individuals. It is not difficult to imagine some likely consequences of what is often characterized as "a mere loss of income": parents are less able to provide for the education of their children; a delay in replacing the worn tires on a car results in an auto accident; attendance at a symphony concert must be forgone; doctor visits must be cut; and so on—the consequences may be of great or small importance in terms of people's prosperity; the point is that they are quite real at the individual, specific level. (The reason they do not make good headlines or special television news reports is obvious—they are seldom drastic or easily traceable to their origins.)

Yet there is an even more basic issue at stake: individuals in society ought to have an individual sphere of self-responsibility. Within this sphere they ought to enjoy the liberty (from others) to act in morally responsible or irresponsible ways, quite irrespective of what they may do for others. Striving valiantly at some occupation or profession in the arts, sciences, or business, or simply getting by or even succumbing to a failure are all morally significant aspects of any person's life. When someone's personal sphere is infringed upon, the opportunity to exercise this basic self-responsibility, to pursue one's life well or badly, has been diminished. To put the matter bluntly, such intrusions violate a person's basic human dignity.[21]

For example, if manufacturers are subjected to regulatory provisions concerning whatever product or service they want to provide in the marketplace, their nature as moral agents is denied by the regulatory process; their liberty to make their own choices and reap the consequences is abridged. Yet they have not been found guilty of any violation of others' rights. It has been determined only that they *might* commit a crime — that is, in cases where such as possibility cannot be ruled out — a risk we encounter in our dealings with any (free) human being.[22]

These and related consequences of government regulatory decisions for individuals vary enormously. Most such decisions will appear on first sight to have but the mildest impact on the lives of the regulated — mild, that is, in comparison to the more blatantly tyrannical policies of governments such as expropriation of land for purposes of building freeways, or the interning of Japanese–American citizens because there is a specious suspicion that they will cooperate with citizens of their ancestors' country in time of war. Nonetheless, these mild forms of tyranny — although petty — are bona fide tyrannies. They impose the sort of undeserved burdens on individuals and groups that would rightly be considered unjust if used for protecting ourselves from criminals.

That government regulation is characterized by the imposition of undeserved burdens will be made clear by a few additional cases. I am not picking sensational regulatory flops as illustrations — for example, the cyclamate- or saccharin-banning incidents — nor what are regarded as major regulatory victories — for instance, the thalidomide case. If my argument is sound, these are not as crucial for assessing government regulation as they are often claimed to be.[23]

21. See Tibor R. Machan, "Human Dignity and the Law," *DePaul Law Review* 26 (Summer 1977): 807–832.

22. It should be obvious that this claim depends to a large extent on the truth of the position that human beings are capable of choosing their own conduct, that they have what is generally called freedom of the will. I must make clear that this freedom does not involve the rejection of causality but merely the expansion of that concept so that it includes self-determination by human beings. See my *The Pseudo-Science of B. F. Skinner* for more on this. See also, R. W. Sperry, "Mind, Brain and Humanistic Values," J. R. Platt, *New Views on the Nature of Man* (Chicago: University of Chicago Press, 1965).

23. The reason is that the case for a certain government function cannot rest on occasional emergencies or tragedies, only on the demonstration that justice in general requires that function. For a discussion of this see my "Prima Facie versus Natural (Human) Rights," *Journal of Value Inquiry* 10 (Summer 1976): 119–31.

For some time now the Federal Trade Commission has required cigarette manufacturers to place on each package of cigarettes a notice concerning the hazards of consuming their products. This may seem a trivial burden and the gains may be considerable, assuming that the practice is successful in its aim. Nevertheless, here again government regulation produces burdens for specific individuals who have not been tried for a crime and found deserving of condemnation and punishment. This conclusion is not mitigated by the fact, if it is a fact, that cigarette smoking is harmful to people. Unless the product is misrepresented, a producer does not violate anyone's right by offering for sale — for *voluntary purchase* — a potentially dangerous item. So although a cigarette maker whose product is advertised as wonderful and life-enhancing might be sued for fraud, that producer cannot *in justice* be penalized simply for selling a product whose consequences in use are knowable by any consumer who has not been living in a cave for the past thirty years!

Regulation with respect to cigarettes has been extended so that burdens are imposed on others also. In 1967 the FCC was successfully urged by John Banshaff to compel broadcasters to provide air time to groups that advocate the quitting of cigarette smoking. In this instance the regulation that ensued is muddied by the fact that the electromagnetic spectrum is "publicly owned" and is managed for the public by the FCC. Accordingly, government regulation of broadcasting might be more appropriately viewed as proprietary management, with all the attendant confusions stemming from lack of a genuine market, restricted entry, oligopolistic tenancy, and so on.

Nevertheless, government regulation of cigarette advertising on radio and television could and, judging by current practices, would exist without state ownership of the airwaves. After all, warning messages are required on cigarette advertisements published in newspapers, regardless of the First Amendment and the ideals of a free press. What needs to be mentioned, however, is that practices imposed or required by law under the "fairness doctrine" or the FCC's "equal time" provisions pertaining to the airing of controversial opinions could just as easily be adopted by broadcasters. And when government owns the airwaves, its imposition of such measures is, strictly speaking, a matter of proprietary management. True, many such controversial topics were not treated as cigarette advertising was — for example, commercials for beer, wine, meat, cosmetics, U.S.

Saving Bonds, Vista, the Peace Corps (some of which later became subjects for litigation)[24]—leaving the impression that politics had considerable influence in these managerial decisions.[25]

By now, of course, cigarette advertising has been banned on the broadcast media. Its regulation alone, however, reveals elements of injustice essentially tied to government regulation. Those whose lives and prosperity depended upon the work involved in broadcasting such ads—on air time that now had to be given to antismoking groups—clearly must have experienced significant, even severe hardship, although once again no evidence had shown they deserved it. Of course, similar losses are experienced whenever business is voluntarily withdrawn from some producer, but here this was clearly not the case. Interruption of trade came about coercively.

Obviously, the present discussion does not bear simply on *federal* government regulation. Building codes, zoning laws, Sunday "blue laws," and similar rules imposed on people and groups by the governing bodies of local communities can be included in the present area of analysis.[26] In these and related cases the crucial point is that goals found desirable by others become the justification for the forcible regulation of the lives and special activities of various (groups of) human beings. In many states, an individual who wishes to engage in certain kinds of business—extermination, for example—must first post with the government a large sum of money. This requirement is aimed at preventing irresponsible dabbling in the profession but may make it extremely difficult for some people, especially the less affluent, to enter the business. (Some of the support for such laws is no doubt provided with this fact well in mind!) No proof of prior irresponsibility by the individuals involved is required.

It should also be noted that the issue here is not whether existing members of a certain industry, for example, the extermination industry, welcome the particular regulatory measures imposed on them by various governmental bodies. Thus it may well be true, as Beatrice Trum Hunter has documented, that many Food and Drug Administration regulations are welcomed by members of the drug indus-

---

24. Early 1980 saw the Gray Panthers file suit against the government for broadcasting misleading U.S. Saving Bonds ads.

25. See Tibor R. Machan, "One-Sided Fairness," *Barron's*, 22 April 1968.

26. For a discussion of zoning along present lines, see Bernard Seigan, *Land Use Without Zoning* (Lexington, Mass.: D.C. Heath, Lexington Books, 1972).

try.[27] If there is one (actual or potential) member of the industry who does not welcome them, the regulation, as here understood, constitutes an unjust imposition of burdens upon that party.

But what if all welcome the measure? Could there be any purpose in requiring it as a matter of law? And would it not be possible to object to such requirement, even under so unlikely a circumstance, on grounds that citizens should not have to fund a government activity like regulation?[28]

I raise these matters here without delving into them. I simply wish to observe that where compliance is mandatory—that is, no one can be a member of the profession or industry without abiding by the regulatory provisions (as opposed to privately generated professional codes)—widespread acceptance is entirely irrelevant. What could obscure this fact is the frequent unqualified endorsement of democracy by those who also value political liberty. But it is only procedural democracy that is compatible with political liberty, the sort that spells out the means by which administrators are to be selected. Substantive democracy, leading to the determination of principles of justice by majority vote, is not. (Consider the difference between the following two systems: in one, the sheriff and judge are elected but must follow due process of law in dealing with crime, while in the other, the establishment of guilt or innocence is left to direct election, as illustrated by lynchings.)

To provide further illustration, let me now consider another federal-government regulatory body, the National Labor Relations Board, which has ruled that a firm may not discontinue production in a plant because the plant is unionized. Imposed on hundreds of businesses each year, this ruling treats employees as part owners of the firm, although ordinarily they are not. Stopping the owners' efforts to close the affected plant, without first establishing that someone's basic human rights have been violated, is again an instance of injustice. Here again, the government has imposed burdens outright without demonstrating that the imposition was deserved. Regulation here is designed to achieve a goal such as the well-being (e.g., employment) of members of organized labor. Furthermore, it may

27. Beatrice Trum Hunter, *Food Additives and Federal Policy* (New York: Scribner's, 1975).

28. Even if unanimously desired, such regulation would involve a distortion of the proper function of government.

be claimed that the closing of such plants could be little more than employer retaliation against what should be regarded as a perfectly legitimate effort of employees to achieve bargaining strength. These objections lose their moral and political force once we remember that (1) the employees do not own the plant; and (2) no matter how strongly they believe it should be kept open, they have no moral justification for coercing the owner(s) into taking such action. The liberty of the commercially engaged citizen is sacrified in the process of yielding to these morally invalid grounds via the NLRB's rulings.[29]

In this case, as in so many others, the same goal (i.e., keeping a plant in operation subsequent to unionization) may be achieved without violating the firm owners' rights. The laborers could resolve to boycott the firm's other products; they could persuade potential customers to join such an effort; they could pool their resources and purchase the business; they could start their own firm and begin to compete with the firm's other branches and lead the firm to reconsider its decision to close. In general, there are numerous steps employees could take without engaging government's coercive powers to induce owners to operate businesses they would rather shut down. But when this coercive power is invoked, the owners' basic human rights are violated. Such coercive power could only be permissibly utilized if the parties had voluntarily entered into a contractual arrangement not to discontinue their business relationship.

In 1964 the federal government enacted legislation requiring manufacturers of television sets to produce only "all channel" (VHF *and* UHF) television sets. In this case of government regulation, manufacturers were being forced to produce something they did not choose to produce, in order to further some goal the legislature considered important. Here no such issues as safety entered the picture—the measure was confined entirely to furthering the goals of some "entrepreneurs"; namely, those who entered or wanted to enter the UHF broadcast market. Congress decided to enact legislation that would give these individuals a special advantage by forcing television manufacturers to make sets suitable to UHF reception. Putting it bluntly, members of Congress thought it advisable to partially inden-

29. For more on this, see Thomas R. Haggard, "Government Regulation of the Employment Relationship," in this volume. See also, Tibor R. Machan, "Some Philosophical Aspects of National Labor Policy," *Harvard Journal of Law and Public Policy* 4 (1981): 67–160.

ture the television manufacturers, in order to accommodate additional viewers. While putting it this way may appear to be overstating the case, it does serve to put things in proper perspective and to illustrate how past injustices have been given "justification."[30] No question can exist as to whether government regulation in the UHF case amounted to a form of petty tyranny.

THE CENTRAL THESIS AND SOME
SECOND THOUGHTS

The argument I have been developing can now be stated in outline form. We should keep in mind that its basic underlying assumption is simply that a just human community must accord with the requirements of morality.

1. Human beings are distinctive in having the moral responsibility to live a good, successful life, namely theirs.
2. The subjection of persons to initiatory, nonretaliatory force destroys some of their moral autonomy and undermines their human dignity as moral agents, whether coercion is accomplished by an individual or a group.
3. Government regulation is the imposition of standards on actions that do not have to have an impact on others – for example, the manufacture or offering for sale of toys and drugs that no one is compelled to purchase.
4. Such imposition is a species of initiatory coercion, a moral authoritarianism that robs individuals of their sphere of moral autonomy.
5. Thus, government regulation constitutes a morally impermissible incapacitation of some people as moral agents, undermines their distinctive human nature, and violates their basic human rights. It is, in short, a form of injustice.

---

30. Although in some cases such justification comes to little more than rationalization of vested interests, when a position is tied to purported general principles of morality or political justice, it may be regarded as a genuine attempt to provide a measure with moral support. Whether it is successful moral support depends on the quality of the framework involved.

How do we answer, from this perspective, Joan Claybrook's impassioned question; namely, "What about the rights of individuals to breathe clean air, to drink clean water, to secure drugs and food that do not have unnecessary side effects or cause illness,"[31] and so forth, as recounted at the outset of this essay? Perhaps one way to provide the answer is by asking a very similar question directed to supporters of government regulation. We might then respond with the query, "What about the rights of individuals to be free of others' interference in their peaceful conduct of economic affairs, to make their own choices about what to produce and sell, not to be restrained in their efforts to make for themselves and their intimates a prosperous life? These are the rights of the citizenry which the Constitution is designed to defend."

But this will not suffice as an answer. Clearly, the fundamental question is, "What are our basic, individual human rights?" And an adequate response requires analyzing the issue in terms of the rights theory outlined earlier. But first we need to consider what Claybrook could be designating as "gross abuses that the marketplace does not correct." This is difficult, however, because by now many potential "marketplace" solutions to various problems have been preempted by government action, so that it is not a simple matter to sort out what influence is responsible for harms that occur. To take just one example, since 1926 the federal government has assumed responsibility, first through the Bureau of Air Commerce and then through the Federal Aviation Administration, for the safety of aircraft. The familiar role of the insurance industry in setting and maintaining safety standards through its contracts with various businesses in other commercial areas thus has never seriously entered into the design, manufacture, and maintenance of aircraft.[32] So disasters such as the DC-10 failure at Chicago's O'Hare Airport in May 1979, can hardly be called a gross abuse that the marketplace failed to correct. The marketplace has not even been allowed to function in this case.

But assuming we do have a reasonable semblance of a free marketplace in some areas, what could Claybrook mean? First, there are certain risks of production failure that, short of completely stopping production, cannot be prevented, although they can be minimized.

---

31. "Joan Claybrook Responds."
32. Robert W. Poole, Jr., "Is This Any Way to Run an Airway?" *Reason* (January 1979): 18–32.

Here, if someone is harmed by such a failure, the role of the courts is crucial in determining whether the harm arose from negligence or whether it was unpreventable within the bounds of reasonable precautions. A system of such judicial enforcement would not provide absolute guarantees against future dangers. But regulation itself has never and could never completely do away with unforeseen problems. Second, there are instances (like the famous thalidomide case) where a product is marketed and consumed even though its dangers very likely could have been known beforehand. But we have courts, not marketplaces, to handle such problems. If it were preventable beforehand, the matter is actionable in the courts, whose province it is to consider all the available facts, weigh degrees of responsibility, and assign liability where that is warranted (including reparations, if applicable).

Could regulation do better than the judicial system, by preventing tragedies rather than imposing penalties in their aftermath? The now massive evidence concerning drug regulation, considerably stricter since the thalidomide case, indicates that such prevention carries its own risks, namely, keeping off the market or delaying the introduction of many lifesaving drugs. Abuses of the marketplace are being exchanged for abuses of regulation, market failures for political ones. Moreover, such preventive regulation carries not just the risk but the *certainty* of imposing burdens on people who have not been found guilty of any wrongdoing. Finally, Claybrook may consider it "a gross abuse that the marketplace does not correct," for example, situations involving auto manufacturers who have not added certain safety features to their cars—even though consumers have been refusing to purchase cars with such features (i.e., have been unwilling to pay the resulting higher prices). If anything, however, this should be labeled a gross abuse on the part of consumers and not of the marketplace. And again, to mandate such features via regulation is to impose burdens—in this case not only on manufacturers but on unwilling consumers.

On Claybrook's second point, while government regulation is often *designed* "to prevent the recurrence of certain harm, not to punish," the *effect* of such regulation is in fact to impose undeserved burdens. Ironically, such regulation does not often enough prevent harm or does so only by incurring measurable costs that are greater than the measurable benefits. But the point here is that burdens imposed without being deserved, for whatever purposes, amount to a form of unjust punishment, for what citizens "might do." Claybrook is invoking that famed excuse of many well-meaning wrongdoers: "But our intentions were good." If that is a legitimate excuse, it means that human beings are not responsible for *failing* to consider the consequences of their conduct. Yet one of the allegations of those who support government regulation is that regulation is required by virtue of the *negligence* of many who are engaged in commercial endeavors, and negligence is precisely the failure to have thought of avoiding some harmful consequences!

A very different reason for government regulation is suggested by Kenneth Arrow, who argues that sometimes "public intervention . . . is necessary to change the way in which resources are used." He tells us that "dumping wastes in a stream may ruin fisheries" and would, "in a proper economic accounting, be charged against the dumper, but it is impractical to do so." He concludes that "the public must intervene in some way, either by charging the dumper for the costs imposed on others or by regulations."[33] This may be construed as the legal-efficiency argument. The harm caused from pollution is sometimes impossible to trace precisely to some perpetrator. So statistically we can tell that acting in certain ways will violate rights, but we may not be able to identify the culprits and tie their actions directly to the victims. Under such circumstances we have a problem that, as Arrow seems to argue, morally requires government regulation.

Inasmuch as such regulation would be an adjunct to the judicial treatment of industrial crimes, it does not quite fit the definition of government regulation I have been employing. And indeed the purpose of such regulation would basically differ from the usual purpose of government regulation. Implementation would also differ from the usual means, namely, the use of prior restraint to prevent someone's legitimate conduct from causing harm. Still, it may be that with such exceptional cases a form of government regulation would have to be deemed morally acceptable. However, what would justify regulation in *this* case would, in turn, rule out virtually all other forms of government regulation that do not involve the sort of judicial motivation Arrow's suggestions call to mind.

---

33. Kenneth J. Arrow, "Two Cheers for Government Regulation," *Harper's* (March 1981): 20.

Arrow also observes that "when it comes to economic rather than moral good, there is no legitimate criterion of policy other than giving people what they want, or should want if they are properly informed."[34] This point has actually been advanced as the main *moral* reason for government regulation by Steven Kelman, as a form of (rare) justified paternalism.[35] However, giving people not what they want but what they *should* want if only they had adequate information—and taking from others to make this giving possible—breaches political morality. The giving assumes a sort of helplessness and social inefficiency as a built-in feature of human community life, something for which no justification is evident, while the taking is a clear case of the violation of human rights.

Finally, getting back to Claybrook's rhetorical question, all that individuals have a right to is not to have *their* air, water, and so forth, contaminated by others. But if I wish to contaminate my lemonade and sell it to adults (without fraudulently claiming that it is uncontaminated), there is nothing that others should do to prevent this, outside of persuasion or boycott. Perhaps I should not have sold such an item (or others), in the various possible and perfectly cogent senses of that term: I might have done better in another endeavor; I might have been more aware of how my customer planned to use this merchandise, and so on. But none of this involves rights, so none of it involves legitimate governmental authority. Rights, in this context, mean enforceable claims against another, not the morality of someone's conduct, as is evident in the case of free-speech rights.

Generally speaking, while Claybrook and others wish to make their case in terms of the rights of individuals, describing their position in such terms is misleading. Their case relies on a conception of rights that is foreign to the American political tradition. For them, a right means a claim to be provided with whatever is wise and prudent and decent for people to possess. Using the vocabulary of freedom, this alternative conception of rights is well expressed in the words of former Supreme Court Justice Abe Fortas.

> The concept of individual freedom has exploded in the last 10 to 20 years and individual freedom means a lot more than technical civil rights and the Bill of Rights. Now it means access and entitlement to a basically decent standard of living; an environment that is agreeable, pleasant and enriching

---

34. Ibid.
35. Steve Kelman, "Regulation and Paternalism," this volume, pp. 217–48.

to individuals, and medical care and a lot of other things that were unimaginable, say, 30 years ago.[36]

If we interpret individual freedom in these terms while still acknowledging that the primary function of government is to secure the right to liberty, a serious change in the role of government is implied. The duties of government then encompass much of what government regulation is all about. The ideal of a free society with a firmly restricted scope of government — namely, protection of the basic rights of human beings (interpreted as what others *may not* do *to* others, not what they *must* do *for* them) — is unappealing today.[37] But what is appealing, especially to theoreticians guided by complicated philosophical doctrines, isn't always correct. Moreover, Fortas's view, though couched in the terminology of modern political theory, if anything, harks back to a conception of the government-citizen relationship more evident in ancient holistic and feudal regimes than in those that view individuals as morally responsible beings.

CONCLUSION

In our time the basic legal documents of the United States are interpreted to embody a concern for both the right to be free from others' interference, including the interference of governments, and a concern with the general welfare, as sketched by Fortas, which requires such interference. (It isn't obvious, of course, that the concept "general welfare" amounts to a concern with living standards, material well-being, safety, etc. Securing the general welfare could well mean nothing more or less than the protection and preservation of so-called negative rights.) Most Western "liberal democracies," as well as the United Nations' charter, follow this dual loyalty faithfully. Philosophers have characterized the result as a sort of balancing of "freedom rights" and "welfare rights."[38] Human beings must

36. Quoted in *Santa Barbara News-Press* (UPI), 3 December 1978.

37. This may seem to trivialize current disdain for the liberal conception of government. Judging from the intuitionist underpinnings of most non-Marxist and even some Marxist criticism of bourgeois society and laissez faire, the term is apt. See my "Wronging Rights," *Policy Review* 17 (Summer 1981): 37–58. Cf., Henry Shue, *Basic Rights* (Princeton, N.J.: Princeton University Press, 1980).

38. For a clear discussion of the distinction, see Gregory Vlastos, "Justice and Equality," in *Human Rights*, ed. A. I. Melden (Belmont, Calif.: Wadsworth Publishing Co., 1970), pp. 76–95.

have both some autonomy and some economic and related security. So government ought to protect their freedom to speak, to engage in artistic, scientific, and especially, political activities; it also ought to take steps to ensure access to medical care, education, a basic standard of living, safe products, a fair distribution of wealth, a healthful workplace, and so on.

This theory, that both freedom rights and welfare rights must be protected by the government, is the most well developed moral position in support of government regulation. I have tried thus far in this essay to develop what is a creditable moral case against government regulation (or *for* the freedom to act — within a given sphere of one's life — according to one's own judgment instead of by the dictates of government). Thus it is important to acknowledge this alternative moral position that several recent treatises in political theory have elaborated, most notably John Rawls's *A Theory of Justice*, Alan Gewirth's *Reason and Morality*, A. I. Melden's *Persons and Rights*, and Ronald Dworkin's *Taking Rights Seriously*.[39] From their very general views about the roughly equal importance of human liberty and human welfare, these theorists derive political institutions to secure both, among which government regulation of commerce can be easily seen as one of the most important.[40] (I am not concerned here with whether these philosophers actually support government regulation in their works, only with the fact that their general moral frameworks provide the most up-to-date theoretical case for such regulation.) But each of these theories has, I believe, serious weaknesses that are avoided by the perspective of the present discussion. These, however, cannot be discussed at the present time.[41] Yet, even without a detailed refutation of contrary views that provide support

39. John Rawls, *A Theory of Justice* (Cambridge, Mass.: Harvard University Press, 1971); Alan Gewirth, *Reason and Morality* (Chicago: University of Chicago Press, 1978); A. I. Meldon, *Persons and Rights* (Berkeley, Calif.: University of California Press, 1977); Ronald Dworkin, *Taking Rights Seriously* (London, England: Duckworth, 1977).

40. For a review and brief criticism of the major human and natural rights theories of the post-World War II period in Anglo-American political philosophy, see Tibor R. Machan, "Some Recent Work in Human Rights Theory," *American Philosophical Quarterly* 17 (April 1980): 103-15.

41. For a more elaborate development of various features of the present position, see my *Human Rights and Human Liberties* (Chicago: Nelson-Hall, 1975). See, also, my "Considerations of the Libertarian Alternative," *Harvard Journal of Law and Public Policy* 2 (1979): 104-24, and "Against Non-Libertarian Natural Rights," *Journal of Libertarian Studies* 3 (1978): 233-238.

for government regulation, there are already good reasons, summarized above, for viewing such regulation in the following light:

1. It denies the essential dignity of human beings because it involves treating persons as, in the last analysis, morally impotent, wards of the state, dependents, or fundamentally incapacitated by their circumstances to prepare for what is, after all, a life with risks, small and great.
2. The policies of government regulation actually diminish the economic welfare of members of society (as established by the overwhelming evidence from studies considering measurable benefits and costs).
3. Justice is obstructed by government regulation through the institution's violation of human rights (including substantive due process of law), its discriminatory practices and statutes, and its destructive effects on the foundation of individual initiative and responsibility in human communities.
4. By making considerateness, compassion, kindness, generosity, and other virtues pertaining to civilized community life matters of government mandate — by rejecting the voluntary human relations that could produce the desired conduct — government regulation is a fundamental threat to the quality of human community life as well as the private lives of its members.

These pervasive and grave flaws of the institution of government regulation rarely have immediate impact. They do not appear in the vivid light to which abuses of justice are often exposed. They are obscured, furthermore, by their close association with widely promulgated and respected ideals that emerge from such moral systems as altruism and utilitarianism. But in reality these moral systems are false and serve as assaults on other, better systems of ideals that stress such values as one's happiness and one's capacity to prosper and enhance the prosperity of one's friends and associates. Altruism is widely advocated — hardly a commencement exercise goes by without the speaker asking youth to go out into the world and sacrifice itself to the general welfare, humanity's destiny, the public interest, meaning, of course, the welfare of *others*. And the prominence of this outlook among intellectuals (although in practice it breeds mostly guilt and vain compromises) has cast government regulatory measures in a morally reputable light.

Yet it is clear enough that altruism and its attendant public policies, including government regulation, breed tyranny, when we consider simply that total states, both ancient and modern, have all had some group's welfare, emancipation, or ultimate triumph as their objective and self-justification. In the case of government regulation, the perilousness of such a general policy is not readily apparent, so we are left with what President Gerald Ford called petty tyrannies. Petty or not, tyrannies they certainly are. Which is why, in the last analysis, government regulation has no proper place within a just legal and political system. Human reason, not force (except in response to force) marks the genuine humanity of a system of law.[42]

42. In my essay, "Human Rights, Feudalism, and Political Change" (*Philosophies of Human Rights*, ed. Alan Rosenbaum [Westport, Conn.: Greenwood Press, 1980], pp. 207–51), I discuss some of the problems related to advancing toward a political system that exhibits the virtues I have stressed here.

INDEX

ABOUT THE EDITORS

Tibor R. Machan, E.C. Harwood Professor of the Behavioral Sciences, Franklin College, Lugano, Switzerland, and Visiting Associate Professor of Economics at the University of California, Santa Barbara, is Senior Editor of *Reason* magazine and Director of Educational Programs at the Reason Foundation. He received his B.A. from Claremont–McKenna College, his M.A. from New York University, and his Ph. D. from the University of California, Santa Barbara. Author of *Human Rights and Human Liberties, The Pseudo-Science of B. F. Skinner*, and *Introduction to Philosphical Inquiries*, Dr. Machan has contributed to numerous volumes and edited three others: *The Libertarian Alternative, The Libertarian Reader*, and *Recent Work in Philosophy* (with K. Lucey). His many articles and reviews have appeared in such publications as *American Journal of Jurisprudence, American Philosophical Quarterly, Barron's, DePaul Law Review, Educational Theory, Harvard Journal of Law and Public Policy, Humanist, Inquiry, Journal of Critical Analysis, Journal of Human Relations, Journal of Social and Political Studies, Journal of Value Inquiry, Los Angeles Times, Modern Age, National Forum, National Review, New York Times, Occasional Review, Personalist, Philosophia, Philosophical Studies, Philosophy of Science, Policy Review, Reason, Review of Metaphysics, Theory and Decision, Wall Street Journal*, and *Western Ontario Law Review*.

M. Bruce Johnson is Research Director for the Pacific Institute for Public Policy Research and Professor of Economics at the University of California, Santa Barbara. He received his B.A. from Carleton College and his M.A. and Ph.D. from Northwestern University. In addition to serving as President of the Western Economics Association (1981–82), Dr. Johnson has been Associate Professor of Economics, University of Washington (1966–68); Acting Director, Institute for Economic Research, University of Washington (1967–68); Chairman, Department of Economics, University of California at Santa Barbara (1970–74); Visiting Professor of Economics, UCLA (1975–76); and Associate Research Director and Professor of Economics, Law and Economics Center, University of Miami (1976–77).

A contributor to over a dozen scholarly volumes, he is the author of *The Economics of America's Third Century, Energy and Jobs: A Long Run Analysis* (with J. Cogan and M. Ward), and *Household Behavior: Consumption, Income and Wealth.* In addition, he is the editor of *Resolving the Housing Crisis: Government Policy, Decontrol, and the Public Interest, The California Coastal Plan: A Critique, Advertising and Free Speech* (with A. Hyman), and *The Attack on Corporate America: The Corporate Issues Sourcebook.*

His articles and reviews have appeared in *American Economic Review, American Spectator, California Real Estate Magazine, Econometrica, Economica, Economic Inquiry, Economic Studies, Environmental Law, Journal of Economic Literature, Law and Liberty, Policy Report, Quarterly Journal of Economics, Reason, Southern California Law Review*, and other popular and scholarly journals.

ABOUT THE AUTHORS

Randall R. Dipert received his B.A. from the University of Michigan and his M.A. and Ph.D. in philosophy from Indiana University. He is currently Assistant Professor of Philosophy and Director of International Education at State University of New York College, Fredonia. Previously, he has been Associate Instructor of both music theory and philosophy at Indiana University (1973–75, 1977). Specializing in the areas of aesthetics, American philosophy, history of philosophy, and logic, Professor Dipert has published articles in the *Canadian Journal of Philosophy, Indiana Music Theory Review, ISIS, Journal of Aesthetics and Art Criticism, Journal of the History of Philosophy, Mathematical Reviews, Mind, Musical Quarterly, Nature and System, Review of Metaphysics,* and many other journals. His current projects include a textbook on logic and computers and an introductory text on the philosophy of the arts.

Thomas R. Haggard received his B.A. in political science from the University of Texas at Austin and his LL.B. from the University of Texas School of Law. Currently he is Professor of Law at the University of South Carolina School of Law. Following an engagement as associate attorney with a private law firm in Washington, D.C. (1967–69), Professor Haggard served as Assistant Professor (1969–72), Associate Professor (1972–74), and Professor (1974–75) at Rutgers University, Camden School of Law; Associate Dean and Professor,

University of South Carolina School of Law (1977–79); and Visiting Professor, Baylor University School of Law (summer 1980). Professor Haggard has contributed to several volumes and his many articles have appeared in *Boston University Law Review, Houston Law Review, Journal of Labor Research, Journal of Social and Political Affairs, Jurimetrics, Nebraska Law Review, North Carolina Law Review, Reason, Rutgers–Camden Law Journal, South Carolina Law Review,* and *Texas Law Review.*

Norman Karlin is Professor of Law at Southwestern University School of Law. He received his J. D. from the University of Chicago, engaged in private law practice, and later became a partner in the law firm of Siegan and Karlin, where he specialized in zoning and land use law. He has written and lectured extensively on the subject of land use law, constitutional law, and law and economics. A contributor to the volumes *Resolving the Housing Crisis, Multiple Use Land Development: Real Property and Tax Problems,* and *Real Estate in Mid Century,* Professor Karlin has also written articles for several journals, including *Environmental Law* and *Southwestern University Law Review.*

Steven Kelman is Associate Professor of Public Policy at the John Fitzgerald Kennedy School of Government, Harvard University, where he received both his B. A. and Ph. D. He spent two years studying at the University of Stockholm in Sweden (1970–71), and has been Research Associate, Harvard School of Public Health (1975–76) and Associate Director of Management Planning, Federal Trade Commission, Bureau of Consumer Protection (1980–81). Books authored by Professor Kelman are *Regulating America, Regulating Sweden; Improving Doctor Performance; Push Comes to Shove; What Price Incentives?;* and *Behind the Berlin Wall.* He has contributed to the volumes *Incentives for Environmental Regulation* and *The Politics of Regulation,* and his articles have appeared in *The Public Interest, Public Policy, Regulation,* and other journals.

J. Roger Lee received his B. A. and M. A. from State University of New York at Albany, and his Ph. D. from the University of Southern California. He is currently a Lecturer in Philosophy, California State University (Dominguez Hills, Los Angeles, and Northridge). Specializing in the areas of ethics and social/political philosophy and the philosophy of language and mind, he has taught at State University of New York at Albany (1968-69), Sullivan County Community College in New York (1969-70), and the University of Southern California (1974), and has been a Visiting Fellow, Center for Study of Public Choice, VPI (1982). A contributor to several volumes, including *The Libertarian Alternative: Readings in Social and Political Philosophy* and *The Libertarian Reader*, Dr. Lee has also written articles and reviews for *Philosophical Studies* and *Reason.*

Nicholas Rescher is University Professor of Philosophy at the University of Pittsburgh where he has served as Chairman of his department and currently is Director of the Center of Philosophy of Science. From 1969 to 1975 Professor Rescher served a term as Secretary General of the International Union of History and Philosophy of Science (an organ of UNESCO). He has been editor of the *American Philosophical Quarterly* since 1964 and was awarded an honorary L. H. D. degree by Loyola University of Chicago. He is the author of over forty books in the theory of knowledge, methaphysics, social philosophy, logic, the philosophy of science and technology, and the history of philosophy. Among his most recent titles are *Risk, Skepticism,* and *Scientific Progress.*

Rolf Sartorius is Professor of Philosophy at the University of Minnesota, Minneapolis. He received his B.A. from the University of Pennsylvania and his M.A. and Ph.D. in philosophy from Princeton University. Specializing in the areas of legal philosophy, political philosophy, and ethics, Professor Sartorius has previously been Assistant Instructor, Princeton University (1962); Assistant Professor, Wayne State University (1964-66); Assistant Professor, Case Western Reserve University (1966-69); and Visiting Professor, University of Utah (1979-80). He is contributor to numerous volumes and his articles have appeared in *American Philosophical Quarterly, Archives for Philosophy of Law and Social Philosophy, Canadian Journal of Philosophy, Ethics, Georgia Law Review, Harvard Law Review, Journal of Philosophy, Midwest Studies in Philosophy, Philosophy and Public Affairs, Psychiatry, University of Minnesota Law Review, Utah Law Review, Virginia Law Review,* and *Yale Law Journal.*

J. C. Smith received his LL.B. from the University of British Columbia and his LL.M. from Yale University. Currently Professor of Law at the University of British Columbia, he previously has been a Visiting Professor in the Department of Jurisprudence, Faculty of Law, University of Sydney in Australia. He has served as Adjudicator and Conciliation Commissioner for several Canadian governmental agencies and as arbitrator in labor disputes. His areas of special interest include legal philosophy, the law of torts, and comparative law. He is the author of *Content and Form* (with S. Coral) and *Legal Obligation*, and the editor of *The Western Idea of Law* (with D. Weisstub). His articles and reviews have appeared in *American Journal of Jurisprudence, Cambridge Law Journal, Canadian Bar Review, Ethics, International Journal of Law and Psychiatry, Modern Law Review, Osgoode Hall Law Journal, University of British Columbia Review, University of Pennsylvania Law Review*, and *University of Toronto Law Journal*, and in several anthologies.

Judith Jarvis Thomson is Professor of Philosophy at Massachusetts Institute of Technology. She received a B.A. from Barnard College, a B.A. and M.A. from Cambridge University, and her Ph.D. from Columbia University. Previously, she has been Lecturer (1956–59), Instructor (1959–60), and Assistant Professor (1960–62) at Barnard College; Assistant Professor, Boston University (1963–64); Visiting Fellow, Australian National University (1968); and Visiting Professor, University of Pittsburgh (1976). Dr. Thomson has contributed to numerous scholarly volumes and is the author of *Acts and Other Events* and the editor of *Ethics* (with G. Dworkin). In addition to serving as Consulting Editor to *American Philosophical Quarterly, Australian Journal of Philosophy, Philosophical Forum, Philosophical Studies*, and *Philosophy and Public Affairs*, she has written articles for *Arizona Law Review, Australian Journal of Philosophy, Journal of Philosophy, Mind, The Monist, Philosophical Quarterly*, and *Philosophy and Public Affiars.*

Leland B. Yeager is Paul Goodloe McIntire Professor of Economics at the University of Virginia. Past President of the Southern Economic Association, he has previously been an editor of *Southern Economic Journal* (1960–63) and is currently editor of *Atlantic Economic Journal* (1973–present). Dr. Yeager received his A.B. from Oberlin College and his M.A. and Ph.D. from Columbia University.

In addition to currently serving as Visiting Professor at Auburn University (1983), he has taught at Texas A&M University (1949–50), the University of Maryland (1952–57), Southern Methodist University (1962), UCLA (1975), and New York University (1979). He has contributed to numerous volumes and scholarly journals, and is the editor of *In Search of a Monetary Constitution* and the author of *Free Trade, Foreign Trade and U.S. Policy* (with D. Tuerck), *The International Monetary Mechanism, International Monetary Relations, Monetary Policy and Economic Performance, Proposals for Government Credit Allocation, Trade Policy and the Price System* (with D. Tuerck), and *Experiences With Stopping Inflation* (with associates).